Learn VB .NET Through Game Programming

Matthew Tagliaferri

Learn VB .NET Through Game Programming
Copyright ©2003 by Matthew Tagliaferri

ISBN (pbk): 1-59059-114-3

Printed and bound in the United States of America 12345678910

Trademarked names may appear in this book. Rather than use a trademark symbol with every occurrence of a trademarked name, we use the names only in an editorial fashion and to the benefit of the trademark owner, with no intention of infringement of the trademark.

Technical Reviewer: Mike Burgess

Editorial Board: Dan Appleman, Craig Berry, Gary Cornell, Tony Davis, Steven Rycroft, Julian Skinner, Martin Streicher, Jim Sumser, Karen Watterson, Gavin Wray, John Zukowski

Assistant Publisher: Grace Wong

Project Managers: Laura Cheu and Nate McFadden

Copy Editor: Kim Wimpsett

Production Manager: Kari Brooks

Production Editor: Janet Vail

Proofreader and Indexer: Carol Burbo

Compositor: Kinetic Publishing Services, LLC

Artist: Dina Quan

Cover Designer: Kurt Krames

Manufacturing Manager: Tom Debolski

Distributed to the book trade in the United States by Springer-Verlag New York, Inc., 175 Fifth Avenue, New York, NY, 10010 and outside the United States by Springer-Verlag GmbH & Co. KG, Tiergartenstr. 17, 69112 Heidelberg, Germany.

In the United States: phone 1-800-SPRINGER, email orders@springer-ny.com, or visit http://www.springer-ny.com. Outside the United States: fax +49 6221 345229, email orders@springer.de, or visit http://www.springer.de.

For information on translations, please contact Apress directly at 2560 Ninth Street, Suite 219, Berkeley, CA 94710. Phone 510-549-5930, fax 510-549-5939, email info@apress.com, or visit http://www.apress.com.

The source code for this book is available to readers at http://www.apress.com in the Downloads section.

To my mom and dad, who got me here

Contents at a Glance

Contents

About the Author

 **matt tagliaferri** has been developing software since his high school obtained its first computers—six TRS-80 Model 3s—in 1982. matt (who prefers his name in lowercase) has developed software in several industries, including retail, insurance, corporate finance, and trucking before (somewhat miraculously) landing a senior analyst position with the Cleveland Indians baseball organization. matt has been with the Indians for six years and is now the manager of application development.

Currently, matt lives in the Cleveland area with his wife and two daughters. He enjoys collecting *The Simpsons* action figures and "family stuff" such as *American Idol* and Friday Pizza Nights.

About the Technical Reviewer

MIKE BURGESS started writing software on computers back when they took up whole rooms and had less memory than an average digital watch today. He has worked for small to large corporations (including Microsoft) and has been working with Visual Basic since the beta of version 1. He's written many different types of software including small business accounting and inventory, real estate, emergency management, corporate communication, multimedia, medical diagnosis, and some hush-hush stuff for the government.

He currently resides in northern Utah with his wife and five (yes, five) children. He enjoys Family Game Night, Mountain Dew, and a good round of Ghost Recon with his kids and brothers.

Acknowledgments

WRITING A BOOK IS DEFINITELY not a solo project—and there are numerous people to thank for the opportunity and the work put into this project. I'd like to thank the entire Apress team. This is my first Apress title, and I've found it to be a first-class organization. Individually, my list of acknowledgments probably reads like the internal Apress organizational chart: thanks to Gary Cornell for listening to and shaping my initial pitch, thanks to Dan Appleman for some overall direction in finding the correct audience, and thanks to Laura Cheu and Nate McFadden for serving as project managers and keeping the project on track. Mike Burgess served as technical editor for the book and did a great job not only making sure the code was complete and that everything compiled but also making suggestions to help improve code clarity and readability. Kim Wimpsett filled the role of editor, keeping my i's dotted and my gerunds gerunding. Finally, Beth Christmas filled a multitude of roles from making sure I had the correct screen-capture software to getting me advance copies of Visual Studio. I thank all of them for turning a simple idea into the organized pile of pages you now hold in your hands.

On the home front, no project gets far without the understanding of my wife, Janet, who has to put up with me running to the computer to check email as soon as I get home from work and with the *clack clack* of the keyboard as she tries to read every evening. I hope she doesn't need to read this to know how much her love and support mean to me.

Introduction

A FEW YEARS AGO, Microsoft raised a few eyebrows (my own included) when it announced that the next version of Visual Basic (VB) would not be backward compatible with the current version, VB 6. There were many valid reasons for breaking the compatibility, but many people still thought Microsoft was taking a considerable gamble. After all, there were thousands of VB programmers cranking out millions of lines of code in the modern workforce, and suddenly Microsoft was announcing that this mountain of code would someday be considered "old" technology.

Introducing the New VB

Would the development community take to the new VB? The answer to that, of course, depended on what the new language had to offer. Community revolt would be the result if it were perceived that VB was changing simply for the sake of change. No, Microsoft had to make sure that the new VB was bringing enough to the table to get developers to want to make the change and make a concerted effort to plan upgrade paths for their production VB code.

Fortunately (for Microsoft and its stockholders), the new VB delivered against these goals. The new VB, called *Visual Basic .NET*, supported a full object-oriented paradigm—much better than the object-oriented features "bolted on" to VB along its prior development cycle. Furthermore, VB was only one of many possible languages that built upon the .NET Framework—an enormous library of classes from which your new programs would be based. Browser-based development took a major leap forward in the new release, as well—allowing the developer to do much of the development outside of the Web page in "standard" classes that could be accessed from the browser. These classes could be accessed through standard means or referenced remotely using Web Services, which allow full .NET Framework objects to be passed via Extensible Markup Language (XML) across the Internet. So much to learn! Where to start?

I've had many different people ask me about the best way to get into programming or the best way to learn a new language such as VB .NET. I've always found that I can't learn a new language unless I have a specific task that I want to solve by writing a program. I'm not of the camp that believes one can sit down with the compiler, the development environment, and the help file and then stand up many hours later an "expert" in the language. I need to learn by doing.

With that in mind, an important choice becomes the type of program to develop. Choose a program too small, and you won't have enough opportunity to learn anything. A program too large doesn't work, either—you end up spending too much time bogged down in the complexity of the task, which takes away time from learning the features of the language. Like Goldilocks, you're looking for the program not too small, not too big, but instead "just right."

I discovered a few years ago that the "small game" program fit nicely into the "just right" category for learning the basics of a programming language. A small game is one that fits on a single screen and can usually be played by a single player in a few minutes. Examples of a small game include card games, dice games, and some simple board games. Many qualities make programs such as these good learning subjects. Programs of this type usually need to keep track of one or more types of game piece, and these pieces are often required to change state (such as a die rolling or a board element changing color). These game elements often come in groups (52 cards in a deck, five dice for Yahtzee), so you'll have to learn how the language stores a group of similar elements. The user interface requirements of such games are usually more interesting (and therefore more challenging) than the usual button/listbox/combobox interface. Finally, when you've succeeded and completed the program, you've got a fun game to play.

The goal of this book is to teach you how to get started programming in Visual Basic .NET by developing games. This book doesn't intend to be a complete treatise of all the features and capabilities of this latest version of VB. Instead, it provides a series of example programs that illustrate basic features of the language and begins the huge task of introducing you to the contents of the .NET Framework. In addition, I introduce one more important programming concept—the concept of *design*. Now that object-oriented languages are more common, people have found that the various objects in a program can be designed to interact with each other in different ways; these interactions can make the program more or less complex or more or less adaptable to future features or enhancements. To illustrate the importance of design on a program, I've taken the time to walk you through the development process of several of these programs rather than simply presenting you with the final version of the game. By learning how to solve a program one way, then improving upon that design in a second or third version of the program, you'll begin to recognize when your own designs might be headed down a wrong path and some redesign is in order.

Where Are You Now?

This book assumes you've had at least some experience in software development before diving into the first chapter and that you now want to learn Visual Basic .NET. Perhaps you're a VB 6 programmer, for example, in which case this book will help describe the syntactical differences between the languages, as well as introduce you to the .NET Framework classes that will be new to you. Perhaps you're experienced in an older technology such as mainframe programming and are looking to update your skill set to something more modern. Or perhaps you've picked up software development as a secondary skill at your job (you're the office "Excel macros guru"), and now you want to learn something more formally. Whatever the case, my assumption is that as you crack open Chapter 1, "Developing Your First Game," you've written programs in some other language so that you have a jumping-off point. Specifically, the following concepts should be familiar to you:

- Simple variables such as integers and strings to hold pieces of information

- Manipulation of data through expressions using elements such as mathematical operators (plus, minus, multiply, divide) or string operations (left, right, substring, uppercase/lowercase)

- Flow statements such as If..Then..Else blocks, For loops, and While statements

- The use of procedures and functions and how to get information into and out of them

- The event-driven nature of Windows programming and how many programs remain in an "idle state" until the user does something, at which point some type of code runs

Getting Up to Speed

If the previous little review list gives you a queasy feeling, or you simply think you might need a refresher on some of these topics, then you'll be happy to know that Appendix A, "The Basics of Visual Basic" contains some introductory material. Specifically, it covers these topics while describing how to write a simple Visual Basic .NET program. Becoming familiar with the topics in the appendix should give you enough background to dive into Chapter 1, "Developing Your First Game," and start the game writing.

Downloading the Code

If you want to follow along with the examples in the book, you can download the code for all the games developed in the book. It's available from the Downloads section of the Apress Web site (http://www.apress.com). The code is divided into the chapter folders described in Table 1.

Table 1. Download the Source Code

FOLDER NAME	USED IN
Art	Graphics/sounds used throughout the book
BMPStitch	Appendix C
CellularAutomata	Chapter 5
CellularAutomataWithSave	Chapter 9
Common	Modules/classes used by multiple projects
DicePanel	Chapter 2
DicePanelNew	Bonus, used by the Yahtzee game
DirectXDemo	Chapter 8
FirstApplication	Appendix A
GarbageDemoOne	Chapter 9
GarbageDemoTwo	Chapter 9
GuessTheDieRoll	Chapter 1
GuessTheDieRoll2	Chapter 2
GuessTheDieRoll3	Chapter 2
InterfaceExample	Chapter 6
NetReversi	Chapter 7
NineTiles	Chapter 3
PCOpponent	Chapter 6
PolymorphismExample	Chapter 5
ShapeTileGames	Chapter 4
SpaceRocks	Chapter 8
ThreadParametersOne	Chapter 9
ThreadParametersThree	Chapter 9
ThreadParametersTwo (broken)	Chapter 9
Yahtzee	Bonus game

Developing Your First Game

To GET THINGS ROLLING right from the start, you'll write a complete (albeit small in scope) game in this chapter. This game will consist of a single die rolling around in a black panel and an end user guessing the outcome of the die (see Figure 1-1). If you consider yourself at a beginner level and think this chapter rushes through some of the Visual Basic (VB) fundamentals, then refer to Appendix A, "The Basics of Visual Basic," to create a simple project in a step-by-step fashion.

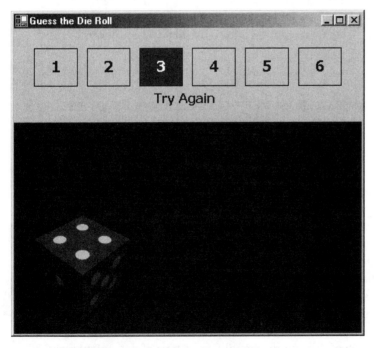

Figure 1-1. The Guess the Die Roll game in all its glory

NOTE *As you go through the code for this first program, you may find you don't agree with all the design decisions made along the way or with how the code is organized. As it turns out, I've gone out of my way on this first program to write the code in a distinctly non-object-oriented style. I've done this so you'll have a point of comparison when you rewrite the same game in Chapter 2, "Writing Your First Game, Again." So, if you're new to the .NET language, concentrate on the individual language elements and constructs, as well as the features of Visual Studio (VS), and pay less attention to the form and structure of this first program.*

When you saw Figure 1-1 with its slick 3D-rendered die, I hope you said to yourself "Oooh, that's pretty cool." This book covers the VB .NET language and object-oriented development using simple games as examples. In other words, this book doesn't teach how to develop the next Quake killer. However, a small game can still become extremely popular if it's done well and if it's fun to play. *Done well* means that the graphics, sounds, and overall design of the game are interesting, unique, funny, or all three. *Fun to play* is of course a matter of opinion, so the games you write will have to at least pass your own "fun meter"—and then perhaps you can try them out on family, friends, and coworkers to get their input.

Learning the Basics of Object-Oriented Programming

Older, procedural-driven languages were difficult on developers in terms of code organization. As projects in these languages grew, it became hard to manage the source code. Larger projects could be split up into different source files, but many times the variable or procedure declarations would collide if they had similar names (which is just one example of the problems that the lack of organization produced). Programmers found they had to name their constructs uniquely to avoid collisions, which meant the variable and procedure names got longer and longer. Having procedure names such as `StockItemSaveMonthlyPaymentToDatabase` certainly didn't help make the code more readable.

Part of the issue was simply *finding* things in a large project. As a natural step, developers began putting procedures that handled similar functions together, sometimes in a single source module. Therefore, all the reports might reside together, or all of the routines handling one type of data might reside together.

The object-oriented programming approach was developed, in part, to allow developers to organize the code by grouping together code constructs that handle similar functions. In fact, the object-oriented programming methodology forces the developer into grouping code in a natural way and into doing so from the beginning of the coding process. Programmers new to this approach might find this methodology difficult at first because they often can't simply jump into their editors and start writing lines of code. Instead, before you start coding, you must plan how you'll organize the code and group it into units and, to some extent, how these units will interact.

What Are Classes and Objects, Anyway?

The basic grouping mechanism in an object-oriented programming approach is known as a *class*. A class is a grouped collection of code and data that models something in life—either a concrete item or a concept. For example, if you're going to write a program that collects information about people (a human resources application, perhaps), then you'll probably create a class in your application that models a person and another class that models a group of people (such as all those in a department or all those managed by one supervisor). If your application instead tracks information for a library, then you'll most likely create classes to model books, magazines, videotapes, CDs, and anything else people can check out of the library. If your program is going to track baseball games, then it would be natural to create classes for players, pitchers, games, teams, leagues, and seasons.

As you can see, the minute you describe a program, even with a single sentence ("a program to track baseball games"), the object-oriented approach asks you to begin modeling the real or theoretical concepts of your program into distinct classes.

One way to think of a class is as a recipe to create something. An *object*, on the other hand, is an actual something. In other words, if a class is a recipe for a cake, then an object is the cake you create from the recipe. You can use the recipe to create many different cakes, and the cakes can be the same (the same flavor, the same frosting, the same number of tiers), or they can be different. Extending the analogy into the programming world, the class is the recipe, and it doesn't maintain any real presence in memory—all the class can do for you is create one or more instances of whatever it models. These instances are called *objects*. Each object has its own memory space and is independent. So, if you have a BaseballPlayer class, then you can create one, two, or 25 instances of that class to represent all the players on a team. You might also have a BaseballTeam class that contains the 25 BaseballPlayer instances. You could then have 30 instances of the BaseballTeam class, each representing a different team in a league. These 30 BaseballTeam instances might be stored in two instances of the BaseballLeague class, representing the American and National Leagues (assuming major league baseball players are being modeled). Notice how the organization of the classes and objects model the relationship of these constructs in "real life."

Why Object-Oriented Programming Is Valuable

This object organization is a powerful concept in that it's both self-documenting and extendable. It would be easy to draw a graphical representation of the classes previously described; people create such graphical representations all the time—the official name for such a drawing is a *UML class diagram*. (UML stands for *Unified Modeling Language*.) In addition, the relationship of the classes makes it easy to know where to "put things" when the developer adds functionality to the program. Suppose version 2.0 of the baseball program has to also model front-office personnel (to store their contract information, for example). It's easy to see that you can create a `FrontOfficeMember` class, and you can place instances of that class where they belong—as part of the `BaseballTeam` class (perhaps now renaming it to something more appropriate such as `BaseballOrganization`). If the program has to track some new advanced statistic for each player, it's evident that this new statistic will become a member of the `BaseballPlayer` class so that every instance of this object has a place to store this statistic.

One other important thing to know about classes is that their definitions can be hierarchical in nature, which is to say that you can create a class by first starting off with another class and then extending the functionality of that base class to create something new. When you do this, the base class is called the *ancestor*, and the new class is called the *descendant*. You can also say that the new class is a *subclass* of the base class. The .NET class hierarchy is a giant family tree in which you can trace every class back to a single ancestor. That "patient zero" ancestor is the class that has the (somewhat unfortunate) name of `Object`.

Subclassing gives you a powerful way to share functionality between classes that are somewhat, but not entirely, similar. Getting back to the baseball example, the program has to represent both pitchers and hitters. Pitchers and hitters share many common traits—for instance, they both belong to teams, they both have uniform numbers, and they both have a height, weight, age, and birthplace. Many of them went to school and played baseball there, which is another piece of information you'll want to store.

However, hitters and pitchers also contain many differences that you need to keep distinct. Pitchers have a separate statistical set than hitters; for pitchers, the program has to keep track of innings pitched, earned run average, and number of starts, wins, and losses (among other statistics). For hitters, relevant statistics include batting average and number of hits, walks, and strikeouts.

NOTE *This example is modeling American League baseball, where pitchers don't usually hit. The relationship (and therefore the class structure) would be different if the program had to model the National League rules, where the pitcher bats. Furthermore, the design would require even more complexity if the program had to model both sets of rules.*

You can easily model this relationship by using the subclassing ability of an object-oriented language. You could model these constructs by creating an ancestor class named `BaseballPlayer` and creating two subclasses from this class named `BaseballOffensivePlayer` and `BaseballPitcher`. The common pieces of information such as height, weight, age, and school would reside in the ancestor class, and the specific pieces of information unique to hitters and pitchers would reside in the appropriate subclass.

You'll start looking at VB classes to see examples of all these concepts soon, but you have one stop to make first—the .NET Framework.

Overview of the .NET Framework

Before cranking out and explaining reams of code, this section discusses some of the underpinnings of this new language and development platform. VB .NET is what's known as a *.NET Framework language*. The .NET Framework consists of two major components—the .NET Framework class library and the common language runtime. The former is a set of classes (recipes) that provide support for all of the languages in the .NET family. From the viewpoint of a former VB developer, it's accurate to say that the .NET Framework class library will in most cases replace the application programming interface (API) calls and user interface toolbox elements of your old language. That is, the classes in the .NET Framework class library will replace all the forms, buttons, listboxes, treeviews, labels, and checkboxes. But it also goes much deeper than that—basically, the Windows API is also encapsulated into an object-oriented framework. One quick example (and one relevant to this book) is the availability of graphics-related classes such as pens, brushes, and bitmaps. These concepts are easy to encapsulate into a class.

Understanding the Common Language Runtime

You can think of the common language runtime as the foundation upon which .NET programs are built. The common language runtime handles the overall memory management of your program, as well as the thread management. It also handles the line-by-line execution of your program. As a beginner to .NET languages, you don't need to know much about the common language runtime. It's always there doing work for you (running your programs), but you don't need to know much else—much like you don't really need to know how the internal combustion process in your engine works to drive a car or how a processor can talk to a graphics card to use your computer.

Understanding the .NET Framework Class Library

The .NET Framework class library, on the other hand, is something you'll become slowly familiar with as you learn VB .NET. In fact, much of the learning process is becoming familiar with the classes in the .NET Framework—much more than learning the syntax of the language, which has changed a bit but not dramatically from previous versions of VB.

The classes that make up the .NET Framework are organized in a hierarchical set of structures known as *namespaces*. There really isn't anything to compare namespaces to in older versions of VB, so you can think of them as groups of objects compiled into a sort of directory structure. The highest level of the directory structure is a namespace, and it's represented by a DLL on the computer. Within that DLL, however, can be other namespaces, each with its own set of classes, and those child namespaces can also contain namespaces within them.

The physical DLL that contains one or more namespaces is called an *assembly*. For your project to use any of the classes in a namespace, it must reference that assembly. A new project has a default set of references that you can see when you begin a new project. You'll learn how to add additional references to your project in Chapter 2, "Writing Your First Game, Again."

With this introduction to the .NET Framework out of the way, let's look at your first class.

Class Is in Session

The Guess the Die Roll program will begin its life as a standard Windows Application solution. You can create this type of project and give it any name you like now. Or, if you'd rather study my version of the project, refer to the project named GuessTheDieRoll. If you haven't downloaded the source code for the book yet, you can do so in the Downloads area of the Apress Web site (http://www.apress.com).

 NOTE *Please refer to Appendix A, "The Basics of Visual Basic," if you want to learn (or review) how to create a new solution in Visual Studio .NET and find your way around the environment.*

If you select Form1.vb in the Solution Explorer for this new project and then click the View Code button at the top of the Solution Explorer, the main window of Visual Studio will open and show you the code that makes up the default form in your project (see Figure 1-2).

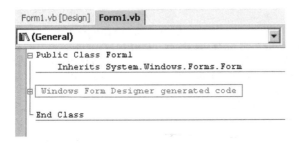

Figure 1-2. *The auto-generated code for the default form in a Windows Forms project*

It doesn't look like much at first, does it? The tiny amount of code declares a class named Form1, which is a subclass of something called System.Windows.Forms.Form. This represents the full name of a class, including the namespace in which that class resides. The ancestor class name is Form, but it resides inside a namespace named System.Windows.Forms.

NOTE   *The dot notation for the* System.Windows.Forms *namespace doesn't imply that there's a namespace named* Forms *contained within a namespace named* Windows *contained within a namespace named* System. *Instead, there's a single assembly named* System.Windows.Forms.dll *on your computer (it might take a while to get used to filenames that have multiple periods in them). There's a* System *namespace, as well, contained in the assembly* System.dll, *but obviously because these two assemblies are contained in different files, the namespaces aren't considered one within the other.*

So, the default project has a class named Form1, which is an ancestor of a class named Form. What does that mean? Well, for starters, it means that the Form1 class automatically gains all the functionality of its ancestor. For an idea of just what type of functionality this is, select View ➤ Class View from the Visual Studio menu, navigate down to Form1, open Bases and Interfaces, and then open Form. Your Class View's treeview will quickly fill up with all the available *members* of the Form class, as shown in Figure 1-3. A member is a field, property, event, or method attached to a class.

NOTE *You'll learn the definition of all these terms as you go. For now, it's important simply to note the sheer quantity of members found in the* Form *class and know that the* Form1 *class you're about to build upon already contains the functionality of* Form *simply because it's declared as an ancestor of the* Form *class. This "borrowing" of functionality is one of the truly powerful aspects of object-oriented programming.*

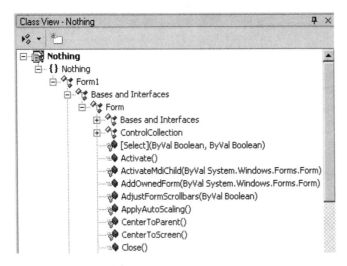

Figure 1-3. The Class View, showing all the functionality received for free because Form1 *is a subclass of the class* Form. *I love free stuff, don't you?*

Understanding Properties

Properties store a piece of information that helps describe an object. Think of a property as a variable that describes some aspect of the object to which it's attached. The Form class, for example, has properties to describe its size (height and width) and location on the screen (top and bottom). Changing the value of any of these four properties changes the appearance of the form.

Note that a property helps to describe an object, not a class. It's important to understand the distinction between those two terms. The class (recipe) helps to define the presence of the property and can declare a starting value, but the property itself is associated with each instance of the object. This means, of course, that each instance can have a different value for the same property. If a cake class has a property named IcingFlavor, then of course each actual cake can have a different value in this property, meaning that each cake can have a different flavor of icing. If a cake class has a property named NumberOfLayers, then each cake can be a single-decker, double-decker, or quintuple-decker, depending on the value that this property contains for each instance of the cake class.

In Visual Studio, you can view and edit the properties for all of the visual objects you create (your user interface elements such as forms, buttons, and labels) with the Properties window. You can open this window using the F4 key from within Visual Studio. The Properties window is a two-column grid (see Figure 1-4).

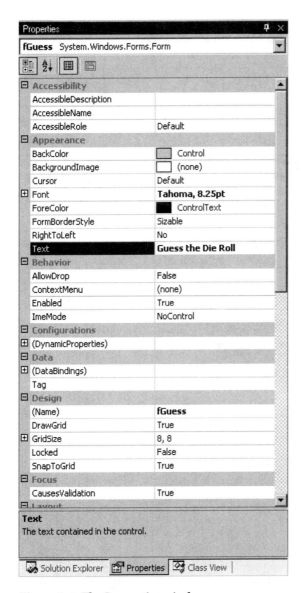

Figure 1-4. The Properties window

The left column of the grid displays the name of each property, and the right side displays the current value of each property. The Properties window shows the properties for a single object at a time. To change which object is being displayed, you can click a new object in the Form Designer, or you can select that object from the drop-down box at the top of the Properties window.

You can change a property by clicking the row that contains that property and then, depending on the type of variable that the property represents, typing a value, selecting it from a list, or sometimes selecting it from an extended selector.

TIP   *If a property has enumerated values (with a drop-down list to select them), you can cycle through the possible values by double-clicking the property name.*

Figure 1-5 shows the StartPosition property on the Form1 object in the example project being changed from the value WindowsDefaultLocation to the value CenterScreen. This property is an enumerated type, meaning it has a finite number of possible values, with each value represented by an easily remembered word. As you can see in Figure 1-5, you change the value of the property by selecting the desired value from a drop-down box. Once changed, the property value displays in bold if it's different from that property's default value.

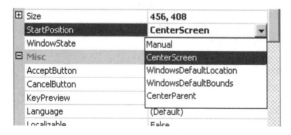

Figure 1-5. Changing a property value in the Properties window

Understanding Fields

A *field* on an object is so similar to a property (at least from the outside of the object) that it's almost impossible to tell the difference between the two, so this chapter won't cover them in any detail. Like a property, a field is like a variable attached to an object instance that describes some aspect of the object. The difference between fields and properties is in how they're declared; because you're not quite ready to learn about declaring, let's continue.

Exploring More Auto-Generated Code

Besides the class declaration and the corresponding End Class statement, the rest of the auto-generated code shown in Figure 1-2 is a single line that reads *Windows Form Designer generated code*. This line at first looks pretty innocuous (perhaps because it's light gray), but the little plus sign to the left of it is a clue that there's something going on underneath. Clicking that plus sign yields some more Visual Studio auto-generated code and demonstrates a cool new feature of Visual Studio: the ability to group code into blocks and then collapse that block to make it easier to manage large modules. If you expand the collapsed region in the Visual Studio code editor, you'll see the VB code shown in Listing 1-1.

Listing 1-1. Auto-Generated Form Initialization and Cleanup Code

```
#Region " Windows Form Designer generated code "

    Public Sub New()
        MyBase.New()

        'This call is required by the Windows Form Designer.
        InitializeComponent()

        'Add any initialization after the InitializeComponent() call

    End Sub

    'Form overrides dispose to clean up the component list.
    Protected Overloads Overrides Sub Dispose(ByVal disposing As Boolean)
        If disposing Then
            If Not (components Is Nothing) Then
                components.Dispose()
            End If
        End If
        MyBase.Dispose(disposing)
    End Sub

    'Required by the Windows Form Designer
    Private components As System.ComponentModel.IContainer

    'NOTE: The following procedure is required by the Windows Form Designer
    'It can be modified using the Windows Form Designer.
    'Do not modify it using the code editor.
```

```
<System.Diagnostics.DebuggerStepThrough()> Private Sub InitializeComponent()
    '
    'Form1
    '
    Me.AutoScaleBaseSize = New System.Drawing.Size(5, 13)
    Me.ClientSize = New System.Drawing.Size(292, 273)
    Me.Name = "Form1"
    Me.StartPosition = System.Windows.Forms.FormStartPosition.CenterScreen
    Me.Text = "Form1"


End Sub

#End Region
```

Visual Studio generated all of this code, including the comments, when you created your project. There's a good deal of stuff in Listing 1-1 that isn't explainable right away, but one thing worth mentioning is toward the bottom, where several properties of this form object appear (AutoScaleBaseSize, ClientSize, Name, StartPosition, and Text).

Note how all of these properties are referenced with the Me keyword—for the ClientSize property, for example, this keyword means "the property attached to Me named ClientSize." Also, notice that the property you changed in the prior section, StartPosition, is one of the properties listed. This is because the property is no longer at its default value. If you change it back to the default value WindowsDefaultLocation in the Properties window, this line of code disappears. Likewise, if you delete this line of code, the Properties window reflects this change. It's best to get into the habit of not modifying this auto-generated code directly, however, because you might (in the worst case) confuse the compiler or corrupt your form to the point where Visual Studio can't read it anymore. When modifying the value of properties, always use the Properties window.

 NOTE *You can add things to the auto-generated code; for example, you might want to add some resource cleanup code to the* Dispose *method shown previously or some initialization code to the* New *method, as the comment suggests.*

Designing the Die Roller Form

One of the first things you should do when starting a new project or adding a form to the existing project is to rename the form. The name Form1 is obviously not very descriptive, and although it seems like no big deal in this small project, the name will lose what little meaning it has as soon as you add a second form to the project ("Which form is Form1 again?"). You can change the name of a form or any other visual control in the Properties window. The label for the Name property is enclosed in parentheses, as shown in Figure 1-6 (Microsoft does this so that the Name property remains at the top of the Properties window when you sort the properties alphabetically). For this example, enter the name fGuess as your form name.

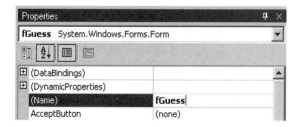

Figure 1-6. Changing the name of your form

Form Renaming Gotcha

When renaming the initial form in a project, you'll get an error message from Visual Studio the next time you try to compile and run your project. For this example, this error message reads as follows:

```
'Sub Main' was not found in 'GuessTheDieRoll.Form1'.
```

What this rather confusing error message is trying to tell you is that the project no longer knows which piece of code to run first. The project was originally instructed to run Form1 on startup, but you just renamed Form1 out of existence.

To fix this error, you'll need to right-click the project name (*not* the solution name) in the Solution Explorer, select Properties, and change the Startup Object in the drop-down box (you can also select Project ➤ Properties from the menu to get to the same dialog box). In a beginning project like this one, there will be only two choices for startup, either fGuess (the renamed Form1) or Sub Main. Sub Main is only available if you don't want to load a form in the beginning of the project. Of course, you must have a Sub Main somewhere in your program to choose this option.

VB got its name because designing forms is a visual process. That is, the programmer can arrange the user interface at design time by adding controls to a form and then moving and sizing them into their desired positions. This was the first Windows language that allowed the graphical arrangement of controls at design time. VB .NET is certainly no exception to this feature—you design forms visually. Specifically, you place controls on a form by using the Toolbox, which is docked (by default) on the left side of Visual Studio (see Figure 1-7).

Figure 1-7. The Visual Studio Toolbox. Now where's that screwdriver...?

The Toolbox contains a series of *controls* commonly used to create applications. A control is a certain type of object in the .NET Framework. Most controls have a visual representation (such as a button or label), and they have built-in code to handle user input (clicks, key presses, and so on).

To begin visually designing a form in your project, locate that form in the Solution Explorer and double-click it. You can also highlight the form in the Solution Explorer and click the View Designer button (second from the left) at the top of the Solution Explorer, as shown in Figure 1-8. Once you have chosen either of these options, the visual designer for this form will display.

To add a control to a form, simply locate the desired control in the Toolbox and drag it onto the form. Alternately, you can double-click the control name in the Toolbox, which will add an instance of it to the form. Once added, you can move and size the control in the manner you'd expect—by clicking the control to select it, by dragging it from the center to move it, and by using the sizing handles around the edge to size it.

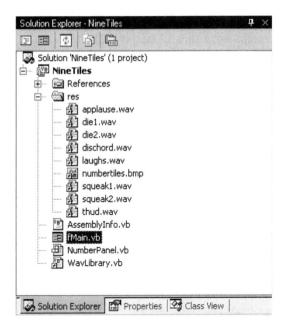

Figure 1-8. The Solution Explorer, showing the View Code button and the View Designer button on the toolbar (the first and second buttons from the left, respectively)

Once you place a control on a form and select it, you can use the Properties window to change that control's appearance and behavior, just as you changed the form's properties earlier.

TIP *You can select multiple controls in the designer by dragging a rectangle around them or by Ctrl+clicking on them in sequence. You can then edit the common properties of multiple controls in the Properties window.*

The Guess the Die Roll game form has seven label controls on it. Six of the controls are similar—they're the numbered "buttons" the user will click to make a guess. This game will use label controls for these buttons mainly because they're easier to color and because they don't give the 3D "clicking" effect. The choice was purely aesthetic. The seventh label control tells users whether they won or lost the game.

The fastest way to add these controls to a form is to add the first label, set its properties so that it looks just the way you want it to look, and then copy and paste it five more times (you can copy and paste controls just like in Word or Excel). You'll then have to change the names of the six labels to lbOne, lbTwo, lbThree, lbFour, lbFive, and lbSix.

Table 1-1 describes the numbered labels and their common properties. (When you view their values in the Properties window, they look slightly different.)

Table 1-1. Label Properties

PROPERTY NAME	VALUE
BorderStyle	System.Windows.Forms.BorderStyle.FixedSingle
Cursor	System.Windows.Forms.Cursors.Hand
Font	New System.Drawing.Font("Tahoma", 14.25!, System.Drawing.FontStyle.Bold)
Size	New System.Drawing.Size(56, 48)
Tag	"Yes"
TextAlign	System.Drawing.ContentAlignment.MiddleCenter

Observe how some of these properties are object instances themselves—the Size and the Font properties have a New keyword in front of them. This is how you create a new instance of an object in code. The BorderStyle, Cursor, and TextAlign properties are all an enumerated type. The name of the enumerated type is the second-from-the-last word in the value (BorderStyle, Cursors, ContentAlignment, respectively). The value of the property is the last word (FixedSingle, Hand, and MiddleCenter, respectively). The remaining portion of the property value is the namespace in which that enumerated type resides (System.Windows.Forms, System.Windows.Forms again, and System.Drawing, respectively). Enumerated types are designed so that their values are self-explanatory rather than having some arbitrary integer value represent the property (in other words, BorderStyle = 1 isn't quite as self-documenting as BorderStyle = FixedSingle).

The only property left to explain in Table 1-1 is the Tag property. If you have experience in VB 6 development, the Tag property was kind of a catchall place to put any user-specific data. The first beta versions of VB .NET left out the Tag property, but Microsoft put it back in because of developer feedback (mainly for backward-compatibility reasons). The six labels have a "Yes" value to easily differentiate them from the single-user feedback label. You'll see why in the next section.

The only remaining design-time object left to put on the form is the user feedback label. This label's name is lbResult, and it goes under the six buttons. Figure 1-9 shows the form in the designer after adding the seven label controls.

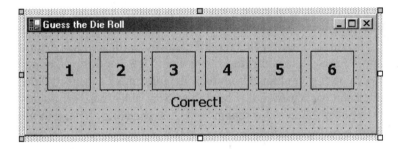

Figure 1-9. The Guess the Die Roll program at design time

Coding the Die Roller

The routine shown in Listing 1-2, named UpdateGuessButtons, takes care of coloring the label on which the user clicks.

Listing 1-2. Coloring the Guess Buttons

```
Private Sub UpdateGuessButtons()

    Dim ctl As Control
    Dim clrBack As Color = Color.Blue
    Dim clrFore As Color = Color.White

    For Each ctl In Me.Controls
        If TypeOf ctl Is Label Then
            With ctl
                If .Tag = "Yes" Then
                    If CInt(.Text) = Guess Then
                        .BackColor = clrBack
                        .ForeColor = clrFore
                    Else
                        .BackColor = Color.FromKnownColor(KnownColor.Control)
                        .ForeColor = Color.Black
                    End If
                End If
            End With
        End If
    Next
End Sub
```

There's quite a bit to look at in this relatively small routine, whether you're new to VB or a VB 6 programmer learning .NET. First, three variables are declared at the top of the procedure. The two color variables are also initialized to a default value, which is something you wouldn't be able to do in VB 6. For this program, these two variable values never change from their default values, so you could theoretically make them constants. In this case, they're variables in case the game ever expands to support variable color schemes, such as the ability to load user-selected colors from a configuration file.

 TIP *The* Color *data type is actually a structure rather than a class. Within it are dozens of static members that return colors by name. You can also specify colors by Red-Green-Blue (RGB) values. Don't worry if any of the terms such as* structure *or* static member *are confusing at this point in the game—it'll all be clear eventually.*

The rest of the routine is a loop that iterates through all of the controls found in the collection Me.Controls. Me is a special keyword in VB that refers to the current object in which this code resides. In this case, the code is inside the form fGuess, so the loop iterates through all the controls that are part of that form. This includes the seven label controls.

The next If statement checks if the current control in the loop is a label (there could be other classes of controls on the form besides the seven labels, and in fact there will be other nonlabel controls by the time this project is complete). If the current control is a label, then a With statement begins. A With statement is a form of shorthand that allows you to avoid having to enter a control's name repeatedly in a block of code. A With statement begins with the keyword With and then contains a control name. The statements within the block can then omit the control name and refer to properties and other members with only a period and the member name. The With statement allows you to omit the control name to make code shorter and more readable.

The rest of the code inside the loop checks first to see if the currently considered label has a Tag property value of "Yes" (so that the lbResult label is never considered in this coloring code). If it does have a Tag value of "Yes", then the code performs a check to see if the Text (formerly called the Caption property in VB 6 and prior) of the currently considered label control matches that of an integer variable named Guess (whose declaration you'll see later). If this label has a Text value of 2 and the current value of Guess is 2, then the background and foreground colors of this label change to the values of the two color variables initialized at the beginning of the routine. If the Text value and variable value aren't equal, then the colors change to the system colors (using yet another built-in .NET Framework enumeration named KnownColor and a function to convert this enumeration to a color data type named FromKnownColor).

The purpose of this routine is to color the six numbered labels so that the label that matches the value of the Guess variable is blue and the other five labels remain black on gray. If one assumes that the value of Guess can only be 1 through 6, then this code will always color exactly one label white on blue and the other five black on gray.

Adding Your Own Property

For simplification, the previous section mentioned that an integer variable named Guess stores the number (1 through 6) that the user guesses for the next die roll. In truth, this was a little lie. Guess is actually a property added to the form. Listing 1-3 shows the code that defines this new property.

Listing 1-3. A Property Added to the fGuess *Form Class*

```
Private FGuess As Integer
Property Guess() As Integer
    Get
        Return FGuess
    End Get

    Set(ByVal Value As Integer)
        FGuess = Value
    End Set
End Property
```

There are actually two declarations in Listing 1-3, but they're related. The first is a private integer variable named FGuess. By declaring a variable private, you hide that variable from any code outside of this form class. Even if someone knew there was a variable named FGuess and tried to refer to it from outside the class, the compiler would complain and state that this variable was unknown.

The second declaration is for the Guess property itself. This declaration is more complex than the simple FGuess integer declaration. A property is defined in a block that has (up to) two subblocks within it: a Get function and a Set procedure. The Get function returns the value of the property whenever someone references it. That is, if a piece of code like the following executes:

```
If CInt(.Text) = Guess Then
    ....do stuff
Else
    ...do other stuff
End If
```

then the property's Get routine executes when it's time to evaluate the value of the Guess property. Note that the code doesn't simply have to return the value of a variable—it could go through any type or length of VB code to calculate or derive the value of the function before returning the current value.

> **CAUTION**   *By convention, I've always used a capital F as the first letter of private form-level variables, as in this example's integer variable* FGuess. *This could initially be confusing from the standpoint that the form in this project is named* fGuess, *coincidentally having the same name as the form-level variable.*

The Set procedure of a property does just the opposite—its purpose is to store the value whenever the property is written to. So, if code is written like this:

```
Guess = 1
```

then the property Set procedure executes. In the case of this property, the private FGuess variable is set to the value passed into the Set procedure and is returned as the current value of the Get function. This is the simplest, most trivial type of property to set up.

The astute reader might ask the following: "Why set up a property in this way?" This property is functionally equivalent to this declaration:

```
Public Guess as Integer
```

Here, a simple integer variable is declared, but it's specified as public instead of private. A public declaration means that the variable is visible to code outside of the class. Therefore, something functionally equivalent was created in fewer lines of code. Isn't that better?

> **TIP**   *A public variable declared on a class is also called a* field.

Under most circumstances, shorter code that does the same thing is indeed better, but in this situation that's not 100-percent correct. The reason is that setting up properties, even if they don't look like they're going to do much for the program yet, are much more powerful and allow you to conserve code later. You won't see this in action until the next chapter when you'll rewrite the Guess the Die Roll program. At this point, just know that properties are better than fields in helping you write more structured object-oriented code.

Setting Up Events, or Making the Program Do Something

The program now has a form class named fGuess that contains seven labels, a property named Guess, and a routine named UpdateGuessButtons that colors the six numbered labels to match the value in the property. What the program doesn't have yet is something that calls this routine. You want the UpdateGuessButtons routine to execute when a user clicks one of the six numbered labels. To accomplish the execution of code, the program needs an *event handler.*

Windows programs operate using an event-driven model, meaning that the program usually just sits around waiting for something (an *event*) to happen. This something is most commonly a mouse click or a key press. The type of mouse click (where clicked, which button, button going up or down) or the type of key press (which key, key going down or up) determines what the program does. Many of these events are preprogrammed—for instance, clicking in the title bar of a window and dragging it moves that window around on the desktop. You don't have to program that functionality into VB .NET programs because the functionality is built into the operating system. Ditto for sizing a window by dragging the lower-right corner—that functionality is built into the operating system.

However, coloring the six buttons (actually, labels) when one of them is clicked on isn't standard functionality, so you'll have to code that functionality. This means you have to write an event handler for the Click event of the six label controls. Listing 1-4 shows the code for that event handler.

Listing 1-4. Click *Event Handler for the Numbered Labels*

```
Private Sub cbButtonClick(ByVal sender As System.Object, _
    ByVal e As System.EventArgs) Handles lbOne.Click, _
    lbTwo.Click, lbThree.Click, lbFour.Click, lbFive.Click, lbSix.Click

    Guess = CInt(CType(sender, Label).Text)
    Call UpdateGuessButtons()
    Call RollTheDie()

    If dieResult = Guess Then
        lbResult.Text = "Correct!"
    Else
        lbResult.Text = "Try Again"
    End If
End Sub
```

An event handler in VB is just a standard procedure (declared Sub). They're also declared private, meaning that they're not callable from the outside of this class. This is desirable because event handler routines are usually not called directly in a program anyway—they're called as a result of the desired events occurring.

In this case, the desired event is one of the six labels being clicked. You can see that the declaration of this event handler states that this event is "attached" to the events lbOne.Click, lbTwo.Click, and so on all the way to lbSix.Click using the Handles keyword.

To set up an event handler, you use the code editor. At the top of the code-editing window are two drop-down boxes. The left drop-down box lists all controls on the current form. Once you select a control, the right drop-down list shows all the event handlers available for this control (see Figure 1-10). Selecting one of these event handlers adds an empty event handler procedure to your code.

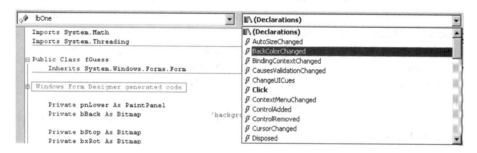

Figure 1-10. Viewing available event handlers for a control using the two drop-down boxes in the code editor

As you can see in Listing 1-4, you can make the same event handler handle events on multiple controls by listing those events after the Handles clause. This is easy to do manually.

The event handler in Listing 1-4 does a few things. The first thing it does is set the Guess property discussed in the previous section to some value. It obtains that value by casting the variable sender (which is passed into the event handler and represents the label that the user clicked) to a label type, then obtaining the value of the Text property of that label, and in turn converting that text (string) value to an integer. All of those things happen in a single line of code:

```
Guess = CInt(CType(sender, Label).Text)
```

Stated another way, when the user clicks the 3 label, this code converts the passed-in sender parameter to a label, converts the text of that label to an integer value, and stores it in the Guess property.

Code Size vs. Complexity

The previous lone line of code functions perfectly, but it does quite a few things at one time, which could be confusing to another programmer trying to figure out what the code is doing. There's a constant battle between keeping a program "short and sweet" and keeping it easy to read. You could rewrite the single line of code in the following, more verbose way:

```
Dim lb as Label
lb = CType(sender, Label)
Guess = Cint(lb.Text)
```

As always, it's up to the developer to decide whether to go for compactness or readability. Factors helping to determine this decision include whether other developers might someday be responsible for your code, your company, or your department coding standards and how you feel that day.

After the Guess integer is populated based on the clicked label, the next line of code calls the UpdateGuessButtons procedure (which has already been discussed). This procedure, as you might recall, colors the six labels in such a way that the one matching the value of the Guess property turns blue. The complete effect is the user clicking one of the labels and having that label change color.

The following line calls a procedure named RollTheDie. You'll learn more about this procedure in the "Tying the Functionality Together" section.

Finally, a new variable named dieResult, is compared with the value of the Guess property. If the values are equal, the seventh label changes to read *Correct!*, meaning the user correctly guessed the value of the die roll. If the value of the two variables isn't equal, the message *Try Again* displays in the seventh label.

This simple event handler represents the complete "flow" of the Guess the Die Roll game. When one of the numbered labels is clicked, the value is stored, the correct label is colored, the die is rolled, and the user is notified whether she won or lost. The game then waits for the user to click one of the labels again, and the process repeats.

Setting Up Methods

The procedures discussed in the previous section, UpdateGuessButtons, are called *methods*. A method is a procedure or function associated with a class. In the case of the Guess the Die Roll program, the UpdateGuessButtons method is associated with the fGuess class, which is a subclass of the .NET Framework form class.

Methods are often thought of as the "do work" code for a class. Because of this, it's common that a method name is an action phrase or a verb. Look at all of the method names associated with the final (version 1) fGuess class in the Guess the Die Roll program, and you'll see a pattern:

- RollTheDie

- UpdateDiePosition

- DrawDie

- UpdateGuessButtons

Each of the method names has a verb in it, and thus it's self-evident what task each method performs.

Rolling the Die

Okay, the mundane part of the game has been covered—selecting the number from 1–6, highlighting the selected button (label), and declaring whether the user wins or loses. Now for the graphics! Getting the die to bounce around at the bottom of the form takes several different techniques.

Introducing the Graphics

The die is an animation comprised of three sets of 36 frames, 108 frames in total. There's a set of 26 frames that shows the die rotating along its x-axis, a second set that shows rotation along its y-axis, and a third set that renders each of the six possible values rotating into its final position (each one of the six values comprises six frames). Each of the 36 frame sets exists in a 6×6 bitmap. Figure 1-11 shows the x-rotation bitmap. For instructions on how to create these bitmaps, refer to Appendix B, "Using POV-RAY and Moray," and Appendix C, "Using the BMPStich Utility."

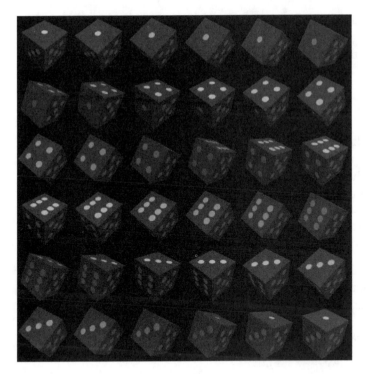

Figure 1-11. One of the three sets of 36 frames of die-rolling animations

Drawing the Graphics

The die rolling works something like a cartoon—the program first decides where on the screen it's going to draw the die. Then it selects one of the 108 frames for drawing, and finally it draws that frame to the screen.

Well, that's almost correct. Instead of drawing that frame directly to the screen, the program instead draws the frame to an intermediate bitmap and then draws *that* bitmap to the screen. Why this extra step? The main reason is screen flicker—copying graphics to a visible surface causes visual problems. This becomes important as more and more objects are rendered (like later when the program draws two dice instead of one die). If you draw to the final visible surface, you can run into screen-flickering issues that aren't appealing to users' eyes.

Describing the Die

Obviously, the program must know several pieces of information to correctly render the die on the form:

- The width and height of a frame

- Which frame to draw at a given time (and how to figure out which frame to draw next)

- The current location of the die on the form (as x and y coordinates)

- The current direction the die is moving

The width and height of a frame are constants, and you can declare them as such at the top of the fGuess form:

```
Const HGT As Integer = 144
Const WID As Integer = 144
```

These values depend on how the frames of the die were created. The current location of the die is also held in a pair of integer values:

```
Private diexPos As Integer
Private dieyPos As Integer
```

A lowercase die designates that these are variables describing the die, and xPos and yPos are abbreviations for the x position and y position.

 NOTE *Variable naming is certainly more art than science; I like to be somewhat consistent in my naming conventions, and I almost always use descriptive variable names except for loop variables or in short blocks of code where the declaration is clearly visible (I'll point out these exceptions along the way).*

Next are the two variables that represent the direction in which the die is moving:

```
Private diexDir As Integer          '-8 to 8
Private dieyDir As Integer          '-8 to 8, indicates direction moving
```

As the comments indicate, these two variables hold a value between –8 and 8 (but never 0). A die moving left has a negative x direction; a positive x direction indicates it's moving right. Likewise, negative and positive y directions indicate upward and downward movement, respectively. Because neither direction can ever be 0, the die is always moving in some sort of diagonal. This is intentional because the animated frames of the bitmap indicate movement along the "diag-onal" of the pseudo-3D surface upon which the die is rolling (in other words, it looks better if the die doesn't move straight up, down, left, or right).

There are three final variables to record the state of the die, the final result of the roll (1–6), the current frame being displayed (0–35), and a status variable to describe in which state the die is. You might recall from Listing 1-4 that the result variable is named dieResult. The other two variables are also appropriately named as follows:

```
Private dieResult As Integer        'result of the die, 1-6
Private dieFrame As Integer
Private dieStatus As DieMovementStatus = DieMovementStatus.dsLanding
```

All of the variables declared to this point have been simple integer types. Look at the type of the dieStatus variable—it's a type named DieMovementStatus. It's also being initialized to a value of dsLanding. Can it be that there's a variable type built into the .NET Framework that explicitly lists the possible status values for a rolling die? Sadly, no. Instead, you have to make you own variable type, called DieMovementStatus, and list the possible values with the declaration. As mentioned earlier, this is known as an *enumerated type*. Fortunately, it's easy to create your own:

```
Private Enum DieMovementStatus
    dmsStopped = 0
    dmsRolling = 1
    dmsLanding = 2
End Enum
Private dieStatus As DieMovementStatus = DieMovementStatus.dmsLanding
```

Enumerated types work just like integers under the hood, but they're much easier to use for two reasons. First, the code is much more readable as follows:

```
dieStatus = DieMovementStatus.Rolling
```

as opposed to the following:

```
dieStatus = 1
```

Second, enumerated types prevent the programmer from using an unknown or out-of-bounds value. The die status type has three possible values: 0, 1, or 2. If you were to use an integer to store the die status, there would be nothing to prevent the code from putting a 3, –3, or 1,203 into that variable. If other parts of that code are expecting only 0–2, there's no telling what bug you just introduced by placing an unexpected value in there.

Getting Down to Graphics

Okay, you've now declared all the variables required to keep track of the state of the die. Listing 1-5 shows the code that actually draws the die onto the background bitmap (named bmBack).

Listing 1-5. The DrawDie Routine

```
Private Sub DrawDie()

    Dim gr As Graphics
    Dim oBitmap As Bitmap

    Dim x As Integer = (dieFrame Mod 6) * WID
    Dim y As Integer = (dieFrame \ 6) * HGT
    Dim r As New System.Drawing.Rectangle(x, y, WID, HGT)

    If dieStatus = DieMovementStatus.dmsRolling Then
        'check quandrant rolling toward based on sign of xdir*ydir
        If (diexDir * dieyDir) > 0 Then
            oBitmap = bmyRot
        Else
            oBitmap = bmxRot
        End If
    Else
        oBitmap = bmStop
    End If

    gr = Graphics.FromImage(bmBack)
    Try
        gr.Clear(Color.Black)
        gr.DrawImage(oBitmap, diexPos, dieyPos, r, GraphicsUnit.Pixel)
    Finally
        gr.Dispose()
    End Try

    pnLower.Invalidate()
    Application.DoEvents()

End Sub
```

As usual, this rather tiny routine is doing quite a bit of work. The variables x and y are set up first. These variables represent the upper-left corner of one of the 36 frames within one of the three die animation bitmaps. The variable dieFrame holds the frame number, and the two equations shown in the declaration of variables x and y calculate the x and y coordinates of that frame. The backward slash in a math statement such as this one refers to an integer divide (where any decimal is truncated), and the Mod operator is the remainder operator after an integer divide. You can check out the math if you like with an example. Suppose dieFrame holds the value 17, then the upper-left corner of frame 17 would turn out to be as follows:

```
x = (17 mod 6) * 144 = 5 * 144 = 720
y = (17 \ 6) * 144 = 5 * 144 = 288
```

Thus, the upper-left corner of frame 17 is the coordinate (720, 288). Next, a .NET Framework class known as a Rectangle is instantiated and filled with these starting coordinates, as well as the constants that represent the width and height of a die frame:

```
Dim r As New System.Drawing.Rectangle(x, y, w, h)
```

This rectangle should now describe one frame of the die within one of the three animation bitmaps.

Now that the program knows the coordinates within the animation bitmaps needed to draw the frame, it needs to select the proper bitmap of the three available bitmaps. Listing 1-6 shows the selection code.

Listing 1-6. Selecting a Die Animation

```
    Dim oBitmap as Bitmap
... (code removed for clarity)
    If dStatus = DieMovementStatus.dmsRolling Then
        'check quandrant rolling towards based on sign of xdir*ydir
        If (diexDir * dieyDir) > 0 Then
            oBitmap = bmyRot
        Else
            oBitmap = bmxRot
        End If
    Else
        oBitmap = bmStop
    End If
```

As you'll recall, the three bitmaps represent the die rolling in the two directions diagonally and coming to a stop on each of the six values. These three bitmaps are held in variables named bmxRot, bmyRot, and bmStop, respectively (you'll see how to load these variables with bitmaps in the next section). When one of the three bitmaps is selected, it's placed in variable oBitmap for later.

The process of selecting which bitmap comes first determines what state the die is in (variable dieStatus). If that status is dmsRolling (the enumerated type value), then more work needs to happen. If the status is any other value (dsStopped or dsLanding), then the choice is easy—the "stopping" is the selected bitmap, which is held in the variable bmStop.

Now, let's get back to the dmsRolling case. What must be decided is if the die is rolling in "upper-left-to-lower-right" diagonal direction or in the "lower-left-to-upper-right" direction. These are the only two cases because the possibility that the die is moving along a true vertical or horizontal has already been eliminated. The direction in which the die is traveling is held in the diexDir and dieyDir variables. The value in these two variables is a random value between −8 to +8, with zero removed as a possibility. You can determine the diagonal direction by multiplying diexDir and dieyDir and looking at the sign of the result (proof that you *can* use geometry in real life). If the sign is negative, then the die is moving along the "lower-left-to-upper-right" diagonal. If the sign is positive, then it's moving along the other one. Figure 1-12 illustrates using the two direction variables to determine the direction of the diagonal.

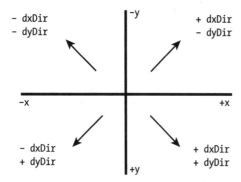

Figure 1-12. Determining which diagonal the die is rolling in by using simple geometry. Special thanks to my 10th-grade geometry teacher, Mr. Cosimi!

The code in Listing 1-6 performs this multiplication and selects either the bitmap bmxRot or bmyRot based on the sign of the result.

Okay, so now there's a source bitmap (one of the three animated die bitmaps), a source rectangle based on which frame to draw, and a destination bitmap (named bmBack). All that remains is to determine where to draw the die on the destination. This is easy, though, because variables that record the position of the die named diexPos and dieyPos already exist. So then, Listing 1-7 shows the code to draw the frame.

Listing 1-7. Drawing a Frame

```
Dim gr As Graphics
...(code removed for clarity)
gr = Graphics.FromImage(bmBack)
Try
    gr.Clear(Color.Black)
    gr.DrawImage(oBitmap, dxPos, dyPos, r, GraphicsUnit.Pixel)
Finally
    gr.Dispose()
End Try

pnLower.Invalidate()
Application.DoEvents()

End Sub
```

Now you're getting back into some .NET Framework stuff. The variable gr is an instance of the Graphics class. This class encapsulates the functionality of a drawing surface—sort of like an electronic piece of paper on which you can draw.

NOTE *Programmers experienced in Windows graphics programming might remember that a graphics surface is known as a* device context *in the Win32 API world.*

To draw on a bitmap (bmBack in this case), you must first create a Graphics object that's associated with the desired Bitmap object. You do this via the FromImage method on the Graphics class. Once you obtain the Graphics object associated with the bitmap, you can use the Clear method to change its color to black and then draw the rectangle from the source bitmap into it using the DrawImage method. Finally, because the graphics object encapsulates exhaustible resources in the operating system, you dispose of the Graphics object using the Dispose method.

Note how the word *Finally* begins the previous sentence, and the word *Finally* also exists in the code in Listing 1-7. The VB .NET keyword Finally is part of something known as a Try...Finally block and is part of a new (to VB, anyway) programming construct known as a *structured exception handler*. (Chapter 9,

"Learning Other Object-Oriented Programming Topics," covers structured exception handlers in detail.) The code after the Finally statement (the Dispose method on the Graphics object) is guaranteed to run, even if there are errors earlier in the method. This allows the programmer to ensure that certain code executes in all cases, even in cases that can't be anticipated—such as machines running out of random access memory (RAM) or networks going down.

The second-to-last line in Listing 1-7 calls the Invalidate method on an object called pnLower. (The next section describes this object.) For now, it's important to know that the Invalidate method on any control forces it to repaint itself. Furthermore, if you've wired up a Paint event to that control, that event will be called as well.

The last line, Application.DoEvents, is equivalent to the DoEvents command in VB 6. It gives the operating system a chance to do its own processing when your code is involved in a loop. It's required in this case so that the window's graphics can update between frames of the die animation.

Where to Draw the Die?

As mentioned earlier, the die frame is being drawn to a background bitmap as opposed to right on the form. So when does the background bitmap get transferred to the form? The final solution to this problem came down to some trial and error. My first attempt was to draw the background bitmap directly onto the form, but the result wasn't adequate. There was a visible flicker as each frame was drawn—in other words, the animation wasn't smooth.

I didn't know the immediate answer for controlling this flicker, so I did some research in the Usenet newsgroups via Google (a fabulous programmer's resource, by the way; I'm not sure how I learned anything new before the Internet became the tool it is today). I found several proposed solutions and tried one or two of them until I achieved a flicker-free result.

The problem had to do with something called a *control style* that exists for every window handle in Windows (every control, be it a button, listbox, or checkbox, has a window handle associated with it). The default control style for a form in Windows manages its own painting, meaning that the operating system is repainting the form and causing the flicker.

Fortunately, there's a way to override this behavior by changing these control style flags. Furthermore, there's a way to do this built into the .NET Framework; the Control class (the class upon which all of the user interface classes are built) has a SetStyle method that gives you the ability to manipulate the control flags.

Thinking in object-oriented terms, I decided that it would be useful (for this game and perhaps future games) to have a control that acts as the visible drawing surface for my bitmaps and automatically controls this flicker. I chose the built-in Framework class Panel upon which to base this new control. With only a few lines of code, my new control, the PaintPanel control, was born. The

`PaintPanel` class acts as the destination for all the bitmap drawing you'll be doing (see Listing 1-8).

Listing 1-8. The `PaintPanel` *Class*

```
Public Class PaintPanel
    Inherits Panel

    Public Sub New()
        MyBase.New()

        Me.SetStyle(ControlStyles.UserPaint, True)
        Me.SetStyle(ControlStyles.DoubleBuffer, True)
        Me.SetStyle(ControlStyles.AllPaintingInWmPaint, True)

    End Sub

End Class
```

> **NOTE** *You can add the code for the new class to an existing code module, or you can keep it within its own code module by selecting Add Class from the solution's right-click menu.*

Once again, you can see the power of object-oriented programming from the standpoint of an existing class and all of its functionality serving as the basis for a new class with different behavior. In this case, a method named `New` is declared. The `New` method on any class is a special type of method called the *constructor*. The constructor is called whenever a new instance of an object is created.

The first thing that the constructor for the `PaintPanel` does is call the constructor in the ancestor class (the `Panel` class) using the syntax `MyBase.New()`. This is an important step that makes sure any initialization code in the `Panel` class is also executed by `PaintPanel` class instances.

The remaining three lines call the `SetStyle` method mentioned earlier. The `Me` at the beginning of each `SetStyle` command isn't necessary in this case, but it's included for clarity. It specifies that the `SetStyle` method is attached to the current class (that is, the `PaintPanel` class). Because there's no `SetStyle` present in the `PaintPanel` class itself (Listing 1-8 shows the complete code for the `PaintPanel`), the language knows to look for the method in the base class, `Panel`. If the method isn't present in that class, then the ancestral chain is traced upward until the first `SetStyle` method is found, and that's the method that executes. One of the nice things about this type of organization is that you don't have to know exactly which class the desired method is in to call it. As long as a method exists in a base class, then you can call it from a descendant class.

The SetStyle method takes two parameters. The first is the style to change, listed as a member of an enumerated type named ControlStyles. The second parameter is a Boolean; it's either True to turn the style on or False to turn it off.

The three style bits that are changed in the PaintPanel get rid of the flickering when drawing directly onto the form. These three styles are documented fully in the online help for the ControlStyles enumeration.

Now that you've created a PaintPanel class to serve as the place where the die will be drawn, the next step is to create an instance of one and put it on the fGuess form. There are two ways to do this. The first way is to add the PaintPanel control to the Toolbox (the same place where the buttons, labels, and other such controls are), and then you can add instances of the class to any form on any project. Chapter 2, "Writing Your First Game, Again," demonstrates this method. The second way to add a new control to a form is through code, which was something you usually couldn't do in older versions of VB. Listing 1-9 shows the Load event of the fGuess form class.

Listing 1-9. The Load *Event for the Form*

```
Private Sub fGuess_Load(ByVal sender As System.Object, _
    ByVal e As System.EventArgs) Handles MyBase.Load

    pnLower = New PaintPanel
    pnLower.BackColor = Color.Black
    pnLower.Dock = DockStyle.Bottom
    pnLower.Visible = True
    AddHandler pnLower.Paint, AddressOf pnLower_Paint
    Me.Controls.Add(pnLower)
    pnLower.Height = Me.Height - lbResult.Height - lbResult.Top - 48

    bmBack = New Bitmap(pnLower.Width, pnLower.Height)

    'initialize the random number generator
    oRand = New Random()

    Guess = oRand.Next(1, 7)
    Call UpdateGuessButtons()
    dieFrame = (Guess - 1) * 6

    Dim a As Reflection.Assembly = _
        System.Reflection.Assembly.GetExecutingAssembly()
```

```
    bmxRot = New Bitmap( _
        a.GetManifestResourceStream("GuessTheDieRoll.dicexrot.bmp"))
    bmyRot = New Bitmap( _
        a.GetManifestResourceStream("GuessTheDieRoll.diceyrot.bmp"))
    bmStop = New Bitmap( _
        a.GetManifestResourceStream("GuessTheDieRoll.dicedone.bmp"))

    'initialize the location of the die
    diexPos = oRand.Next(0, pnLower.Width - WID)
    dieyPos = oRand.Next(0, pnLower.Height - HGT)
    DrawDie()

    lbResult.Text = ""
End Sub
```

The first portion of this event creates the PaintPanel instance, named pnLower (which is declared earlier in the fGuess class declaration). It sets a few properties, it sets the BackColor, Dock, and Visible properties to some values, and it "wires up" the Paint event to an event handler using the AddHandler statement. This statement is the runtime equivalent of setting up an event handler with the Handles clause at design time and associating an event with some code to be executed when that event fires. Next, the code adds the pnLower control to the form using the Controls.Add method of the Form class (Controls is a property on the form, which itself has an Add method). This step is required to make the form the owner of the new control.

 NOTE *More "free" functionality—the* BackColor, Dock, *and* Visible *properties, as well as the* Paint *event—aren't declared explicitly in* PaintPanel, *so they must exist in either the* Panel *class or somewhere further up the chain. You don't need to know within which subclass they're declared to use them here.*

The next section of code initializes an instance of a .NET Framework class named Random. This class handles "random" number generation. (Random values on computers are usually pseudo-random values chosen from a predetermined list.) As with all computer-based random values, a seed value gets things started. If a seed value isn't explicitly given, as in this case, then a seed value based on the current time is used.

Once a Random variable (named oRand) is instantiated, the Next method generates random numbers in any range desired. The first task asked of it is to come up with the initial value of the die, stored in the variable Guess. You'll notice that the range used here is 1 to 7, even though a die's range is obviously 1 through 6. The Random variable's Next method generated integer values less than, *but not including*, the upper bound given. Later in the procedure, the same Random class initializes the location of the die in a random spot on the PaintPanel. You may receive a runtime exception if your panel is not at least as wide and high as the form-level constants WID and HGT, which are both defined as 144 for this project.

The next part of the event fills the three bitmap variables bmxRot, bmyRot, and bmStop with bitmaps found in the executable. A variable named a is declared (so much for self-documenting variable names) and is initialized to the assembly that's executing (in other words, the assembly containing this program). The next lines of code load the named bitmaps into the three variables using a method of the Assembly class named GetManifestResourceStream. This method requires a resource name in the format namespace.file.ext. The namespace to use is the name of the project itself. GuessTheDieRoll is the name of this project; the namespace would change if the project had a different name.

TIP *You can add bitmaps and other resources to the project using the Solution Explorer. Once a bitmap is added, you must click it in the Solution Explorer and then switch over to the Properties window to change the Build Action property to* Embedded Resource.

The last piece of code that accomplishes drawing the die to the PaintPanel control is the PaintPanel class's Paint method, shown in Listing 1-10.

Listing 1-10. The Paint *Method of* PaintPanel

```
Private Sub pnLower_Paint(ByVal sender As System.Object, _
    ByVal e As System.Windows.Forms.PaintEventArgs)

    e.Graphics.DrawImage(bmBack, 0, 0)
End Sub
```

The Paint method passes in the Graphics object that's associated with the control being painted. As discussed earlier, the Graphics object is the virtual canvas upon which graphics drawing and painting happens. All that's required in this method is to transfer the background bitmap bBack to the PaintPanel class's canvas. The 0 and 0 parameters specify to draw the background bitmap in the upper-left corner of the PaintPanel class.

To review, this is the complete chain of events for drawing the die:

1. The program calculates the coordinates of the animated die source bitmap based on the current frame.

2. The program selects the correct animated die bitmap based on the state of the die and the direction it's rolling.

3. The program clears the background image.

4. The program draws a single die frame in the correct position on the background image.

5. The program invalidates the `PaintPanel` control, forcing the `Paint` method to be called.

6. The `Paint` method copies the background bitmap (containing the die frame) to the `PaintPanel` class.

Putting the Die in Its Place

The program can now handle drawing a single die frame onto a `PaintPanel` control, but it hasn't decided yet where to draw it or how to select which frame to draw. The initial location of the die is selected in the `Form_Load` event, as shown in Listing 1-11.

Listing 1-11. Choosing the Initial Die Location

```
oRand = New Random(Now.Ticks Mod 100)
<code deleted>
diexPos = oRand.Next(0, pnLower.Width - w)
dieyPos = oRand.Next(0, pnLower.Height - h)
DrawDie()
```

Here, the event uses the variable named oRand. The variables diexPos and dieyPos are initialized to some random number between 0 and the width/height of the panel less the width/height of a die frame (stored in the constants w and h, respectively). If the width/height of a die frame isn't subtracted, the die could easily be plopped partially off the right/bottom edge of the panel, as shown in Figure 1-13.

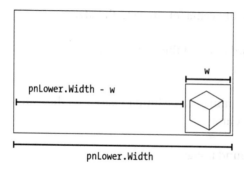

Figure 1-13. This shows why the range for placement of the die is the width of the panel less the width of the die frame. Ditto for the height.

Moving the Die

The UpdateDiePosition method moves the die around within the PaintPanel, as shown in Listing 1-12.

Listing 1-12. The UpdateDiePosition *Method*

```
Private Sub UpdateDiePosition()

        Select Case dieStatus
            Case DieStatus.dsLanding
                'if landing reduce the frame by 1, regardless of direction
                dieFrame -= 1
            Case DieStatus.dsRolling
                'frame goes up or down based on y direction
                dieFrame += Sign(dyDir)
        End Select
        If dieFrame < 0 Then dieFrame += 36
        If dieFrame > 35 Then dieFrame -= 36


        'update the position

        diexPos += diexDir

        'bounce for x
        If diexPos < 0 Then
            diexPos = 0
            diexDir = -diexDir
        End If
```

```
        If diexPos > pnLower.Width - w Then
            diexPos = pnLower.Width - w
            diexDir = -diexDir
        End If

        dieyPos += dieyDir
        'bounce for y
        If dieyPos < 0 Then
            dieyPos = 0
            dieyDir = -dieyDir
        End If
        If dieyPos > pnLower.Height - h Then
            dieyPos = pnLower.Height - h
            dieyDir = -dieyDir
        End If
    End Sub
```

Unlike some of the other code in this chapter, this code actually does less than it appears to do. The main purpose of this routine is to update the variables dieFrame, diexPos, and dieyPos.

dieFrame is the animated frame that the program is going to display. The frames are displayed in order, either from 0–35 or 35–0. If the die is rolling, this direction is determined by looking at the sign of variable dieyDir (which tells whether the die is moving up or down on the PaintPanel). If the die is about to land on a number, then the direction must be backward because of the way the six landing frames are arranged.

The two rolling animations are rendered in such a way so that they loop, meaning that frames 34, 35, and then 0 are played, and the animation looks smooth. Therefore, after updating dieFrame, the program checks to see if it has gone outside the 0–35 boundary. If it's outside the boundary, it's "fixed" by adding or subtracting 36, as shown here:

```
If dieFrame < 0 Then dieFrame += 36
If dieFrame > 35 Then dieFrame -= 36
```

Now, let's tackle the position. The amount of movement of the die in each direction is stored in the variables diexDir and dieyDir (remember, they can be positive or negative but not zero). To update the position, you simply add the direction:

```
diexPos += diexDir
```

The syntax of the preceding line might give you a moment of pause—unless you have some experience in a C-syntax language. The line is equivalent to the following line:

```
diexPos = diexPos + diexDir
```

Like for the frame variable, you must perform some range checking here. What if the die position has just been placed off the boundary of the PaintPanel? The effect you want is that when the die gets to the edge of the PaintPanel, it should bounce into the other direction. This is actually quite simple—when the die needs to bounce off of the left or right side, the sign of the diexDir variable is negated. Likewise, if the die is to bounce off the top or bottom, the value of dieyDir is negated. This is what the rest of the code in Listing 1-12 does. Note that it uses the same right and bottom boundaries that the original placement code does (not the complete width of the PaintPanel but the width less the width of an animated frame).

Tying the Functionality Together

All that remains at this point is to link the die moving and die drawing code into a loop to complete the animated effect. Of course, the loop has to have a built-in mechanism for ending so the die can stop rolling and display the result. Listing 1-13 shows the method RollTheDie, which contains that loop and other functionality.

Listing 1-13. The RollTheDie *Routine*

```
Private Sub RollTheDie()

    Dim iLoop As Integer = 0

    lbResult.Text = ""

    Do
        diexDir = oRand.Next(-8, 9)
    Loop Until Math.Abs(diexDir) > 3
    Do
        dieyDir = oRand.Next(-8, 9)
    Loop Until Math.Abs(dieyDir) > 3

        'decide what the result will be
        dieResult = oRand.Next(1, 7)
```

```
Application.DoEvents()
Me.Cursor = Cursors.WaitCursor

dieStatus = DieMovementStatus.dmsRolling
Do
    UpdateDiePosition()
    DrawDie()
    iLoop += 1

    Select Case dieStatus
        Case DieMovementStatus.dmsRolling
            'after 100 frames, have a 15% chance
            'that the die will stop rolling
            If iLoop > 100 And oRand.Next(1, 100) < 10 Then
                dieStatus = DieMovementStatus.dmsLanding
                iLoop = 0
                dieFrame = dieResult * 6
            End If

        Case DieMovementStatus.dmsLanding
            'die lands for 6 frames and stops
            If iLoop > 5 Then
                dieStatus = DieMovementStatus.dmsStopped
            End If
    End Select

    Loop Until dieStatus = DieMovementStatus.dmsStopped
    Me.Cursor = Cursors.Default
End Sub
```

This routine does the following tasks:

- Clears the result label (*Try Again* or *Correct!*).

- Initializes the diexDir and dieyDir variables. After a bit more experiment-
  ing, I decided the die didn't look right if the values of these variables were
  +/−1 or 2, so the final code initializes the value from +/−3 to +/−8.

- Picks what the die will land on (1–6).

- Sets the cursor to an hourglass.

- Starts the rolling loop. Within each loop iteration, the methods UpdateDiePosition and DrawDie are called.

- Sees if it's time to begin the die landing process. There is a 15-percent chance the die will land after drawing at least 100 frames.

- If the die is already in the landing process, then stop the loop after six frames are drawn (the sixth frame in the landing bitmap is the final frame).

- Sets the cursor back to an arrow.

You should be able to match up the code in Listing 1-13 with each of these tasks.

The End?

So, there it is—your first game! A few cool bitmaps, some animation code, some labels, and your first game is in the can. Before you really take off like a rocket and start writing some more games, let's take a second look at this one in Chapter 2, "Writing Your First Game, Again."

CHAPTER 2

Writing Your First Game, Again

WITH YOUR FIRST GAME out of the way, it's time to start thinking about your next game. It seems reasonable to come up with at least one more dice-related game because you have all those three-dimensional dice renderings and the code to make it bounce around realistically.

So, then, without knowing exactly which game to write next, what you need to do is grab the dice-related code out of the first project and bring it into the second project. The first reaction that strikes many programmers (especially inexperienced ones) is to copy the old project to a new project, hack out all the undesired code, and start over using some of the code from the first project as the starting point. Although this accomplishes the task and may even be easier in the short run, coding in this way can lead to nasty problems down the road. What if, for example, somebody finds a bug in the die-rolling code? For example, somebody reports that the die occasionally gets stuck when it bounces directly into the upper-right corner. After lots of careful debugging, you determine the cause of this bug and that the fix requires a fairly big rewrite to one of the routines. You finally get the bug squashed. Now, how many projects are you going to have to go back into and make the same fix?

Even if you decided to copy the die-rolling code from the first game into a second project, this task is hard because the die-related code is scattered all over the first project. The code contains declarations at the top of the project, bitmap setup code in the form's Load event, and several methods specific to the die rolling. You'd have to remove these individual pieces from the first project to copy them to the second project.

This lack of organization is only one problem with the die-rolling program as it currently exists. Here's another—what if your next game requires two dice rolling around? Or three? If you'll recall, most of the dice information resides in some "loose" variables that are fields on the Form class of the game. What organization would the code take if you wanted to have two dice? Would you simply double the number of loose variables (dieXPos1, dieyPos1, diexPos2, dieyPos2, and so on)? Or, perhaps you'd switch to arrays (diexPos(0) and dieyPos(0)).

Whether you've guessed it by now, this is a problem screaming out for an object-oriented solution. There should be a Die class in the program because the die is a "thing" in the program. One (perhaps overly) simple rule when writing an object-oriented program is to look for the "nouns" in a program and convert those nouns into classes. This is especially true if the nouns in question will be occurring in pairs or groups. By turning the die into a Die class, the program can merely instantiate two Die objects when you require two dice. This solution also scales upward—if some crazy game requires 1,000 dice, then the project could instantiate 1,000 Die class instances.

So, the object-oriented solution looks like it will handle the multiple dice problem. How about the organization problem? Well, if you can place all of the die functionality into a class, then you can probably find any bugs in that functionality in the Die class code, which you've separated from the rest of the program. If, for example, the die occasionally gets stuck in the upper-right corner, you'd know that the Die class—a specific part of the program—is behaving incorrectly. This eliminates the need to hunt for the bug in other parts of the program. Furthermore, if the Die class is compiled into something called an *assembly* (its own DLL file) and multiple files share that assembly, then fixing the bug in that one class will fix it in all programs that use it.

Understanding the Benefits of Rewriting

It sounds like the object-oriented approach is the way to go. However, do you really want to go back and rewrite a working program in another style? Is such an exercise worth the effort? Such an endeavor is most often worthwhile. First, you're really not "rewriting" the code per se; it's more a matter of "reorganizing" the code. It's certainly a different task than figuring out how to make the die bounce or determining what equation is needed to select the next frame in the animation. You did all that work in the previous chapter, and you don't need to repeat it.

 NOTE *Another term for reorganizing existing code is* refactoring.

The idea of refactoring an existing program is often a "one-step-back-two-steps-forward" approach. Imagine for a moment that you refactor the die code into a class, and that class is working perfectly in this die-rolling program. If you can get to that point, then making two dice roll for the next game will be much easier. If you really want to think ahead (to what will be covered at the end of the chapter—no peeking!), imagine a class that encapsulates a *set* of dice bouncing around and that contains a simple property on the class to control the number of dice to display. Now *that* would be useful!

TIP   *The benefit of refactoring existing programs is so great that I'm going to restate it one more time:* **Don't be afraid to rewrite code.**

Okay, that's settled, so you'll now rewrite the Guess the Die Roll program in a more object-oriented style, turning the die into a class. You'll also add a few (small) features as you go—things you can reuse in future chapters and games. Then, you'll once again take a step back to examine what you've got and decide if it's good enough. (Here's a hint: It won't be.)

Creating the Die Class

Your goal is to move all of the die-related code into the Die class and to shield, or *encapsulate*, this information from the outside. Encapsulation is one of the key features of object-oriented programming. The goal is to provide functionality to the user of a class without the user knowing about all of the implementation details that make that functionality work. With that in mind, Listing 2-1 shows the beginning of the Die class definition. If you'd like to follow along in Visual Studio, you can find this project in the folder GuessTheDieRoll2.

 NOTE   *You can download the code from the Downloads section of the Apress Web site (*http://www.apress.com*).*

Listing 2-1. Start of the Die *Class Declaration*

```
Public Class Die

    Private Enum DieStatus
        dsStopped = 0
        dsRolling = 1
        dsLanding = 2
    End Enum

    Private bmStop As Bitmap
    Private bmxRot As Bitmap
    Private bmyRot As Bitmap
    Private bmBack As Bitmap                    'background bitmap
```

```
Private oRand As New Random(Now.Ticks Mod 100)
Private FRollLoop As Integer

Private h As Integer = 144
Private w As Integer = 144

Private diexPos As Integer
Private dieyPos As Integer
Private diexDir As Integer
Private dieyDir As Integer
Private FStatus As DieStatus = DieStatus.dsLanding
Private FPanel As PaintPanel
```

First, note that the declaration of the Die class has no Inherits clause, as shown with the PaintPanel class in Chapter 1, "Developing Your First Game." If no Inherits clause is present, then this class inherits directly from the Object class. (Every class is an ancestor of Object.)

Second, note the declaration of all of the die-related variables. All of these variables are declared as private. As briefly discussed in the previous chapter, private means that these variables aren't visible from outside of the class. For example, the following code fragment isn't legal:

```
Dim d as new Die()
d.diexPos = 0
```

Although the variable diexPos is indeed declared as part of the Die class, because it's listed as private, it can't be accessed from code outside of the class. Because all the variables declared in Listing 2-1 are private, the user of the class can never know about these variables. This is a good start—it looks like all of the die position and direction information will be shielded from the outside programmer.

 TIP *It's useful to think of classes as "black boxes" during their development, where the users of the class (other programmers) are shielded from as much of the implementation details of the class as possible, and you as the class developer expose only what's needed to make the class functional. You should try to think in these terms even if you're the programmer on both sides of the curtain (the class developer and class user). You'll find this useful as you implement your classes in your programs, and you need only set a few properties or call a method or two to get the class up and running.*

Table 2-1 shows each of the variables declared in the Die class and the purposes they serve.

Table 2-1. The Die *Class Private Variables and Their Purposes*

VARIABLE NAME	TYPE	PURPOSE
bmStop	Bitmap	The bitmap that contains the 36 frames of the die stopping at each number (six frames per number).
bmxRot	Bitmap	The bitmap that contains 36 frames of the die rolling along the x-axis.
bmyRot	Bitmap	The bitmap that contains 36 frames of the die rolling along the y-axis.
bmBack	Bitmap	The off-screen, background bitmap upon which drawing is performed before being transferred to the PaintPanel class.
oRand	Random	Random number generator.
FRollLoop	Integer	Counts how many frames have been drawn. This integer determines when to stop rolling.
h	Integer	Constant, set to the height of one die frame (144).
w	Integer	Constant, set to the width of one die frame (144).
diexPos	Integer	The x (horizontal) position of the die on the PaintPanel.
dieyPos	Integer	The y (vertical) position of the die on the PaintPanel.
diexDir	Integer	The x direction the die moves in a frame. Positive means moving right, and negative means moving left. The value can't be 0.
dieyDir	Integer	The y direction the die moves in a frame. Positive means moving down, and negative means moving up. The value cannot be 0.
FStatus	DieStatus (Enumerated)	State of the die (rolling, stopping, stopped).
FPanel	PaintPanel	The PaintPanel class upon which the die is displayed.

Understanding Class Communication

The last declaration in Table 2-1, FPanel, is particularly interesting. Remember that the goal is to encapsulate all of the die rolling and bouncing code inside of this class. To determine when a die bounces off the edge of its container, the program must know some information about that container (the width and height). Thus, a private PaintPanel variable named FPanel is declared, and this variable will point to the PaintPanel used on the main form. This act of pointing to an object instance is a bit strange at first, so an abstract example might be in order:

```
Dim a as someobject
Dim b as someobject
a = new someobject()
b = a
a = nothing
```

In this code fragment, both a and b point to the same object instance in memory. The code following this fragment couldn't have b reference anything because the object being pointed to by the variable b was cleared when the variable a was set to nothing.

In the Die class, it's assumed that a PaintPanel instance will be declared somewhere outside of the class (such as in part of a form) and then passed into the class somehow and pointed to by the variable FPanel, such as the variable b pointing to the object instance a in the previous code fragment. The program will use the FPanel variable when deciding when and how the die will bounce.

Understanding the Power of Properties

You may have noticed there wasn't any private variable declared at the start of the class to store the value of the die (1 through 6). The version of the program written in the previous chapter contained a variable named dieResult. In the RollTheDie code, that variable was set to a random value between 1 and 6.

The Die class will obviously need a way to store the value of the die, and an integer value seems like it'll do the trick. However, it stands to reason that this variable probably can't be private like the variables declared so far. Why not? Well, anyone in need of a Die class will need to be able to query the class for the current value of the die. Therefore, this member will probably need to be declared public instead of private. A public member is accessible to everyone inside and outside of the class.

Your first instinct might be to declare another field but use the public keyword instead of the private keyword used on the other variables:

```
Public Result as Integer
```

This syntax is legal and will create the desired member. However, it can lead to big problems. For example, some other developer who is using your class in his own program could write the following code:

```
Dim d as new Die()
d.Result = 7
```

This code is also legal, but it could lead to some runtime errors at best or unexpected behavior at worst. Die values should be constrained from 1 to 6. You shouldn't allow a value of 7 (or 0, or 23, or −38 for that matter). How can you prevent this?

What's required is the ability to check the value of the field every time it's set and then disallow illegal values. You might be able to achieve this with a private field and a pair of public methods:

```
Private FResult as integer
Public Sub SetResult(I as Integer)
    If I > 0 and  I < 7 then
        FResult = I
      Else
        <trigger error>
    End If
End Sub
Public Function GetResult as Integer
    Return FResult
End Function
```

This is a variable (FResult) declared as private so outsiders can't modify it directly. It contains a method for setting the value (which contains appropriate error checking) and a method for returning the value. This solves the range-checking requirement. Therefore, the user of the class will use the following syntax when setting the value:

```
Dim d as new Die()
d.SetResult(7)
```

and your code will result in an error if the user enters an illegal value. The user would do something like the following to retrieve the value:

```
if d.GetResult() = 3 then
    msgbox "Die Roll is 3"
end if
```

You've solved the problem at the expense of a little syntactical awkwardness. The user of the class will now have to remember different method names every time he wants to set or retrieve the value of a variable attached to the Die class.

Fortunately, there's a better way to handle this, and that's by creating a property on the class. From the outside of the class, properties look no different from public fields. However, you can attach code that runs whenever the property is written to or read from, which means you can perform range checking or similar error checking. Listing 2-2 shows the declaration of one of the two properties on the Die class, the Result property.

Listing 2-2. A Lovely Property on the Lower West Side...

```
Private FResult As Integer        'result of the die, 1-6
Property Result() As Integer
    Get
        Return FResult
    End Get
    Set(ByVal Value As Integer)
        If Value < 1 Or Value > 6 Then
            Throw New Exception("Invalid Die Value")
        Else
            FResult = Value
        End If
    End Set
End Property
```

The declaration of the Result property should look a bit like the SetResult/GetResult solution offered earlier in that a function (named Get) and a sub (named Set) manipulate a value named FResult. The Set function also checks for the die boundaries and causes an error ("throws an exception" in .NET vernacular—more on that in Chapter 9, "Learning Other Object-Oriented Programming Topics"). The only real oddity is that these two procedures are themselves wrapped inside a Property..End Property block.

NOTE *It's a matter of style to declare the private fields* FFrame *and* FResult *in this location rather than at the top of the class with all of the other private fields. I like to keep my private fields near the properties as a matter of style.*

What this block of code produces is something that looks like a field variable from the outside but acts like a public pair of Get/Set methods when the property is written to or read. Thus, the following code:

```
Dim d as new Die()
d.Result = 7
```

actually calls the Set method inside the property, passing in 7 as the parameter. The code checks that parameter to make sure it's in range and throws an exception (generates an error) if the range check fails. If the range check succeeds, then the private field FResult takes the value of the parameter. When some other code attempts to read the value of the Result property, like so:

```
if d.Result = 3 then
    msgbox "Die Roll is 3"
end if
```

then the Get method executes, which in this case simply returns the value stored in the FResult variable.

The Die class has a second property named Frame, which represents the frame of animation from 0 to 35 being displayed from one of the bitmaps. Listing 2-3 shows the declaration of that property.

Listing 2-3. The Frame *Property*

```
Private FFrame As Integer
Property Frame() As Integer
    Get
        Return FFrame
    End Get
    Set(ByVal Value As Integer)
        FFrame = Value

        If FFrame < 0 Then FFrame += 36
        If FFrame > 35 Then FFrame -= 36
    End Set
End Property
```

The basic structure is the same, but there's no strict error checking in the Set method. Instead, if the value of the variable passed in lies outside of the range of 0–35, then it's brought back into that range by adding or subtracting 36 to it. This provides a "rollover" effect so that adding 1 to the value of the Frame property yields the sequence 33...34...35...0...1...2, and subtracting 1 yields the sequence 2...1...0...35...34...33. This works perfectly for the x-axis and y-axis rotation bitmaps because they were designed to animate in a continuous loop from the last frame back to the first.

Excluding the Private Field

Although both of these property examples serve as a wrapper for a private field, the presence of such a field isn't a requirement for creating a property. Consider the example shown in Listing 2-4, which is the declaration of the Guess property on the form.

Listing 2-4. A Property That Doesn't Use a Private Field

```
Property Guess() As Integer
    Get
        Dim c As Control

        For Each c In Me.Controls
            If TypeOf c Is Label Then
                With CType(c, Label)
                    If .BackColor.Equals(FBackColor) Then
                        Return CInt(.Text)
                    End If
                End With
            End If
        Next
    End Get

    Set(ByVal Value As Integer)

        Dim c As Control
        Dim bFound As Boolean = False

        For Each c In Me.Controls
            If TypeOf c Is Label Then
                With c
                    If .Tag = "Yes" AndAlso CInt(.Text) = Value Then
                        .BackColor = FBackColor
                        .ForeColor = FForeColor
                        bFound = True
                    Else
                        .BackColor = Color.FromKnownColor(KnownColor.Control)
                        .ForeColor = Color.Black
                    End If
                End With
            End If
        Next

        If Not bFound Then
            Throw New Exception("Guess must be a number from 1 to 6")
        End If
    End Set
End Property
```

Let's get away from the `Die` class for a moment and into the form that has the six numbered labels that the user clicks to make his guess. In Listing 2-4, the value of the `Guess` property is tied to the six numbered labels on the form.

When the user sets the `Guess` property, the program iterates through all of the controls on the form. When it finds a label control that has a `Tag` property value of "Yes" (your clue that this is one of the six clickable labels), and the `Text` property of the label equals the passed-in parameter value (which is the value that the `Guess` property was just set to), then this label's color changes to white text on a blue background. The other five labels are set to the default color.

When the `Guess` property is queried, the `Get` method runs. In this method, the program iterates through the controls on the form again, and when it finds the blue background label, it passes back the value of the label's `Text` property.

By doing this, you've "linked" the user interface elements with a property on the form, ensuring that they'll always stay in sync. There are many good uses for this, such as linking checks on menus to the value of properties or enabling/disabling user interface elements based on the value of properties. As you can see, having the ability to run code when a user reads or writes a value in your class can be extremely powerful.

Using One-Way Properties

Sometimes, it may be desirable to have a property that can be read but not written to. For example, you might have an `Area` property for a geometric shape that can be queried, but setting this property would be difficult (setting an area of 12 for a rectangle is ambiguous—does the user want a 6×2 rectangle, a 2×6 rectangle, a 3×4 rectangle, or a 4×3 rectangle, and so on?).

NOTE *The opposite—having a property that can be written to but not read—is technically possible but often impractical.*

In this circumstance, you can create a read-only property. The `Die` class has a read-only property named `IsNotRolling`, shown in Listing 2-5.

Listing 2-5. `IsNotRolling,` *a Read-Only Property*

```
ReadOnly Property IsNotRolling() As Boolean
    Get
        Return FStatus = DieStatus.dsStopped
    End Get
End Property
```

The ReadOnly keyword indicates that this property can't be written to, meaning that a Set method isn't required (or even allowed—the compiler will complain if you add a Set method to a read-only property). This is a good example of a property that isn't attached to a private field. In this case, the FStatus variable is checked and a true is returned if it's one of the three possible values. Instead of creating a property wrapped around the FStatus variable, this design allows you to encapsulate the enumerated type DieStatus inside of this class, meaning that the outside programmer won't ever need to know about it. In other words, the user of the class never really needs to know if the die is rolling or stopping, only if it stops. Creating the read-only, Boolean property shown in Listing 2-5 is the perfect solution.

There's one other read-only property in the Die class, which is an encapsulation of the Background bitmap. This is required in the current design because the contents of the background bitmap is copied to the PaintPanel control outside of the Die class, meaning that you have to expose the background bitmap to the outside world somehow. Listing 2-6 shows this declaration.

Listing 2-6. BackgroundPic, *a Second Read-Only Property*

```
ReadOnly Property BackgroundPic() As Bitmap
    Get
        Return bmBack
    End Get
End Property
```

Rearranging Methods

Two of the methods discussed in the first version of the Guess the Die Roll game, DrawDie and UpdateDiePosition, have moved into the Die class for version 2 of the program with barely any change. The first of these two methods, DrawDie, is the same except that two lines at the end of the first version of the method that forced the PaintPanel to redraw have moved out of the Die class. The second method, UpdateDiePosition, is almost the same, with the exception of one little new piece of functionality. See if you can spot the change in Listing 2-7.

Listing 2-7. UpdateDiePosition *Version 2.0*

```
Public Sub UpdateDiePosition()

        Select Case FStatus
            Case DieStatus.dsLanding
                'if landing reduce the frame by 1, regardless of direction
                Frame -= 1
```

```
        Case DieStatus.dsRolling
            'frame goes up or down based on x direction
            Frame += (1 * Sign(dieyDir))
End Select

'update the position
diexPos += diexDir

'bounce for x
If diexPos < 0 Then
    diexPos = 0
    diexDir = -diexDir
    Call WavPlayer.PlayWav("GuessTheDieRoll2.DIE1.WAV")
End If
If diexPos > FPanel.Width - w Then
    diexPos = FPanel.Width - w
    diexDir = -diexDir
    Call WavPlayer.PlayWav("GuessTheDieRoll2.DIE1.WAV")
End If

dieyPos += dieyDir
'bounce for y
If dieyPos < 0 Then
    dieyPos = 0
    dieyDir = -dieyDir
    Call WavPlayer.PlayWav("GuessTheDieRoll2.DIE2.WAV")
End If
If dieyPos > FPanel.Height - h Then
    dieyPos = FPanel.Height - h
    dieyDir = -dieyDir
    Call WavPlayer.PlayWav("GuessTheDieRoll2.DIE2.WAV")
End If

FRollLoop += 1

Select Case FStatus
    Case DieStatus.dsRolling
        'after 100 frames, check for a small
        'chance that the die will stop rolling
        If FRollLoop > 100 And oRand.Next(1, 100) < 10 Then
            FStatus = DieStatus.dsLanding
            FRollLoop = 0
```

```
            Frame = Result * 6
        End If

    Case DieStatus.dsLanding
        'die lands for 6 frames and stops
        If FRollLoop > 5 Then
            FStatus = DieStatus.dsStopped
        End If
    End Select

End Sub
```

Other than the slightly different variable names, this method is line for line like the method from the first version of the program—except for those interesting WavPlayer.PlayWav... lines. What the heck are those? You'll learn about those a bit later in the section "Playing WAV Files"; for now, let's finish talking about the Die class.

In addition to bringing over some existing methods, you created a few new methods when moving the die-rolling code into its own class. The first is InitializeRoll, shown in Listing 2-8.

Listing 2-8. The Public Method InitializeRoll

```
Public Sub InitializeRoll()

    Do
        diexDir = oRand.Next(-8, 9)
    Loop Until Abs(diexDir) > 3
    Do
        dieyDir = oRand.Next(-8, 9)
    Loop Until Abs(dieyDir) > 3
    Result = oRand.Next(1, 7)

    FRollLoop = 0
    FStatus = DieStatus.dsRolling

End Sub
```

As is often the case when refactoring a program, this code isn't new—the same functionality appears at the top of the method RollTheDie in the first version of the program. By splitting it out into its own area and moving it to the Die class, you now have a method that sets up the variables needed before a roll takes place. The horizontal and vertical movement directions are chosen, the loop counter is set back to zero, and the status variable is set to the rolling status.

The second new method in the Die class is InitializeLocation, shown in Listing 2-9. This is called right after an instance of the Die class is created to place it somewhere on the PaintPanel.

Listing 2-9. The Public Method InitializeLocation

```
Public Sub InitializeLocation()
    diexPos = oRand.Next(0, FPanel.Width - w)
    dieyPos = oRand.Next(0, FPanel.Height - h)
End Sub
```

Creating the Constructor

Believe it or not, the Die class is almost complete, built entirely out of code from the first program. This should help illustrate that object-oriented programming is as much a method of arranging code as anything else. When the second version of this program is complete, you'll have written in a distinctly non-object-oriented style and then again in a more object-oriented style, but the basic code is the same.

The last part of the Die class to discuss is the *constructor*. A constructor is a special method that gets called whenever a new instance of the class is created. So, whenever a user of the die class creates an instance, like this:

```
Dim d as new Die()
```

the constructor gets called. In Visual Basic (VB) .NET, constructors all have the name New(). Listing 2-10 shows the constructor for the Die class.

Listing 2-10. The Die *Class Constructor, Called Whenever a New Die Is Created*

```
Public Sub New(ByVal pn As PaintPanel)
    MyBase.New()

    FPanel = pn
    bmBack = New Bitmap(FPanel.Width, FPanel.Height)
```

```
Dim a As Reflection.Assembly = _
   System.Reflection.Assembly.GetExecutingAssembly()
bmxRot = New Bitmap(a.GetManifestResourceStream( _
   "GuessTheDieRoll2.dicexrot.bmp"))
bmyRot = New Bitmap(a.GetManifestResourceStream( _
   "GuessTheDieRoll2.diceyrot.bmp"))
bmStop = New Bitmap(a.GetManifestResourceStream( _
   "GuessTheDieRoll2.dicedone.bmp"))
End Sub
```

As hinted earlier, there's a place where an outside `PaintPanel` is passed in and gets pointed to by the local `PaintPanel` variable `FPanel`. That place is here; as you can see, the parameter on this constructor is of type `PaintPanel`, and the second line of this method sets that variable to the parameter.

The remainder of the method loads the die animation bitmaps out of the executable and into the bitmap variables, as shown in Chapter 1, "Developing Your First Game." The only other interesting line is the first one:

```
MyBase.New()
```

`MyBase` is a keyword that represents the class above this one in the class hierarchy. This line calls the constructor in the base class. This ensures that any initialization needed by this class that's performed in the base class is performed. In this particular class, the call to `MyBase.New` is probably not needed because the `Die` class inherits directly from `Object`, which has no initialization in its constructor. However, making the call certainly doesn't hurt anything, so it's included as a matter of convention.

Playing WAV Files

If you want your game to play sounds, you can use a WAV file to do it. You'll reuse the `WavPlayer` class throughout the book whenever you want to include sound effects in a game. Listing 2-11 shows the code for the class.

Listing 2-11. The WavPlayer *Class*

```
Public Class WavPlayer

   Private Declare Function sndPlaySound Lib "winmm.dll" _
      Alias "sndPlaySoundA" (ByVal szSound As Byte(), _
         ByVal UFlags As Int32) As Int32
```

```
Private Const SND_ASYNC As Integer = 1
Private Const SND_MEMORY As Integer = 4

Public Shared Sub PlayWav(ByVal cResName As String)

    Dim a as System.Reflection.Assembly
    Dim oS As System.IO.Stream

    a = System.Reflection.Assembly.GetExecutingAssembly
    oS = a.GetManifestResourceStream(cResName)

    'couldn't find the sound
    If oS Is Nothing Then Exit Sub
    Dim bstr(oS.Length) As Byte

    Try
        oS.Read(bstr, 0, Int(oS.Length))
        sndPlaySound(bstr, SND_ASYNC Or SND_MEMORY)
    Finally
        bstr = Nothing
        oS = Nothing
    End Try

End Sub
End Class
```

There are two interesting points to notice about this class. First, the class declares a reference to an external function found in a Windows system file named winmm.dll. Those familiar with the VB 6 world should recognize this as an Application Programming Interface (API) declaration. VB .NET also supports interfacing with the Windows API when you can't find the functionality you need in the .NET Framework. This particular declaration is for the sndPlaySound function, which will play a sound in WAV file format either from disk or from memory. This class assumes the passed-in sound is embedded in the current application as a resource (see the bitmap resource example in Chapter 1, "Developing Your First Game," to see how to embed resources in your projects). The class loads the resource into a byte array named bstr and then passes the byte array to the API function.

The second interesting thing about this class is that its lone method, PlayWav, is declared with the Shared keyword on it. The Shared keyword on a method indicates that you can call this method without creating an instance of this class first. That is, instead of having to do this:

```
Dim wp as new WavPlayer()
wp.PlayWav("GuessTheDieRoll2.DIE1.WAV")
```

you can instead simply do this:

```
WavPlayer.PlayWav("GuessTheDieRoll2.DIE1.WAV")
```

You'll encounter various examples of shared methods in the .NET Framework as you learn your way around it.

Putting the Die Class to Work

Now that you've completed the Die class, all that remains is to create an instance of it and let it do the work for you. Truth be told, the form that makes up the game has little code left now that the die code is in its own class.

This chapter has already discussed the Guess property, which stores the guess that the user makes with the six label buttons. The Form_Load event is similar to the first version of the program from Chapter 1, "Developing Your First Game." However, instead of initializing all the die-related variables, an instance of the Die class is instantiated and methods of that class are called. Listing 2-12 shows this new Form_Load event, which sets up the PaintPanel and Die classes.

Listing 2-12. The Form_Load *Event*

```
Private Sub fGuess_Load(ByVal sender As System.Object, _
    ByVal e As System.EventArgs) Handles MyBase.Load

    pnLower = New PaintPanel()
    pnLower.BackColor = Color.Black
    pnLower.Dock = DockStyle.Bottom
    pnLower.Visible = True

    AddHandler pnLower.Paint, AddressOf pnLower_Paint
    Me.Controls.Add(pnLower)
    pnLower.Height = Me.Height - lbResult.Height - lbResult.Top - 48

    Guess = 1

    'start the die on whatever the initial guess is
    d = New Die(pnLower)
    d.Frame = (Guess - 1) * 6
```

```
'initialize the location of the die
d.InitializeLocation()
d.DrawDie()

lbResult.Text = ""
End Sub
```

The Die variable, named simply d in this program (shame on me for bad naming conventions), is instantiated by calling the constructor, as shown in Listing 2-12. Remember that the constructor for the Die class takes a PaintPanel as its parameter. Then, the initial frame of the die is set so that the die is drawn showing the value in the Guess property, which is hard-coded to 1 in this version of the program. Finally, methods on the die are called to initialize its location (within the PaintPanel) and draw it.

The only other major part of the program is the RollTheDie method on the form, which runs the die-rolling code in a loop to handle the moving and drawing of the die in the PaintPanel. Listing 2-13 shows this method, which is basically a loop that calls the die updating/painting methods until the roll ends.

Listing 2-13. RollTheDie *Version 2.0*

```
Private Sub RollTheDie()
    Dim iLoop As Integer = 0

    lbResult.Text = ""

    Application.DoEvents()
    Me.Cursor = Cursors.WaitCursor

    d.InitializeRoll()
    Do
        d.UpdateDiePosition()
        d.DrawDie()
        pnLower.Invalidate()
        Application.DoEvents()
    Loop Until d.IsNotRolling

    If d.Result = Guess Then
        lbResult.Text = "Correct!"
    Else
        lbResult.Text = "Try Again"
    End If
    Me.Cursor = Cursors.Default

End Sub
```

This procedure first clears the result label (and calls the ubiquitous DoEvents to refresh the screen before entering the big loop). The InitializeRoll method on the Die instance is then called, which picks the direction vectors (shown in Listing 2-8), starts the loop counter, and sets the status to dsRolling. In each iteration, the position is updated, the correct frame is drawn, and the PaintPanel is invalidated (which draws the die frame onto it). This loop continues, until the die stops, using the read-only property called IsNotRolling. You can see now why it wasn't required to expose the DieStatus enumeration and Status property—this code only needs to know when to stop the loop.

Once the loop is done, the result of the die is compared to the user's guess, and the label updates to tell the user whether he guessed correctly.

Summarizing Version 2

You've now converted your little game into an object-oriented program. You've encapsulated the major "thing" in the game, the die, into its own class. Therefore, you've hidden most of its functionality in such a way that the outside user doesn't have to worry about the details of how those various functions work anymore.

Are you happy with the code, though? Is the Die class passing the "black box" test? In other words, if you wanted to post the class onto a Web site, sell it, or in some other way make it available to other programmers to use in their own programs, you would have to include a pretty big ReadMe file or at least a sample program to show the programmer how to use it. See, there's still quite a bit of code outside the class that sets up the die and even more code (the big loop shown in Listing 2-13) to get the thing rolling. Not only that, but the die is closely related to another class, the PaintPanel. In fact, you can't use the Die class without also using the PaintPanel class.

In the book *Design Patterns Explained: A New Perspective on Object-Oriented Design* by Alan Shalloway and James R. Trott (Addison-Wesley, 2001), an object in an object-oriented programming framework is defined as an "entity with responsibilities." Furthermore, good object-oriented design dictates that objects should be coded to be responsible for themselves. Making an object responsible for itself means that other objects won't have to be responsible for it.

In version 2 of the program (version 1 of the Die class), you went part of the way to make the object responsible for itself, but you didn't go far enough. The user of the class is still required to do all of the following things to get the die on the screen:

- Instantiate the PaintPanel.

- Instantiate the Die instance.

- Attach the Die to a PaintPanel (this step and the previous one happen together in the constructor).

- Set up the first animation frame to display (this is optional and defaults to 0).

- Wire the Paint event of the PaintPanel to the BackgroundPic found in the die.

- Call InitializeLocation.

- Call DrawDie.

Then, the programmer must create the loop (or one similar to it) shown in Listing 2-13 to get the die rolling and bouncing. It's obvious that this Die class isn't responsible for itself, so you still have some work to do.

Taking a Step Back

You could rewrite this program again, moving a bit more code into the Die class until there's a Roll method on the die and make it so that the user of the Die class knows as little as possible. However, that still wouldn't get you exactly where you'd like this program to go. There would still be at least a little necessary knowledge required to "link up" the Die instance to the PaintPanel.

Furthermore, there would still be some more die-related code left to write. As mentioned, it seems like a logical requirement to have two dice rolling around (you couldn't write a craps game without two dice, now could you?). But why restrict it to two dice? You might want to write a Yahtzee knockoff someday, which means you'd need five dice rattling around on the screen. Clearly, the best solution is to allow an arbitrary number of dice to display. This requirement brings up some new challenges, such as the following:

- **Creating a new class**: You need to write code that stores the multiple instances of the dice, initializes all of them, and gets them all rolling until they stop. This sounds like a new class that contains Die class instances within it.

- **Using multiple graphics**: As written now, each instance of the Die class loads the three animated dice bitmaps. A multiple dice program using the current class would load the same bitmaps into memory multiple times—not very efficient.

- **Preventing overlap**: You don't want one die to obscure another, especially when they come to a stop, or the user won't be able to read one of them. There needs to be a way to prevent this.

It seems obvious that you need some type of "manager" class to manage the multiple instances of dice. The best-sounding implementation would be if the number of dice to be displayed was a simple property set by the programmer. This manager class would store the multiple die instances, encapsulate the rolling code, and perform the drawing onto the `PaintPanel`.

After considering the design of this `DiceManager` for quite awhile, you might have a "eureka" moment—an idea that solves all of the previous requirements and wraps the entire "multiple dice" concept into a neat little package. The solution is this: Combine the `DiceManager` and the `PaintPanel` concept into a single class: the `DicePanel` class.

Version 3: Creating the DicePanel Class

The `DicePanel` class will be a descendant of the .NET Framework `Panel` class (just as the old `PaintPanel` was), which in turn is a descendant of the `Control` class. The entire object hierarchy looks like this:

```
System.Object
    System.MarshalByRefObject
        System.ComponentModel.Component
            System.Windows.Forms.Control
                System.Windows.Forms.ScrollableControl
                    System.Windows.Forms.Panel
                        DicePanel
```

All of the classes listed in this hierarchy (except for the `DicePanel` you're about to write, of course) are part of the .NET Framework. The `Control` class serves as the ancestor to any class with a visual representation. Therefore, all of the buttons, list-boxes, labels, radio buttons, checkboxes, and so forth are all descendants of the `Control` class. You might also notice that the `Panel` class inherits directly from something called `ScrollableControl`, which provides support for scrolling—functionality that won't be used in the `DicePanel` class.

Because the `DicePanel` will be a descendant of the `Control` class, you'll be able to place it into the Toolbox on the left side of Visual Studio, which means a programmer will have the ability to drag a `DicePanel` off of the Toolbox and onto any form (how cool is that?). To set this behavior up, however, it's best to separate the `DicePanel` into its own project.

 NOTE *You can find the* `DicePanel` *project in the source code for this book. If you haven't downloaded the code yet, you can do so in the Downloads section of the Apress Web site* (`http://www.apress.com`).

Creating the DicePanel Project

The Class Library project is the type of project you should use when creating new controls to add to the Toolbox. If desired, you can put multiple classes inside the class library if it makes sense to do so (if the classes have similar or related functionality, for example). In this case, you'll implement just one class in this library.

Figure 2-1 shows how to create a new VB .NET Class Library solution. This is the project into which you should copy the entire `DieStuff.vb` contents from version 2 of the die-rolling program (the `Die` and `PaintPanel` classes). Once you copy the old code into the new project, the refactoring will begin once again.

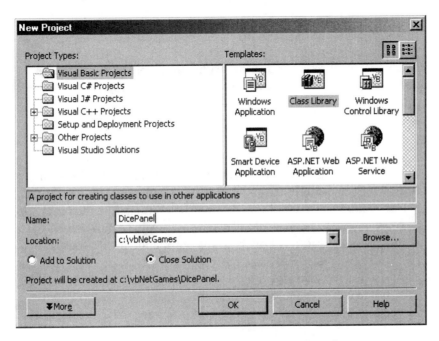

Figure 2-1. Creating a Class Library solution in Visual Studio

Setting Up More Refactoring

The `DicePanel` class will be acting as the "manager" class to some number of individual dice, so it still makes sense to have a `Die` class encapsulate the functionality of a single die. However, you don't ever need to expose this `Die` class to the outside world. Remember, good object-oriented programming dictates that objects should be responsible for themselves and rely on as little outside help as possible. To that end, the DicePanel class will completely encapsulate the functionality of the die initializing, rolling, drawing, and bouncing—meaning that the user of the DicePanel won't ever be exposed to all of that code.

Because the Die class is to be used only by the DicePanel class, you can structure the classes in this way:

```
Class DiceManager
<...stuff>

    Private Class Die
        <...stuff>
    End Class
End Class
```

As you can see, the Die class is declared within the DicePanel class, and it's declared private, meaning that the outside world can't access it.

Moving Code

You've moved several things out of the Die class and into the DicePanel class in this final version. First, you declared and initialized the animated bitmaps in the DicePanel class. This means that only one copy of each bitmap is in memory, regardless of how many dice the panel will display. Also, you've moved the background bitmap (named bmBack) that serves as the destination for off-screen rendering into the DicePanel class.

Furthermore, you've moved the Paint event, which used to be external to the PaintPanel class and on the main form of the game, inside the DicePanel class. This means the user of the class doesn't need to do anything to get the panel to draw correctly. Listing 2-14 shows the Paint functionality.

Listing 2-14. Painting and Resizing Functionality Inside of DicePanel

```
Protected Overrides Sub OnPaint(ByVal e As _
    System.Windows.Forms.PaintEventArgs)
      MyBase.OnPaint(e)

      'happens in design mode
      If bmBack Is Nothing Then
         Call SetupBackgroundAndDice()
      End If
      e.Graphics.DrawImageUnscaled(bmBack, 0, 0)
   End Sub
```

```
Protected Overrides Sub OnResize(ByVal eventargs As System.EventArgs)
    MyBase.OnResize(eventargs)
    Call SetupBackgroundAndDice()
End Sub
```

Actually, I fibbed a bit when I said the Paint *event* moved into the class. In truth, the OnPaint *method* is what's coded here. What's the difference? The programmer of a class can't code event-handling code for that class. If you'll recall, events are notification routines called by the class to the outside world and aren't part of the class itself. For example, the Click event of a button isn't part of the button class; it's the code that the user of the button runs whenever a button in his project is clicked.

Most class events are raised from inside a method whose name corresponds to the event with the prefix On. Thus, the Paint method of a class is raised from a method named OnPaint. So, if you want code to execute when your control is painted, you need to override the OnPaint method of the class.

Note how the first line of the OnPaint method shown in Listing 2-14 calls the OnPaint method in the base class. This is necessary so that events are raised properly. Without this call, users of the class would never receive a Paint event. The remainder of the OnPaint method performs the copy of the background bitmap to the surface of the panel, creating the background bitmap first if it hasn't already been created.

Listing 2-14 shows a second method—the OnResize method, which is called whenever the DicePanel changes size. If the panel changes size, then the size of the background bitmap must change to match; otherwise, it might not be large enough to render the panel correctly. Like the OnPaint method, the OnResize method also calls the base class method of the same name, ensuring that users of the class receive their events.

Examining the Die Class Changes

The Die class itself has several additions, but the original code hasn't changed drastically. Listing 2-15 shows the interface for versions 2 and 3 of the Die class, side by side. The interface is a listing of all the members of a class without showing all of the declarations. (The private fields have been removed from this listing.) Once you've studied the two interfaces, you'll learn about the major differences.

Listing 2-15. Interfaces of the Previous Version of the Die *Class and the New One*

```
Public Class Die  (version 2)
    Public Sub New(ByVal pn As PaintPanel)

    Property Frame() As Integer
    Property Result() As Integer

    Public Sub InitializeLocation()
    Public Sub UpdateDiePosition()
    Public Sub InitializeRoll()
    Public Sub DrawDie()

    ReadOnly Property IsNotRolling() As Boolean
    ReadOnly Property BackgroundPic() As Bitmap

End Class

Private Class Die (version 3)
    Public Sub New(ByVal pn As DicePanel)
    Private Property Frame() As Integer
    Property Result() As Integer

    Private Property xPos() As Integer
    Private Property yPos() As Integer

    Private Sub BounceX()
    Private Sub BounceY()

    Public Sub InitializeLocation()
    Public Sub UpdateDiePosition()
    Public Sub InitializeRoll()
    Public Sub DrawDie(ByVal bDest As Bitmap)

    ReadOnly Property IsNotRolling() As Boolean
    ReadOnly Property IsRolling() As Boolean

    ReadOnly Property Rect() As Rectangle
    Public Function Overlapping(ByVal d As Die) As Boolean
    Public Sub HandleCollision(ByVal d As Die)
    Public Sub HandleBounceX(ByVal d As Die)
    Public Sub HandleBounceY(ByVal d As Die)

End Class
```

The following are the major differences between the two versions:

The Frame property is private in version 3. The Die class is 100-percent responsible for controlling what animated frame it's on, which follows the rule that objects should be responsible for themselves. Declaring a property private makes certain that outside users of class have no ability to modify or use this member.

The variables that control the location of the die, xPos and yPos, are now properties (still private, though). This allows for range checking whenever the property is modified.

There are new (private) methods named BounceX and BounceY. These methods reverse the direction of xPos or yPos and call a method on the DicePanel that serves to raise an event named DieBounced. This allows the DicePanel to communicate to the outside world whenever a die bounces, allowing that program to react by playing a WAV file or performing some other custom action.

The method DrawDie now takes a bitmap parameter, which serves as the bitmap into which the die should be drawn.

The property BackgoundPic has been removed in version 3 because the background bitmap is now declared inside the DicePanel class.

The method IsRolling, the opposite of the existing version 2 method IsNotRolling, is used for clarity (it's clearer to write Do While d.IsRolling than it is to write Do While Not d.IsNotRolling).

The property Rect and the methods Overlapping, HandleCollision, HandleBounceX, and HandleBounceY are new. These are all new members that handle collisions between multiple dice. The "Detecting Collisions" section covers collision handling.

Examining the DicePanel Functionality

Now that you've seen how the Dice class represents a single die, it's time to see how the DicePanel class manages some number of them. How can a variable number of Die classes be stored? One common way in VB 6 to store a variable number of something is to use an array. There's a class in the .NET Framework called the ArrayList that allows for the management of a variable number of classes. The DicePanel declares an ArrayList named aDice. When it's time to create the Die instances and put them in the ArrayList, the GenerateDice method is called. Listing 2-16 shows this method, which is called whenever the Die class instances need to be created.

Listing 2-16. The Method GenerateDice

```
Private Sub GenerateDice()

    Dim d As Die
    Dim dOld As Die
    Dim bDone As Boolean
    Dim iTry As Integer

    aDice = New ArrayList()

    Do While aDice.Count < NumDice
        d = New Die(Me)
        iTry = 0

        Do
            iTry += 1
            bDone = True
            d.InitializeLocation()
            For Each dOld In aDice
                If d.Overlapping(dOld) Then
                    bDone = False
                End If
            Next
        Loop Until bDone Or iTry > 1000
        aDice.Add(d)
    Loop

End Sub
```

This method sets up a loop that runs for a number of iterations equal to the value of the property NumDice. In each iteration, it creates a new Die instance and stores it (temporarily) in the variable d. The program then places this Die instance into its initial location. Once placed, the die location is compared to all previously created dice to see if their locations overlap. If the program finds an overlap, it initializes the current die location again. This happens repeatedly until a "free" location is found or until the location setting is attempted 1,000 times for this die, at which point the loop terminates. The 1,000 upper limit is required because the possibility exists that the panel is simply too small to hold unique locations for the number of dice in the NumDice property. If this was true and the upper bound wasn't present, attempting to put the dice in a unique location would result in an infinite loop.

Let's look at the `NumDice` property in Listing 2-17.

Listing 2-17. Controlling the Number of Dice on the Panel via the `NumDice` *Property*

```
Private FNumDice As Integer = 2
Property NumDice() As Integer
    Get
        Return FNumDice
    End Get
    Set(ByVal Value As Integer)
        FNumDice = Value

        'regen dice, but only if done once before, or else dbl init
        If DiceGenerated() Then
            Dim d As Die
            GenerateDice()
            Clear()
            For Each d In aDice
                d.DrawDie(bmBack)
            Next
            Me.Invalidate()
        End If
    End Set
End Property
```

This looks like many of the other property examples you've seen so far.
A private variable, `FNumDice`, stores the value of the property. When the property
changes, the `GenerateDice` method is called and then each die is drawn onto the
panel. Putting the generation/redrawing code here allows dice to be generated
and drawn at design time, something you'll see once you place the control into
the Toolbox. Listing 2-18 shows the constructor of the `DicePanel`.

Listing 2-18. The `DicePanel` *Constructor*

```
Public Sub New()
    MyBase.New()

    Me.SetStyle(ControlStyles.UserPaint, True)
    Me.SetStyle(ControlStyles.DoubleBuffer, True)
    Me.SetStyle(ControlStyles.AllPaintingInWmPaint, True)
```

```
Me.BackColor = Color.Black

Dim a As Reflection.Assembly = System.Reflection.Assembly.GetExecutingAssembly()
FbmxRot = New Bitmap(a.GetManifestResourceStream("DicePanel.dicexrot.bmp"))
FbmyRot = New Bitmap(a.GetManifestResourceStream("DicePanel.diceyrot.bmp"))
FbmStop = New Bitmap(a.GetManifestResourceStream("DicePanel.dicedone.bmp"))

'NEW. this used to be a major pain in VB6
FbmxRot.MakeTransparent(Color.Black)
FbmyRot.MakeTransparent(Color.Black)
FbmStop.MakeTransparent(Color.Black)


End Sub
```

You've seen much of this code before. The SetStyle commands are necessary to control flicker. The animation bitmaps are loaded dynamically using the GetManifestResourceStream method of the assembly class. Note that the name-space name has changed from the program name to DicePanel, which is declared at the top of this unit. The last three lines convert the color black in the three bitmaps to a transparent color, which means the black isn't drawn. This is neces-sary when two dice are close to each other or else the black border of one die would overlap another, as shown in Figure 2-2. (Making a color transparent in VB 6 requires a series of API calls.)

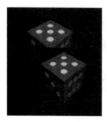

Figure 2-2. Making the black transparent

There are several "mini-members" that perform some simple tasks in Listing 2-19. The Result property, a read-only property, returns the result of all the dice in the panel by iterating through the ArrayList and adding up the Result values of each die. The AllDiceStopped property is used when rolling the dice to determine when all the dice have stopped moving. Finally, the sub OnDieBounced is a protected method that raises the DieBounced event so that the user of the class can react or perform some custom task whenever a die bounces off of an edge or off of another die. Listing 2-19 shows these three members.

NOTE *Chapter 1, "Developing Your First Game," covered public and private members. You can see a protected member in the current class and any subclass of the current class, but it's unavailable (as if it was private) to everyone outside of the class.*

Listing 2-19. Some Miscellaneous Tasks Implemented in the DicePanel

```
ReadOnly Property Result() As Integer
    Get
        Dim d As Die
        Dim i As Integer = 0

        For Each d In aDice
            i += d.Result
        Next
        Return i
    End Get
End Property

Private ReadOnly Property AllDiceStopped() As Boolean
    Get
        Dim d As Die
        Dim r As Boolean

        r = True
        For Each d In aDice
            If d.IsRolling Then
                r = False
            End If
        Next

        Return r
    End Get
End Property

Protected Sub OnDieBounced()
    RaiseEvent DieBounced()
End Sub
```

Detecting Collisions

The last two major topics to discuss are the RollDice method and the members that deal with collision detection in both the Die class and the DicePanel class. This section discusses all the collision detection code because this functionality is new to this version of the die program.

You can handle collision detection in a two-dimensional world in several different ways. In this case, you want the dice to "bounce," or change direction, when they collide either with one of the walls of the panel or with each other. The wall bouncing code has been in place since the first version of the program, so all that remains is the code to check for the dice colliding with each other.

This code can get a little tricky. The challenge is to avoid two dice getting "stuck together." For example, if two dice overlap, you want to change the direction of one or both so they move away from each other.

I tried a few different methods with varying results and finally settled on this basic case-by-case scenario: I decided that if two dice collided, they would either bounce in the x direction or in the y direction, but not both. The direction I chose depended on the position of the dice. If the two dice are closer together in height (along y) than in width (along x), this means they're arranged in more of a horizontal fashion, as opposed to a vertical arrangement. In that case, I decided it would look more natural to have them bounce in the x direction. Similarly, if the dice are closer together in width, then they're arranged in a more vertical orientation, so it looks more natural to have them bounce in the y direction.

Figure 2-3 illustrates the two orientations. You can see two pairs of dice: one pair in a horizontal arrangement and the other pair in a vertical arrangement.

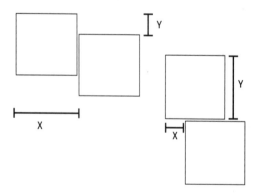

Figure 2-3. Deciding on which way to bounce dice that have just collided

You can determine which of these two orientations to use by comparing the x and y positions of the two dice. As shown in Figure 2-3, if the dice are next to each other, then the difference between x positions will be greater than the difference between y positions. If the dice are one over the other, then the y difference is greater.

Once you've determined if the dice are in the horizontal or vertical orientation, you can decide how they collide. There are three possible outcomes for each orientation. Table 2-2 shows the six possibilities and the action the dice will take.

Table 2-2. Six Cases of Colliding Dice and How to Bounce Them

CASE	DESCRIPTION	RESULT
A	The left and right dice run into each other.	Bounce both dice along x.
B	The leftmost die catches up to rightmost die.	Bounce leftmost die along x.
C	The rightmost die catches up to leftmost die.	Bounce rightmost die along x.
D	The top and bottom dice run into each other.	Bounce both dice along y.
E	The topmost die catches up to the bottommost die.	Bounce topmost die along y.
F	The bottommost die catches up to the topmost die.	Bounce bottommost die along y.

Figure 2-4 illustrates the six cases. (The letter in Table 2-2 matches the letters in the illustration.)

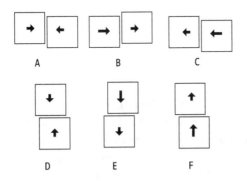

Figure 2-4. The six die collision cases

This solution works well because it automatically prevents the two dice from getting stuck together and bouncing back and forth repeatedly while inside each other's boundaries. The reason this is so is that the six cases aren't all of the possible cases or orientations of dice. For example, it doesn't include the case when the dice in the horizontal orientation are moving away from one another. So, if two dice moving toward each other collide and both bounce away from each other, the next frame won't handle the collision because the two dice are no longer in one of the six cases shown in Table 2-2. In my first attempts at collision detection I had trouble taking into account dice that were close together or overlapping but were moving away from each other.

Now that you've learned about the algorithm in plain English, you'll see it in VB code. Listing 2-20 shows the HandleCollisions method on the DicePanel class.

Listing 2-20. The HandleCollisions *Method*

```
Private Sub HandleCollisions()

    Dim di As Die
    Dim dj As Die
    Dim i As Integer
    Dim j As Integer

   If NumDice = 1 Then Exit Sub

    'can't use foreach loops here,
    'want to start j loop index AFTER first loop
    For i = 0 To aDice.Count - 2
        For j = i + 1 To aDice.Count - 1
            di = aDice.Item(i)
            dj = aDice.Item(j)
            di.HandleCollision(dj)
        Next
    Next
End Sub
```

This routine is nothing special—it's simply a nested loop that handles every pair of dice in the aDice ArrayList. One interesting note is that it doesn't use the For..Each enumerator of the ArrayList because neither of the two loops actually iterates through every item in the list. The first loop starts at the beginning and stops one short of the end, and the second loop starts one more than the beginning of the first loop and goes to the end. Using a For..Each construct for the two loops would result in each pair of dice being checked for collisions twice—clearly an undesired effect.

The "meat" of the collision-handling algorithm happens in the Die class itself in the method HandleCollision (yet another example of making an object responsible for itself). Listing 2-21 shows that method, along with the Overlapping method and the Rect property.

Listing 2-21. Collision-Handling Members on the Die *Class*

```
Public Sub HandleCollision(ByVal d As Die)
    If Me.Overlapping(d) Then
        If Abs(d.yPos - Me.yPos) <= Abs(d.xPos - Me.xPos) Then
            HandleBounceX(d)
        Else
            HandleBounceY(d)
        End If
    End If
End Sub

ReadOnly Property Rect() As Rectangle
    Get
        Return New Rectangle(xPos, yPos, w, h)
    End Get
End Property

Public Function Overlapping(ByVal d As Die) As Boolean
    Return d.Rect.IntersectsWith(Me.Rect)
End Function
```

The Rect and Overlapping members use features already built into the .NET Framework, so the code within them is pretty short. Rect simply returns an instance of the .NET Framework Rectangle class, using the current position, and the constant size of the Die object in question. The Overlapping method leverages the use of the built-in Rectangle.IntersectsWith method.

The HandleCollision method takes a Die instance as a parameter, which might seem odd at first because this method is in the Die class itself. By passing a Die instance into a method on the Die class, you have two Die instances at your disposal—the parameter instance (named d) and the current instance that this code is running for (named Me).

The first line of the HandleCollision method checks to see if the two dice are overlapping. If they aren't overlapping, then of course there's no need to make them bounce off each other. If they're overlapping, however, the next comparison determines whether the two dice are in the horizontal arrangement or the vertical arrangement. (Refer to Figure 2-3 to compare the If statement with the illustration of this comparison.) Once the orientation is determined, one of two private methods named HandleBounceX (horizontal arrangement) or HandleBounceY (vertical arrangement) are called.

Listing 2-22 shows the HandleBounceX method (HandleBounceY is similar). This method creates new die variables named dLeft and dRight and assigns them to the two die (d and Me) for readability (the leftmost die being assigned to dLeft, and the rightmost to dRight, of course). Then, the three cases are checked and acted upon as discussed earlier. If the leftmost die and rightmost die are moving toward each other, both of them are bounced. If instead the dice are moving in the same direction and one has caught the other, then only the faster-moving die is bounced). Other cases (such as the two dice moving away from each other) result in no change in direction.

Listing 2-22. HandleBounceX

```
Private Sub HandleBounceX(ByVal d As Die)

    Dim dLeft As Die
    Dim dRight As Die

    If Me.xPos < d.xPos Then
        dLeft = Me
        dRight = d
    Else
        dLeft = d
        dRight = Me
    End If


    'moving toward each other
    If dLeft.dxDir > 0 And dRight.dxDir < 0 Then
        Me.BounceX()
        d.BounceX()
        Exit Sub
    End If


    'moving right, left one caught up to right one
    If dLeft.dxDir > 0 And dRight.dxDir > 0 Then
        dLeft.BounceX()
        Exit Sub
    End If


    'moving left, right one caught up to left one
    If dLeft.dxDir < 0 And dRight.dxDir < 0 Then
        dRight.BounceX()
    End If


End Sub
```

Testing the Collisions

The collision code might all seem logical enough when being explained in a book, but coming up with this collision system, as mentioned earlier, took a bit of trial and error. Before clearly defining the algorithm outlined previously, I kept getting in situations where the dice would get stuck together and keep bouncing back and forth while inside each other.

While debugging, it was difficult to see exactly which dice were touching (I was using a big test form with the NumDice property cranked up to 7 so that collisions were happening often, as opposed to having only two dice that didn't collide as frequently). I decided it would be useful to be able to see the bounding box of each die, along with a line indicating what direction the die was traveling. This could help me truly see when two dice were overlapping and in what direction they were moving.

You can accomplish this by adding a new property to the DicePanel named DebugDrawMode. This is a simple Boolean property that does nothing fancy or tricky inside its Get or Set members:

```
Private FDebugDrawMode As Boolean = False
Property DebugDrawMode() As Boolean
    Get
        Return FDebugDrawMode
    End Get
    Set(ByVal Value As Boolean)
        FDebugDrawMode = Value
    End Set
End Property
```

TIP *Even though I could have used a field instead of a property on this member, I always choose to spend the extra 10 seconds and set up the property using the Get and Set methods in case I want to attach code for reading/writing to the property later.*

Once set up, all you have to do is add a few short lines to the DrawDie method to add the rectangle and direction line. Listing 2-23 shows the new code in the DrawDie method to show a bounding box and directional line, only if the DebugDrawMode property on the panel is set to True.

Listing 2-23. New Code in the DrawDie *Method*

```
gr = Graphics.FromImage(bDest)
Try
    gr.DrawImage(b, xPos, yPos, r, GraphicsUnit.Pixel)
    If FPanel.DebugDrawMode Then
        Dim p As New Pen(Color.Yellow)
        Dim xc, yc As Single

        xc = xPos + (w \ 2)
        yc = yPos + (h \ 2)

        gr.DrawRectangle(p, Me.Rect)
        gr.DrawLine(p, xc, yc, xc + Sign(dxDir) * (w \ 2), yc + Sign(dyDir) * (h \ 2))
    End If
Finally
    gr.Dispose()
    End Try
```

You can see the new If statement right after the DrawImage method draws the animated die bitmap onto the Graphics instance. This code uses the Pen class in the .NET Framework to set up a yellow pen (you could even get fancy and make the color of the debug drawing configurable). Then, two new methods on the Graphics class are called. The DrawRectangle method draws a rectangle in the location specified. You already have a method named Rect on the Die class that returns a Rectangle instance, so you can simply pass the result of that method into the DrawRectangle method, along with the Pen instance.

Drawing the line takes a bit of math because you want to start at the center of the die and draw out to one of the corners. Once you determine the endpoints of the line, you can simply call the DrawLine method on the Graphics class, passing in these endpoints and the yellow Pen instance as parameters. The result of these few lines of code, shown in Figure 2-5, is instrumental in helping you debug the collision-handling code.

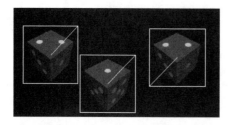

Figure 2-5. Dice drawn with extra lines to denote bounding boxes and direction

Testing the Classes

Because you created this project as a class library, you can't test it by simply clicking the Run button. Instead, you need to create a new solution that contains multiple projects.

One effective way of testing the classes in a class library is to create a "dummy" project that can use the test classes. Creating an empty or nearly empty test project allows you to focus on debugging the code in your class library instead of trying to simultaneously work with code both inside and outside of the class library. Only when you've gotten your class library classes working as desired should you use the classes in a real project.

To create a new test application, select File ➤ New ➤ Project from the Visual Studio .NET application menu. Select a Windows Application under Visual Basic Projects (unless you feel like switching over to the dark side of curly-braced C# programming, that is).

Once you've created this blank project (and solution), the next step is to add the DicePanel project to the solution. You accomplish this by right-clicking the solution name in the Solution Explorer and selecting Add ➤ Existing Project from the context menu. Figure 2-6 shows the menu layout when the solution is selected. Once selected, navigate to the DicePanel.vbProj filename and select it.

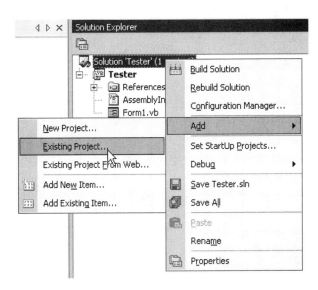

Figure 2-6. Creating a multiproject solution by adding a project to an existing solution

The next step is to create a reference in the tester project to the DicePanel project. To do this, right-click References in the tester project (make sure you get the correct project now that you have two of them) and select Add Reference. Then, select the Projects tab and select the DicePanel project.

Once you add the reference, you can create and use the DicePanel class in your projects. Listing 2-24 shows the code that makes up the tester project, which creates a DicePanel and links it up to roll when clicked.

Listing 2-24. The Tester Project

```
Public Class Form1
    Inherits System.Windows.Forms.Form

#Windows Form Designer generated code

    Private d As DicePanel.DicePanel.DicePanel

    Private Sub Form1_Load(ByVal sender As System.Object, _
        ByVal e As System.EventArgs) Handles MyBase.Load

        d = New DicePanel.DicePanel.DicePanel()

        With d
            .Dock = DockStyle.Fill
            .Height = Me.Height - 32
            .NumDice = 3
            .DebugDrawMode = True
        End With
        AddHandler d.Click, AddressOf ClickIt
        Me.Controls.Add(d)

    End Sub

    Private Sub ClickIt(ByVal sender As Object, _
        ByVal e As System.EventArgs)

        d.RollDice()
    End Sub
End Class
```

It might look a bit odd that the variable d is declared as DicePanel.DicePanel.DicePanel. The three words represent the assembly name (DLL name), the namespace, and then the class name. In hindsight, it might be better to name some of these things differently or perhaps even remove the namespace from inside the assembly (which would probably require "fixing" the bitmap loading code because it refers to the assembly/namespace names). The rest of the code creates the DicePanel instance, sets a few properties, and adds it to the form's `Controls` collection (a required step whenever you add visual controls to a form at runtime). The `AddHandler` statement "wires up" the `Click` event to a procedure named `ClickIt`, which calls the `RollDice` method on the `DicePanel` instance.

Now that you've set up the two projects in a single solution and linked them via their references, you can set breakpoints in the class library and do "live" debugging to get your classes working.

Adding the DicePanel Class to the Toolbox

The runtime addition of controls to a form is one way to get things done; however, as promised earlier in the chapter, you can add the `DicePanel` class to the Visual Studio Toolbox.

You can customize the Visual Studio Toolbox by right-clicking on it. You can choose to add a new tab to the Toolbox to differentiate your controls from the default .NET controls. Selecting Add Tab from the menu accomplishes this and brings up an editor so you can type in the name of your new tab.

Once you add the new tab, right-click again and select Add/Remove Items from the menu. The Customize Toolbox dialog box, shown in Figure 2-7, will display (make sure to be patient because this dialog box can take quite a while to load).

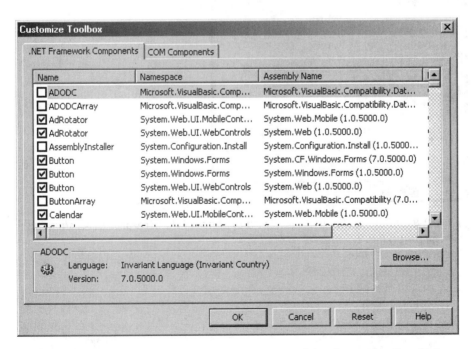

Figure 2-7. The Customize Toolbox dialog box, one of the slowest-loading dialog boxes in Visual Studio

Click the Browse button to add your new class library to the list of available class library references (first click the .NET Components tab at the top of the dialog box). Then, navigate to the DicePanel.dll file in the bin directory of the DicePanel project folder. Once added, you can select OK and the DicePanel will appear in the Toolbox! Now you can simply drag it from the Toolbox onto any form of any project. Doing so automatically creates a reference in that project to DicePanel.dll, similar to the way you created the reference manually in the previous example. Figure 2-8 shows the Properties window in design mode including all of the "for free" properties of the Panel class and the new properties of the DicePanel class, specifically NumDice, DebugDrawMode, and Result (shown in gray because it's a read-only property).

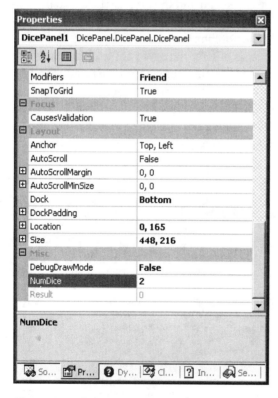

Figure 2-8. The Properties window for an instance of the DicePanel *class, showing the new properties. Try that in VB 6!*

TIP *You can choose to add the* DicePanel *project to a blank solution as in the previous section if you plan to debug the* DicePanel *code. You don't have to add the source code projects of your Toolbox classes just to use the class on a form, just like you don't have to add a class library project containing the* Button *class just to use the* Button *class on a form.*

Having the new class properties display in the Properties window is really cool, but Figure 2-8 demonstrates a few minor problems. First, notice that all three of the new properties appear under the heading *Misc.* It would be nice if you could customize that heading for each property. Also, the little help box at the bottom of the Properties window doesn't show any help, except for the name of the property in bold. It would be useful to add help for the programmers using your class.

You can accomplish both of these tasks by using something called *attributes.* An attribute is a special type of class that can document, describe, or categorize your code. This is a new concept to pre-.NET programmers, so it requires some clarification. An attribute is an instance of a class that's created and "attached" to various elements of your project; you can associate an attribute with a class or any member of a class such as a property, event, or method. These attributes can help document the author of the code and the last time it was modified, and they can define security constraints. One example of the usefulness of attributes is the ability to write a program that takes your compiled code as input, extracts the documentation-specific attributes, and outputs them into a specific format (Extensible Markup Language, Word document, and so on).

Several built-in attributes help document class properties. Listing 2-25 shows the NumDice property on the DicePanel with three attributes attached to it.

Listing 2-25. NumDice *Property with Attributes*

```
<Description("Number of Dice in the Panel"), _
    Category("Dice"), _
    DefaultValue(2)> _
    Property NumDice() As Integer
        Get
            Return FNumDice
        End Get
    <... code removed ...>
    End Property
```

CAUTION   *You'll need to add* System.ComponentModel *to the* Imports *section at the top of any code file that you want to extend through attributes.*

You define the attributes between brackets before the property name. Note the line-continuation characters, meaning that the attributes are actually on the same line as the member name (something I hope Microsoft changes in future versions of VB .NET, but oh well...).

There are three attributes here: The Description attribute defines the little help text at the bottom of the Properties window, the Category attribute defines the name of the branch under which the attribute will sit in the Properties window, and the DefaultValue attribute defines, of all things, the default value of the property. After setting up all three of the DicePanel properties, the result is an improved Properties window, as shown in Figure 2-9.

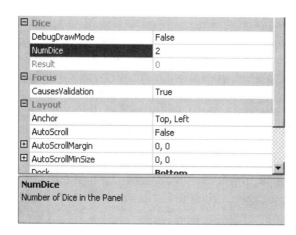

Figure 2-9. The Properties window, showing how you now have complete mastery of creating properties, putting them in categories, and writing help, all by using attributes

As mentioned, attributes are a powerful concept. Consult the online help for more information. Use *attributes* and *metadata* as your search criteria to get you started.

Now That's Reusable Stuff!

It might have taken seemingly forever to get there, but this chapter has pounded this DicePanel class into submission; you've created a truly reusable class. It uses encapsulation to hide as many details as possible so that the outside user of the class doesn't need to know anything about its internal operation—the user simply adds an instance to a form, sets some properties, and off he goes.

The next chapter takes the DicePanel class and uses it in some more complex games, showing how to use the classes you build as the foundation for new, larger projects. These next games will even be fun to play for more than five seconds, I promise. . . .

NOTE *You can find a final version of the dice-rolling program, named* GuessTheDieRoll3, *in the source code for the book. This project differs from the previous project; it uses the Toolbox version of the* DicePanel *class, and it uses two dice, meaning that the player has to guess a number from 2–12 rather than from 1–6.*

Understanding Object-Oriented Programming from the Start

YOU'VE SPENT A LOT OF TIME perfecting the DicePanel class, and now you're going to put that time to good use. In this chapter, you'll write a new game that uses the DicePanel class. This game requires two dice and a set of numbered "tiles" that disappear based on the dice value. This game has dozens of variations; this one is called *NineTiles* (see Figure 3-1).

Figure 3-1. NineTiles

The object of NineTiles is to remove tiles that add up to the result shown on the two dice. In Figure 3-1, the dice result is 8, so you could get rid of the 8 tile, the 5 and 3 tiles, the 6 and 2 tiles, or the 7 and 1 tiles. The dice then roll again, and you repeat the process. You win the game if you get rid of all nine tiles, and you lose the game if the remaining tiles don't add up to the dice result. In a slightly devious twist, the game automatically restarts after you win or lose, which gives it a somewhat addictive quality (you want your games to be played over and over, right?).

Starting the NineTiles Project

Believe it or not, about half of the NineTiles project is already written. You're half done, and you haven't even started! Of course, this is because you slavishly spent time refining the DicePanel class in Chapter 1, "Developing Your First Game," and Chapter 2, "Writing Your First Game, Again." Now that the DicePanel class is a Toolbox control, you can simply drop it on a form and use it.

That's exactly what you should do to start the NineTiles project. Create a new Windows Forms project in Visual Studio .NET and then drop a DicePanel instance onto the default form. You can see how this might look in Figure 3-2. If you'd rather look at the completed code that comes with the book, you can download the NineTiles project.

NOTE *You can download the code from the Downloads section of the Apress Web site (*http://www.apress.com*).*

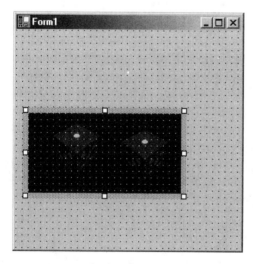

Figure 3-2. A new project with a DicePanel *control*

As mentioned previously, because DicePanel is an ancestor of the Panel control, you get all the functionality of the parent control in the descendant "for free." So, use some of the Panel functionality in the NineTiles game by setting the Dock property of the DicePanel instance to Bottom and the Name property to oDice. You can also make the default height a bit larger by using the Properties window or by resizing the actual control in design mode.

As for the form in the project, rename it to fMain (also remember to change the startup Object of the project as shown in Chapter 1, "Developing Your First Game"). In addition, you can also change the Size property, making the form much higher than wide, change the Text property (which becomes the window caption on a form instance) to NineTiles, change the font to 8-point Tahoma (my favorite font), and change the FormBorderStyle property to Fixed3D. These decisions are all personal preference, of course. As the designer of this game, you can choose the font, title, border style, and where to put the dice. You can also decide how the dice will look; for instance, instead of the 3D, slightly transparent red color, you could just as easily go with ivory or green and a 2D-only look.

Once you've set up these initial properties, you can test run the project to see how it looks. Once satisfied that the form is set up and the DicePanel looks okay, it's time to tackle the numbered tiles.

NOTE *I'm the type of programmer who test runs the program continuously throughout its development, both checking how it looks and checking if the various features I'm coding are working.*

Creating More Classes

It seems reasonable to encapsulate the functionality of the nine numbered tiles inside of its own class, just like the DicePanel class encapsulates the dice functionality. The structure of this new class will be served well if it's similar to DicePanel from the standpoint that a single "manager" class will handle several instances of some type of "tile" data class. There are a few differences, however. One is that the "tile manager" class has a fixed number of tiles to manage (nine), so you don't need a property to control the number of items to manage (such as the NumDice property on the DicePanel class). Another major difference is that the tiles don't move around within the panel, meaning you don't have to worry about position, direction, or collision-handling code. It's for these reasons that you'll create new classes for the numbered tiles functionality as opposed to somehow combining the functionality of the DicePanel class and this new class.

NOTE *See the "Looking Back on the Design" section at the end of this chapter for alternate ways of organizing this project.*

Creating a NumberPanel Class

The manager class in the NineTiles game is NumberPanel. Some of the functionality of the NumberPanel class is similar to the DicePanel class, including the following:

- Inheriting the control from the .NET Framework Panel control and using the SetStyle method to eliminate flicker

- Loading the graphics from a bitmap embedded in the executable

- Using a background bitmap where drawing takes place and overriding the Panel control's OnPaint method to copy the background bitmap to the foreground

- Using an embedded class that manages the individual instances of the "managed" objects, which in this case are the nine tiles

Because these parts of the NumberPanel class are so similar to the DicePanel class, this chapter won't cover their functionality. It focuses instead on the new topics.

Manipulating the Tiles: Left-Clicking

Users manipulate the tiles by clicking them. When a tile is left-clicked, it toggles between facing forward and backward, with an animated sequence moving from one state to the other. If a numbered panel is right-clicked, then all the backward tiles disappear from the panel—but only if these backward tiles add up to the numbers on the dice (this is perhaps better demonstrated than explained; you'll get it in about two seconds if you play the game). Figure 3-3 shows the game in progress, demonstrating the three states of the tiles. In this game, the 5, 7, and 9 tiles have already been removed, and the 4 and 3 tiles have been flipped over to match the amount rolled on the dice. A right-click at this point of the game removes the 4 and 3 tiles.

Figure 3-3. NineTiles in action

Listing 3-1 shows the code within the NumberPanel class that handles the left-click portion of the tile movement. The OnMouseDown method determines exactly which tile was clicked with the help of the private TileFromPoint method. Once the program determines the clicked-on tile, it calls the ToggleFacing method on the TileData object (this is the class that encapsulates a single tile object, discussed in the "Creating the TileData Class" section).

Listing 3-1. Manipulating a Tile

```
Private Function TileFromPoint(ByVal x As Long, _
    ByVal y As Long) As Integer
    TileFromPoint = ((y \ IRAD) * 3) + (x \ IRAD)
End Function
```

```
Protected Overrides Sub OnMouseDown(ByVal e As _
    System.Windows.Forms.MouseEventArgs)
    MyBase.OnMouseDown(e)

    If e.Button = MouseButtons.Left Then
        If Not FInAnimation Then
            FInAnimation = True

            Try
                Dim aTile As TileData
                Dim iTile As Integer = TileFromPoint(e.X, e.Y)

                aTile = oTiles(iTile)
                aTile.ToggleFacing
            Catch oEX As Exception
                Throw oEX
            Finally
                FInAnimation = False
            End Try

        End If
    End If
End Sub
ReadOnly Property bInAnimation()
    Get
        Return FInAnimation
    End Get
End Property
```

A private variable named FInAnimation is checked and set at the beginning and end of the OnMouseDown method. This Boolean variable indicates that the NumberPanel is currently in an animation loop and helps prevent further user action while this action is occurring. This helps prevent, for example, a double-click from animating a tile twice. As you can see, the variable is set back to False at the end of the method within a Finally block, which guarantees that this line will run regardless of errors that might occur in Listing 3-1.

This FInAnimation variable is exposed to the outside world via the read-only property bInAnimation, also shown in Listing 3-1.

NOTE *The code uses the* OnMouseDown *method instead of* OnClick *because* OnMouseDown *makes available the button or buttons that were used, and* OnClick *doesn't.*

Manipulating the Tiles: Right-Clicking

When the NumberPanel is right-clicked, the reversed tiles need to disappear. There's one important trick to this functionality that greatly affects the design of the program, however. The backward tiles disappear from the panel *only if* they add up to the value on the two dice. For example, if the two dice add up to 7 (perhaps a 4 and a 3) and the game player flips over the 8 tile, then the panel needs to reject the right-click.

It's this important fact that prevents you from handling the right-click code in the same OnMouseDown method shown in Listing 3-1. Currently, the NumberPanel class has no way of determining the value of the DicePanel class; in fact, the NumberPanel class has no knowledge of the existence of a DicePanel class at all. Clearly, the code will eventually need to compare the value of the NumberPanel class's backward tiles to the value of the DicePanel class's dice. In effect, you need to create some type of "linkage" between the classes.

These class linkage decisions are often important design decisions in large projects, depending on how you connect the two classes. For example, you may force those two classes to exist together whenever they're used in the program. Let's move away from the current game for a minute to look at an abstract example. Say you have designed and written a human resources application for your company, and version 1.0 of this application has been in use for a year or so. As the designer and chief developer on this project, you've spent a great deal of time creating the Employee class. This class encapsulates all of the information and responsibilities of a single employee being tracked by the application.

Later, the human resources department asks if you can connect your program to the external, third-party payroll program for the purpose of some new payroll-based reporting. One of the large requirements of this new functionality is security; most people in the company shouldn't be able to access any of the payroll information.

You design and develop a class (named PayrollInfo) that encapsulates the connection and retrieval of payroll data from the third-party system, and now you need a way to "connect" some of the information in the Employee class (perhaps the employee's married status or how long she's been with the company) to the data in the PayrollInfo class so that you can create the new desired report. This is where you need to address the big "linkage" design decision. You could, for example, simply add a property onto the Employee class of type PayrollInfo (class properties and fields can be objects of other types, as you've already seen with the declaration of the PaintPanel member on the Die class in Chapter 2, "Writing Your First Game, Again"). With this decision, an instance of the PayrollInfo class is "carried around" with every instance of the Employee class. With this decision, you've possibly introduced many problems into your application, including the following:

Security: Is the information contained in the `PayrollInfo` class useful or required every time an `Employee` class is instantiated? Probably not because the `Employee` class is probably used in some 90-plus percent of the program. Is embedding the "supersecret" class inside the most well-used and important class of the program a good idea? It isn't if a team of programmers works on this program. What if your application becomes so important to the company that it promotes you to manager and hires three entry-level developers to work under you? Do these first-year programmers need access to the `PayrollInfo` code? Probably not. Of course, you can hide the code for this class by putting it in a separate DLL and giving them access to the object code only. But how hard would it be for a programmer to write a test program that instantiates an instance of the `Employee` class, calls the code that loads the `PayrollInfo` data, and then displays the employee's salary in the Visual Studio console window? The programmer doesn't need access to the source code; she only needs to know the implementation details of this class (provided all too happily by Visual Studio's Intellisense). To counteract this, you need to build user-based security inside the `PayrollInfo` class.

Overhead: Even if the data involved in the new functionality isn't supersecret, do you need to carry it around in memory every time you create an `Employee` class? Probably not; after all, this program has existed for a year without this data. The functionality has been working fine without the new data, so why add to the memory requirement of these old functions?

The degree of connectivity between functionality (classes) in the object-oriented world is called *coupling*. Good object-oriented design dictates keeping coupling between objects *loose*. In the human resources application, embedding the `PayrollInfo` class inside the `Employee` class is an example of tight coupling— you've linked their functionality together forever by putting one inside the other, and the two problems described previously are examples of why this is bad. Instead, you need to come up with a solution that's more loosely coupled.

In this example, you can achieve a more loosely coupled solution by reversing the original concept. Instead of a `PayrollInfo` property attached to the `Employee` class, attach an `Employee` property to the `PayrollInfo` class.

The benefits of this solution are many. From a security standpoint, you can continue to keep your new `PayrollInfo` source code (and perhaps even compiled code) away from your first-year developers by putting it in a place on the network where they don't have access. You (as the sole developer of this high-security code and data) will have access to this source code area. All developers can access the area where the `Employee` class resides. This solves the overhead problem because the often-used `Employee` class doesn't "bloat up" with the code and data providing this new functionality. Instead, the PayrollInfo class, when it's used, creates the equivalent Employee object so it has access to data such as a hire date or married status.

You can see how such a seemingly innocuous design decision (which class to make a property of the other) can have possible wide-ranging effects on both the security and memory requirements of the final application.

Enough discussion about human resources applications (yuck!); let's get back to discussing the NineTiles project. There are two classes, the DicePanel and NumberPanel classes, and some part of the program will need access to both the value of the dice and the value of the reversed tiles so that they can be compared. One way to do this is to create a property on the NumberPanel class that refers to the DicePanel class. This allows you to check the public Result property in the protected OnMouseDown method. This solution exhibits tight coupling between the two classes, however. What if, down the road, someone introduced a new game (or even nongame) program where the NumberPanel class might be useful but didn't require a DicePanel class? This would be too bad for you—the file DicePanel.dll would be required because of the reference to the DicePanel class as a property, meaning you would be installing a DLL on the end user's computer that might never be used.

Instead, you can choose a solution that decouples the DicePanel and NumberPanel classes. This solution is to handle the right-click handling code in the external MouseDown event of the NumberPanel class (see Listing 3-2).

Listing 3-2. Tile Right-Click, Handled Outside the NumberPanel *Class*

```
Private Sub NumPanelMouseDown(ByVal sender As Object, _
   ByVal e As System.Windows.Forms.MouseEventArgs)

  If oNumPanel.bInAnimation Then Exit Sub

  If e.Button = MouseButtons.Right Then
     If oDice.Result = oNumPanel.Result Then

        oNumPanel.HideBackward()
        oWav.Play("thud", 400)

        If oNumPanel.TilesVisible = 0 Then
          oWav.Play("applause", bSync:=True)
           StartGame()
        Else
           oDice.RollDice()
```

```
              If Not oNumPanel.ResultAvailable(oDice.Result) Then
                oWav.Play("laughs", bSync:=True)
                    StartGame()
              End If
          End If
      Else
          oWav.Play("dischord")
      End If
    End If
End Sub
```

This event is defined in the game's form, just as you might handle the Click event of a button. It runs whenever the user clicks the mouse on the panel with either mouse button. Because this code runs from the form, it has access to the NumberPanel instance (named oNumPanel) and the DicePanel instance (named oDice), so the comparison can be done between the two values.

In truth, this single event handler comprises almost all of the game functionality. Let's trace through it to see what it's doing. First, it checks to see if the NumberPanel is already engaged in an animation via the bInAnimation property shown in Listing 3-1. If this property is True, then the event handler exits immediately (it doesn't want to do further processing until the animation loop is complete). If this property is False, the code continues.

If the user right-clicks, you want to run the "make-tiles-disappear" code. The previously alluded to comparison happens between the DicePanel class's Result property and the NumberPanel class's Result property. If they're unequal, then the knucklehead user has right-clicked with the backward tiles not equaling the result on the dice, and the line of code oWav.Play("dischord") executes. (This will be discussed later; suffice to say that a nasty-sounding WAV file plays to indicate that the user made an error.) If the two values are in fact equal, then the program removes the tiles (the HideBackward method on the NumberPanel), and a little sound effect plays (named thud).

The rest of the event deals with what happens after this turn is over. There are two possibilities—the user has won the game because there are no tiles left or the user continues to play because some tiles remain, in which case the dice roll again. After this new roll, the program checks to see if this new roll can be satisfied by the remaining tiles (the ResultAvailable method). If it can, the code ends for now (it will wait for the user to flip over tiles and keep playing). If the result can't be satisfied, then the user has lost.

If the player has either won the game or lost it in this event handler, the same two actions are performed. First, a sound effect plays (some applause for the winner or mocking laughter for the loser), and then the game restarts. This auto-restart of the game is key to its addictive nature (at least I find it hard to stop playing).

Creating One Click but Multiple Methods

You might have noticed something interesting about Listings 3-1 and 3-2. There's an OnMouseDown method *inside* the NumberPanel class and a MouseDown event *outside* of the class, and both pieces of code run when the player clicks on the panel. The functionality between these two procedures is mutually exclusive (one performs actions upon a left-click, the other on a right-click), but this is by choice. It's possible to have multiple pieces of code run in response to the same event. How is this linked together? Listing 3-3 shows a greatly simplified version of the NumberPanel and its ancestor class, the Panel, to try to explain.

Listing 3-3. Relationship Between an Event (MouseDown) and the Method That Calls It (OnMouseDown) in an Ancestor Class

```
Class Panel
    Public Event MouseDown

    Protected Sub OnMouseDown
      RaiseEvent MouseDown
    End Sub

End Class

Class NumberPanel
    inherits Panel

    Protected Overrides Sub OnMouseDown
      MyBase.OnMouseDown()
      ... (left click code)
    End Sub

End Class
```

The Panel class contains an event named MouseDown that's raised from within the method named OnMouseDown. This method is protected, meaning that it's available in descendant classes. In your descendant class, NumberPanel, the intent was to add functionality inside the class to handle the animation of a tile when it was left-clicked. To accomplish this, you can override the OnMouseDown method and place the tile-moving code in that method. The one thing you must remember to include is the MyBase.OnMouseDown call. This important line runs the OnMouseDown code in the base class (Panel), which is the code that raises the event to the outside world or to the form using the NumberPanel class. The right-click handling code is placed in this event handler.

NOTE *Because Microsoft doesn't currently make the .NET Framework source code available, Listing 3-3 doesn't necessarily accurately reflect the exact structure of the* Panel *class. Instead, it represents a "best guess" as to its structure.*

If you'd like a demonstration of how the event and protected methods are linked, try commenting out the MyBase.OnMouseDown line in the NumberPanel class's OnMouseDown event and run the program. What you'll find is that the right-click handling event code on the form is no longer executed. You've prevented the RaiseEvent line in the Panel class from running because the Panel class's OnMouseDown is never called.

Understanding Decoupling vs. Encapsulation

This chapter and the previous one have thrown two important object-oriented principles at you. Chapter 2, "Writing Your First Game, Again," described the concept of encapsulation and making an object responsible for itself. This chapter has discussed the desire for loose coupling between classes so that they can work on their own.

These two principles are actually working against each other in this project. It would be better for the sake of encapsulation if you could bring the right-click handling code inside of the NumberPanel class. To accomplish this, though, you'd need to somehow bring the value of the dice into the NumberPanel class so you could check to see if it's okay to hide the tiles on which the user has clicked.

There are ways to solve this particular problem to achieve better encapsulation but still keep the two classes decoupled. (A hint: The solution requires a new event on the NumberPanel class). This chapter won't cover this solution for now, though, because although it might solve the problem of comparing the dice value to the NumberPanel value, there are other reasons to couple the two classes later, such as getting the dice to reroll after hiding the backward tiles or after the user has won or lost the game.

The point is that there isn't always a "perfect" design. The current design has some problems (the lack of encapsulation of the NumberPanel right-click functionality), but solving that problem by coupling the two classes might bring on new problems in the future—for instance, if you decided to create a second game with the NumberPanel that didn't require a die.

It often turns out that the solution you come up with now may prove to hinder some aspect of your coding down the road. If you chose to add a DicePanel property on the NumberPanel class, thinking this was the only NumberPanel game you were to ever write, you'd have a problem in the future because of the unnecessary requirement you created by tightly coupling the two classes.

NOTE *This, of course, leads back to matt tag's first law of coding:* ***Don't be afraid to rewrite code.***

Nobody can predict the future (if I could, I'd know the winners of the next 10 World Series and Super Bowls, which would pretty much ruin any interest I have in sports). Therefore, it's quite possible you may not come up with the best design for a project today because you don't know how you might reuse the elements in that project (or future projects) tomorrow. When you do find you've made a shortsighted decision that you can correct with some refactoring, and you know this refactoring will improve the code for a future project, then you should do the refactoring. The result is better code with higher reusability.

Getting Back to the NumberPanel Class

The right-click event shown in Listing 3-2 references a number of members found in the NumberPanel class (see Table 3-1).

Table 3-1. Important Members of the NumberPanel *Class*

MEMBER NAME	TYPE	PURPOSE
Result	Property (read-only)	Returns summed value of flipped-over tiles
HideBackward	Method	Marks all flipped-over tiles as invisible and redraws the panel so they disappear
TilesVisible	Method (returns Integer)	Returns number of tiles left showing and determines if the game has been won
ResultAvailable	Method (returns Boolean)	Returns if the visible tiles can be combined to add up to the value passed in as a parameter and determines if the game has been lost

The first three members in Table 3-1 have a similar structure in that they loop through all of the tile objects and check some data within them or perform some action on them. Listing 3-4 shows the code for all three members.

Listing 3-4. NumberPanel *Members That Loop Through the* ArrayList *of* TileData *Objects to Do Something*

```
Public Function TilesVisible() As Boolean

    Dim aTile As TileData
    Dim i As Integer = 0

    For Each aTile In oTiles
        If aTile.pVisible Then
            i += 1
        End If
    Next
    Return i

End Function

ReadOnly Property Result() As Integer
    Get
        Dim aTile As TileData
        Dim i As Integer = 0

        For Each aTile In oTiles
            If aTile.pVisible And aTile.pBackwards Then
                i += aTile.pTileNum
            End If
        Next
        Return i
    End Get
End Property

Public Sub HideBackward()
    Dim aTile As TileData

    For Each aTile In oTiles
        If aTile.pVisible And aTile.pBackwards Then
            aTile.pVisible = False
        End If
    Next
    Me.Invalidate()
    Application.DoEvents()
End Sub
```

In all three of these members, the ArrayList named oTiles is iterated against to obtain each TileData object contained within it. Each instance (held in the variable aTile in all cases) is then checked for visibility (in all three members, hidden tiles are ignored). The work done on each tile is slightly different in each case and corresponds to the function each member performs as listed in Table 3-1.

The last member, ResultAvailable, is more of a "brute-force" loop that determines if a given value can be obtained by adding up the visible tiles. This routine makes use of the fact that no more than four tiles could ever be summed up to obtain a value rolled on two dice (2 to 12). The five lowest tiles add up to 15, and 1+2+3+4 could be used on a roll of 10. Listing 3-5 shows the beginning of this routine (the remainder of the routine contains a great deal of duplication; you can check it out in its entirely in the project if you're curious). The method returns True if the passed-in value can be obtained with some combination of visible tiles.

Listing 3-5. The ResultAvailable *Method*

```
'checks all combinations of 1, 2, 3, and 4 visible tiles
Public Function ResultAvailable(ByVal iDesired As Integer) As Boolean

    Dim i, j, k, l As Integer
    Dim aTilei, aTilej, aTilek, aTilel As TileData

    'one-bangers
    For i = 0 To oTiles.Count - 1
        aTilei = oTiles(i)
        If aTilei.pVisible Then
            If aTilei.pTileNum = iDesired Then
                Return True
            End If
        End If
    Next

    '2-bangers
    For i = 0 To oTiles.Count - 2
        For j = i + 1 To oTiles.Count - 1
            aTilei = oTiles(i)
            aTilej = oTiles(j)
            If aTilei.pVisible And _
                aTilej.pVisible Then

                If aTilei.pTileNum + aTilej.pTileNum = iDesired Then
                    Return True
                End If
```

```
              End If
           Next
        Next
... <3 and 4 tile checks removed>
```

Creating the TileData Class

As mentioned earlier, the NumberPanel class acts as a manager to nine instances
of a TileData class. This class contains the information necessary to track one of
the nine colored, numbered tiles. Listing 3-6 shows the public interface of the
TileData class.

Listing 3-6. The Class TileData

```
Private Class TileData

    Public Sub New(ByVal oPanel As NumberPanel, _
      ByVal iTileNum As Integer)

    ReadOnly Property pTileNum() As Integer
    Property pVisible() As Boolean
    Property pBackwards() As Boolean

    Public Sub Reset
    Public Sub ToggleFacing
End Class
```

Looking at the public interface for a class is a good way to study its functionality and behavior without getting bogged down or confused by how this behavior
is implemented. You'll do this quite often when studying the classes in the .NET
Framework. These classes are described in the help documentation in terms of
their public interface and what function each member of that public interface
performs. To use a class in the .NET Framework, you need only understand its
public interface.

TIP *When it comes time to extend the functionality of a .NET
Framework class through inheritance, you then need to understand
the base class's protected interface.*

Table 3-2 describes the public members on the TileData class.

Table 3-2. TileData *Members*

MEMBER NAME	TYPE	PURPOSE
pTileNum	Property	Returns the number on the tile, 1–9. This is read-only because it's set via the constructor.
pVisible	Property	Sets/returns whether the tile is visible. The user wins the game when pVisible = False for all nine tiles.
pBackwards	Property	Sets/returns whether tile is facing forward or backward.
Reset	Method	Sets tile to face forward, visible.
ToggleFacing	Method	Plays animation loop of tile moving from forward to backward or vice versa.

If you're comparing the TileData class to the Die class discussed in Chapter 2, "Writing Your First Game, Again," you might find a member or two conspicuously absent from its interface. In particular, where is the Draw method? Doesn't the NumberPanel class need a way to draw a tile onto itself? Also missing is the pFrame property. How does the TileData know which frame it's going to draw during the animation or simply when it's drawing the tile at rest, either forward or backward?

The answer is that these two members aren't missing; they're simply not public. Remember that Listing 3-6 describes only the public interface for the class. Any functionality declared as private isn't described, so you as the potential user of this class can be spared from the implementation details.

This public/private shielding is rather a moot point in the discussion of the TileData class because the entire class is declared as private inside the NumberPanel class, meaning that you as the user of the NumberPanel would never have access to it anyway. That doesn't prevent you as the coder from attempting to make the object as responsible for itself as you can, though, if for no other reason than keeping good design methods in practice.

Exploring the Animation Details

Each animated tile is represented by 10 frames rotating from a front-facing to a rear-facing position. Figure 3-4 shows the master bitmap used as the source of the animated frames.

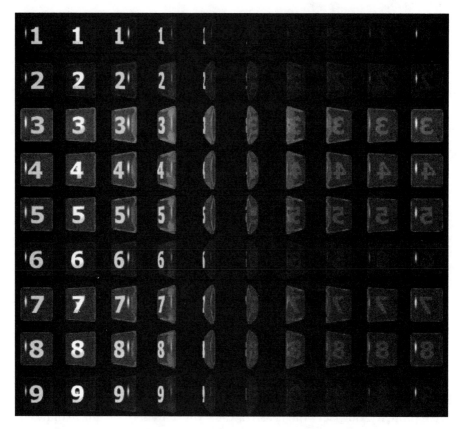

Figure 3-4. The 90 animated frames used to render the nine tiles

As you can see, if you're responsible for rendering one of the nine tiles, you'll render along a horizontal row on the source bitmap. In other words, the source y coordinate won't change from frame to frame; all that changes is the x coordinate. You can determine the changing x coordinate by which of the 10 frames (numbered 0–9) is to be drawn. You can calculate the coordinate by multiplying the current frame value by the width of one animated frame (the constant 112). Another constant in rendering is where the tile is to be drawn on the destination panel because the numbered tiles don't move around like dice do.

These three fixed values are stored in private variables on the TileData class. Listing 3-7 shows the declaration of these three values, as well as the constructor for the class, which shows where these values are initially calculated and stored.

Listing 3-7. Private Variables and Constructor for the TileData *Class*

```
Private Class TileData

    Private FPanel As NumberPanel

    'don't need separate height/width, sprite is square
    Private Const IRAD As Integer = 112

    'tiles are always drawn in the same place on the panel
    Private FxPos, FyPos As Integer
    Private FySrc As Integer

    Public Sub New(ByVal oPanel As NumberPanel, _
      ByVal iTileNum As Integer)

        MyBase.New()

        Dim iTilePos As Integer

        FPanel = oPanel
        FTileNum = iTileNum

        iTilePos = iTileNum - 1          '0-8, one less than tile number

        'coordinates to draw tile on panel are fixed
        FxPos = (iTilePos Mod 3) * IRAD
        FyPos = (iTilePos \ 3) * IRAD

        'y coord in source bitmap fixed (see bitmap)
        FySrc = iTilePos * IRAD
    End Sub
```

The constructor takes a NumberPanel and a tile variable (integer 1–9) as a parameter. The NumberPanel is referenced by the private variable FPanel, which is similar to the setup that was used in the Die class to hold an instance of the DicePanel class. The FPanel variable will be used later to gain access to required members of that class for drawing. You use the tile number integer as the basis to calculate the destination point on the panel (FxPos and FyPos) and the source y coordinate in the animation frame's bitmap (FySrc).

The Frame property (which is private) tells the class which of the 10 frames to draw. If you think about it, it's easy to determine the frame. If the tile is facing forward, the frame is 0. If the tile is facing backward, the frame is 9. If the tile is being animated in either direction, the frame is iterating from 0 to 9 or 9 to 0 in a loop.

This gives you enough information to draw a tile onto a bitmap. Listing 3-8 shows the (private) Draw method of the TileData class. Note this method is private, meaning the NumberPanel class can't call it. Who calls it, then?

Listing 3-8. The TileData *Class's* Draw *Method*

```
Private Sub Draw()

    Dim gr As Graphics
    Dim r As System.Drawing.Rectangle
    Dim xSrc As Integer

    Dim bDest As Bitmap = FPanel.bBack

    gr = Graphics.FromImage(bDest)
    Try
        If FVisible Then
            xSrc = FFrame * IRAD
            r = New System.Drawing.Rectangle(xSrc, FySrc, IRAD + 1, IRAD + 1)
            gr.DrawImage(FPanel.fbNum, FxPos, FyPos, r, GraphicsUnit.Pixel)
        Else
            'draw a black square
            r = New System.Drawing.Rectangle(FxPos, FyPos, IRAD, IRAD)
            gr.FillRectangle(New SolidBrush(Color.Black), r)
        End If
    Finally
        gr.Dispose()
    End Try

End Sub
```

The Draw method for the tile is somewhat similar to the like-named method of the Die class shown in Chapter 2, "Writing Your First Game, Again." One difference is that this class has to be able to "draw" an invisible tile, which it does by drawing a filled black rectangle instead of one of the source bitmap frames. Another difference is that this method doesn't pass in the destination bitmap as a parameter. Instead, the background bitmap associated with the NumberPanel is obtained directly by using the FPanel variable. This is a design choice and doesn't really provide any design benefit.

You've now seen the Draw method, but you still haven't seen what calls it yet. You can make a reasonable guess, though. Because the method is private, it has to be called from within the TileData class. In fact, two places in the class call the code. Listing 3-9 shows both calling members.

Listing 3-9. The TileData *Class's* pVisible *Property and* ToggleFacing *Method*

```
Private FVisible As Boolean = True
Property pVisible() As Boolean
    Get
        Return FVisible
    End Get

    Set(ByVal Value As Boolean)
        FVisible = Value
        Me.Draw()
    End Set
End Property


Public Sub ToggleFacing()

    Dim iStart, iEnd As Integer
    Dim iDir, iLoop As Integer

    If Not FVisible Then Exit Sub

    If pBackwards Then
        iStart = 9
        iEnd = 0
        iDir = -1
    Else
        iStart = 0
        iEnd = 9
        iDir = 1
    End If

    FPanel.OnTileMoving(pBackwards)
    For iLoop = iStart To iEnd Step iDir
        pFrame = iLoop
        Me.Draw()
        FPanel.Invalidate()
        Application.DoEvents()
    Next
    pBackwards = Not pBackwards
End Sub
```

The pVisible property is a great example of connecting code execution to the changing state of an object. When an outside call changes the pVisible property, the Set method calls the Draw method, which redraws the tile on the panel.

The ToggleFacing method handles the animated loop of a tile moving forward or backward when clicked. The animated frames are iterated from 0 to 9 if the tile is currently facing forward and from 9 down to 0 if the tile is currently facing backward. Furthermore, note how this method makes a call to the FPanel.OnTileMoving method, which in turn raises a public TileMoving event on the NumberPanel. This event allows the NumberPanel to notify the calling form that a tile is moving so that it can react by playing a sound, for example.

Connecting It All Together

The NumberPanel class is complete; all that remains is to slap one on the main form, wire it up, and start playing. You could put the NumberPanel class into its own project, compile it into a DLL, and add it to the Visual Studio Toolbox, just as you did the DicePanel. However, because this new class doesn't seem as "general purpose" as the DicePanel is, adding it to the Visual Studio Toolbox won't necessarily benefit you in later projects. Therefore, you can leave the class inside this project and then create one and add it to the form on the fly. Listing 3-10 shows how you do this. This isn't quite as clean (or fun) as adding the control to the Toolbox, but it serves the purpose of this game well enough.

Listing 3-10. Adding a NumberPanel *to a Form on the Fly*

```
Public Class fMain
    Inherits System.Windows.Forms.Form

    Private oNumPanel As NumberPanel
    Private oWav As WavLibrary
    Private oRand As Random

    Private Sub fMain_Load(ByVal sender As System.Object, _
        ByVal e As System.EventArgs) Handles MyBase.Load

        oNumPanel = New NumberPanel
        oNumPanel.Dock = DockStyle.Top
        AddHandler oNumPanel.MouseDown, AddressOf NumPanelMouseDown
        AddHandler oNumPanel.TileMoving, AddressOf NumPanelTileMoving
        Me.Controls.Add(oNumPanel)

        SetupWavLibrary()
        oRand = New Random

    End Sub
```

Listing 3-10 shows the Form.Load event of the main form and a few private variables on the form. This event shows a NumberPanel object being instantiated and added to the form via the form's Controls.Add method. You can also see how the right-click code event handler (shown way back in Listing 3-2) is wired up to this object via the AddHandler statement and how a second method named TileMoving is wired up to another method named NumPanelTileMoving. This method simply plays a WAV file while a tile is animating backward or forward.

Speaking of playing WAV files, the next section discusses a new, improved WAV-playing library and how to use that code in multiple programs.

Using WavPlayer Release 2.0: The WavLibrary

You saw a simple class that used a Win32 application programming interface (API) call to play a WAV file in Chapter 2, "Writing Your First Game, Again" (refer to Listing 2-11 if you'd like to review it). Although the basic engine of playing the WAV file appears to function well enough, version 1.0 of the class has two problems:

- **Unwieldy names for the WAV files**: Because the WAV files are embedded in the executable as resources, they end up having names that include the namespace name, such as GuessTheDieRoll2.DIE1.WAV. These long names tend to be distracting on a line of code; it'd be better to refer to a sound by a nickname, such as die1.

- **Unnecessary memory move**: If you study Listing 2-11, you'll see there's a memory copy from the embedded resource into a byte array named bstr every time the WAV plays. Even though there weren't any noticeable performance problems, it seemed more efficient to perform this memory move only once per WAV file and then store the byte array in memory until the end of the program.

These two new requirements gave rise to a new version of the WavPlayer class. The concept behind this new design should be familiar to you by now; you can encapsulate a single WAV file as a class and then wrap that class with a manager class that handles the setup and storage of the individual components. This new class is called WavLibrary.

Using the Manager Pattern

I seem to be stuck on this "manager/embedded class" design methodology in the early stages of this book, but I'm certainly not advocating using this style of design over any other. I find this design useful when I have some number of "things" (such as dice, tiles, or WAV files) that I need to keep track of but have no use for the "things" to be accessed as individuals in the outside world. In other words, I can embed the class that tracks the things inside a manager class and allow that manager class to be the interface to the outside world.

This was especially useful in the case of the DicePanel and TilePanel classes because the manager class was also providing the visual representation of the object (because both were descendants of the .NET Framework Panel class). If you're familiar with the concept of design patterns, this common pattern is known (appropriately enough) as the Manager pattern.

The WavLibrary class contains a private class named WavFile, which contains the byte array into which each WAV resource is loaded, as well as a Name property that will allow you to refer to each sound using a short "handle." Listing 3-11 shows the public interface for the WavFile class, which encapsulates a single sound used by the game.

Listing 3-11. Public Interface for the WavFile Class

```
Private Class WavFile

    Public Sub New(ByVal cName As String)
    Public Sub Dispose()
    Property Name() As String

    Public Function LoadFromResource(ByVal cResName As String) As Boolean

    Public Overloads Sub Play(ByVal bSync As Boolean)

    Public Overloads Sub Play(ByVal mSec As Integer, _
        ByVal bSync As Boolean)

End Class
```

Chapter 2, "Writing Your First Game, Again," already discussed how a WAV resource is loaded from the executable into a byte array and how that byte array is passed the Win32 API function sndPlaySound, so this chapter won't cover that material again. What has changed is when the byte array is loaded: Instead of loading it every time a sound is played, a separate method named LoadFromResource has been added, with the intent that this method be called before the WAV file is played the first time but is then kept in memory for subsequent plays.

Another difference in this class is that there are three methods for playing the sound. The first two are both named Play, which is a new feature to Visual Basic .NET. Previous versions of Visual Basic didn't allow two methods with the same name. True object-oriented languages allow this as long as the method signature (parameter list) of each like-named method is different. In object-oriented programming, this is known as *method overloading*. You'll notice that Visual Basic requires the use of the Overloads keyword on any method that you plan to overload with multiple implementations. Method overloading is much easier on the user of your class because she doesn't have to remember multiple method names such as Play and PlayWithPause.

The two different Play methods allow a single method name to provide different functionality. In this case, the second method allows the entry of an integer value that represents a number of milliseconds that the player should pause after playing the WAV file. This allows the user of the WAV library to time her sound effects with the actions they're augmenting. A parameter named bSync on both Play implementations allows the sound to be played synchronously instead of asynchronously, meaning that all action stops while the sound is being played. This feature is used in NineTiles when the derisive laughter or light applause plays at the end of the game.

The WavLibrary class is the manager class for the individual WAV files. It's small enough that Listing 3-12 shows most of it.

Listing 3-12. The WavLibrary *Class, the Manager for the* WavFile *Classes*

```
Public Class WavLibrary
    Private FSounds As Hashtable

    Public Sub New()
        MyBase.New()
        FSounds = New Hashtable
    End Sub

    Public Sub Dispose()

        Dim w As WavFile
```

```
            For Each w In FSounds.Values
                  w.Dispose()
            Next
        End Sub


        Public Function LoadFromResource(ByVal cResName As String,_
            ByVal cName As String) As Boolean

            Dim w As WavFile

            w = New WavFile(cName)
            If w.LoadFromResource(cResName) Then
                FSounds.Add(w.Name, w)
            End If

        End Function

        Public Overloads Sub Play(ByVal cName As String, _
            Optional ByVal bSync As Boolean = False)

            Dim w As WavFile

            w = FSounds.Item(cName)
            If w Is Nothing Then
                Throw New Exception("Sound name " & cName & " not found")
            Else
                w.Play(bSync)
            End If
        End Sub


        <overloaded Play method removed (very similar to first Play method)
        <Wav File declaration removed>


    End Class
```

The first interesting thing about this manager class vs. the others you've seen is that this class uses a Hashtable to store its component objects rather than an ArrayList. A Hashtable is a different type of collection class that allows a unique key to be stored along with each object. This satisfies the requirement of being able to name each sound with a "handle" to which it can be referred, rather than the ungainly full name of the WAV file that includes the program's namespace. You can see the line of code that adds a new WavFile instance to the Hashtable in the LoadFromResource method. The objects contained within a Hashtable can then be retrieved by name, which is shown in the Play method. Note that if a handle is passed into the `Play` method that doesn't exist in the `Hashtable`, meaning that the caller of the library tried to play a WAV file that hasn't been set up, an exception is thrown. Otherwise, the named sound has been found, and the `Play` method on the corresponding `WavFile` instance is called.

Another interesting thing about the `Play` method is the use of an optional parameter named `bSync`. If the caller omits this parameter, its value is defined to be `false`. The combination of the optional parameter and the overloaded `Play` method allows the caller to call this one method four different ways to achieve different combinations of functions:

```
oWav.Play("snd")
oWav.Play("snd", bSync:=true)
oWav.Play("snd", 100)
oWav.Play("snd", 100, bSync:=true)
```

Here, the WAV file plays four different ways: with no pause, synchronously, with a 100-millisecond pause, and both synchronously and with a 100-millisecond pause (kind of overkill, but what the heck).

Setting Up the WavLibrary

You can use the `WavLibrary` class in a program with a few short setup routines. Listing 3-13 shows how the NineTiles program uses this class. All that's required is loading each WAV resource and calling the `Play` method at the appropriate time.

Listing 3-13. Using the WavLibrary *Class*

```
Private oWav As WavLibrary
Private oRand As Random
Private Sub fMain_Load(ByVal sender As System.Object, _
    ByVal e As System.EventArgs) Handles MyBase.Load

    <unrelated code removed>
    SetupWavLibrary()
    oRand = New Random

End Sub

Private Sub SetupWavLibrary()
```

```
oWav = New WavLibrary
oWav.LoadFromResource("NineTiles.die1.wav", "die1")
oWav.LoadFromResource("NineTiles.die2.wav", "die2")
oWav.LoadFromResource("NineTiles.squeak1.wav", "squeak1")
oWav.LoadFromResource("NineTiles.squeak2.wav", "squeak2")
oWav.LoadFromResource("NineTiles.thud.wav", "thud")
oWav.LoadFromResource("NineTiles.applause.wav", "applause")
oWav.LoadFromResource("NineTiles.laughs.wav", "laughs")
oWav.LoadFromResource("NineTiles.dischord.wav", "dischord")

End Sub


Private Sub oDice_DieBounced() Handles oDice.DieBounced

    Dim cWav As String
    If oRand.Next(0, 1000) Mod 2 = 0 Then
        cWav = "die1"
    Else
        cWav = "die2"
    End If
    oWav.Play(cWav)

End Sub
```

Listing 3-13 shows how the WAV library is declared, instantiated, and then loaded with the WAV resource embedded in the program. You can see how each resource is connected to a "handle," which in this case is simply the filename of each file without the namespace or the extension. You can give any handle to any WAV file.

The oDice_DieBounced method shows how one of two available die "clicking" noises plays whenever one of the dice bounces against a wall or against another die.

It's also interesting that the WavLibrary class is used only in the main form and not in any of the classes in this project (DicePanel, NumberPanel). When sounds are to be played in combination to actions happening in these classes, an event is raised back to the main program to play the sound, just as the DieBounced event shown previously. This is another example of reducing coupling between classes.

Creating One Library, Multiple Projects

You might imagine that a class such as WavLibrary has wide-ranging utility, and therefore it might be something you can reuse in multiple projects. When you've written a potentially often-used piece of code like this, you can move the source file to a common folder so that you're not copying the same source file into multiple application folders.

However, Visual Studio has a somewhat nasty habit when dealing with source files in other folders. Whenever you add a file to a Visual Studio project that isn't in the project's source folder, the file is *automatically copied* into the project's source folder. Therefore, if you decide to put the WavLibrary source file into a common folder and then you go and add it to your NineTiles project or any other project, Visual Studio makes a copy of that file and puts the copy into the NineTiles folder.

Why is this a bad habit? Well, suppose you find a bug in the WavLibrary class or decide to add new functionality to it. You open your project and make the required changes. Unfortunately, if this "common" source file is used in many projects, then you've only changed the single copy of the library, and all of the other copies remain unaltered.

NOTE *I used to work with a guy who had a "common" string library, but it was copied into every project's source folder, which I didn't realize when I first started working there. Over time, both of us were adding useful functions to what I thought was a common function library. I eventually realized that there were in fact a dozen copies of the "common" library, and I had a full-scale mess on my hands trying to combine all the changes into a single useful library module.*

Fortunately, there's a way to override this functionality and to instead create a *link* to a file in a folder other than the project's folder, but it's a bit hidden. The key is that when you select Project ➤ Add Existing Item, the common dialog box that comes up has a slight modification to it: a little drop-down button to the right of the Open button. Clicking this drop-down button presents you with three options: Open File (the default), Open File With (allowing you to open the file in some other program), and Link File (see Figure 3-5). This last option is the one you want here. The result is to create a shortcut to the file without copying it to the project folder. This allows you to create common, often-used libraries of code that you can share between applications.

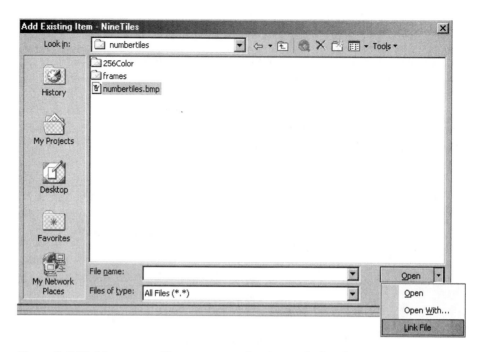

Figure 3-5. Linking source files to your project instead of making copies of them

You can see that a file is linked to a project by the (very) little shortcut symbol in the lower left of the icon for that file in the Solution Explorer. Feel free to use this linking for items other than source files, as well.

TIP *I often use this linking technique for embedded resources such as bitmaps and WAV files so that I can keep these in a common folder.*

Looking Back on the Design

It's often helpful to revisit the design decisions you've made after completing a project or set of projects to see if you might learn something from them. Let's look at the NineTiles project from a design viewpoint and see what might come from it.

The NineTiles game is comprised of two major classes: the DicePanel and NumberPanel classes. These two classes contain a great deal of similarity:

- Each class inherits from the .NET Framework class System.Windows.Forms.Panel.

- Each class calls the SetStyle method in its constructor to change some default window styles and control flicker.

- Each class uses a background bitmap for drawing.

- Each class acts as a manager class for a number of subordinate classes.

In addition to this, the two subordinate classes have a ton in common, including the following:

- Each class is visualized through a series of animated frames found in one or more bitmaps.

- Each instance of the subordinate class has a fixed height and width.

- Each class is drawn to the background bitmap of the manager class.

- Each class contains information as to its position on the panel/background bitmap.

Those of you familiar with object-oriented design are probably jumping up and down right now as a seemingly obvious issue smacks you in the face: Why don't you further abstract the subordinate/manager classes into a Sprite/SpritePanel class and then implement the existing classes and descendants of these new abstraction classes? Figure 3-6 shows the proposed relationship.

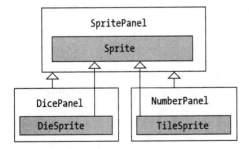

Figure 3-6. A new proposal combining the common functionality of the two Panel *classes and the two "subordinate" classes into an inheritence hierarchy*

This new level of abstraction is perfectly valid and may provide all the benefits that good object-oriented design gives you. Having this abstract SpritePanel/Sprite class combination could be a great building block to any number of future games. There are three reasons you should stick with the current design, however.

First, your current plans don't include any further bitmap-based sprite-style games. Although refactoring is a good thing, refactoring a working program with little promise for future benefit may not be the best use of your time in a real-world situation filled with deadlines and deliverables.

Second, there appears to be a bug, or at least an inconsistency, in Visual Basic .NET when using embedded classes. VB .NET doesn't allow you to create a class within another class and then reference that class through inheritance unless the embedded class is public. The following code fragment illustrates this:

```
Public Class SpritePanel

    Protected Class Sprite
    End Class
End Class

Public Class DicePanel
    Inherits SpritePanel

    Protected Class DieSprite
        Inherits SpritePanel.Sprite    ← error
    End Class
End Class
```

This code fragment declares the SpritePanel and Sprite classes within it and then attempts to inherit from both with the classes DicePanel and DieSprite (exactly as Figure 3-6 illustrates). This code produces an error in Visual Basic .NET, however. The error reads "TestInherit.SpritePanel.Sprite is not accessible in this context because it is Protected." Huh? Wasn't the purpose of making something protected to make it available in descendant classes? So why isn't the protected Sprite class available in the descendant DicePanel class?

This is probably a bug because the same construct is legal in the other .NET language, C#:

```
public class SpritePanel
{
        protected class Sprite
        {
        }
}
```

```
public class DicePanel: SpritePanel
{
        protected class DieSprite: SpritePanel.Sprite
        {
        }
}
```

There are no compiler errors here (although it does take me about three times longer to successfully enter this little test as I try and get all my matching braces correct).

Anyway, this bug vanishes in Visual Basic if you change the Sprite class to public, but you really don't want to do that from a design perspective. One of the design goals of this arrangement was to shield the user of the manager class from having to know anything about the objects being managed, and making the Sprite class public would go against that design goal. If a new program does suggest the need for access to the individual sprite classes, you could change the arrangement and take the Sprite class out of the SpritePanel class altogether, thereby removing the "embedded" class design concept. Again, however, you have no need to do that at this point, so the current design is adequate.

Finally, you may have noticed that the performance of these bitmap-based animations isn't exactly what you would call "state of the art." In fact, the original NineTiles game had an opening animated sequence where all nine tiles moved from their backward state to facing forward at one time, but this sequence was simply too slow. Some online research revealed that these early versions of the GDI+ classes .NET Framework (such as the classes Bitmap and Graphics) aren't hardware optimized, and there's often a great deal of behind-the-scenes format conversions going on when copying bitmaps from place to place. The poor performance as the number of simultaneous moving objects increases is probably because of the nonoptimized nature of the GDI+ functions in this current version of the .NET Framework.

You can do a number of things to improve the performance of the graphics. The first is to "drop down" to the Win32 API and use the good old BitBlt function. A second option is to explore using DirectX functionality (Chapter 8, "Using DirectX," covers this technology). Either of these options will probably require a nice chunk of refactoring (for example, DirectX uses a "surface," which probably needs to be created in the manager object). In any event, if you're going to make further use of this SpritePanel/Sprite functionality, you'll probably be doing something to improve performance, especially if the new project requires moving dozens of sprites, so you can tackle that refactoring project at the same time that you change the existing two classes to inherit from a common ancestor.

CHAPTER 4

More OOPing Around

Inheritance is a powerful concept, and you can use it in many different ways to solve a problem. However, inheritance can also be misused, or used in the wrong way. Such misuse can lead to overly complex solutions or ones that don't scale well. This chapter demonstrates this type of poor design choice.

The three games in this chapter use a game element called a *tile*, a small square piece containing one of four shapes—a square, a circle, a triangle, or a diamond. A shape can be one of four colors—red, blue, yellow, or green. Figure 4-1 shows each of the four shapes.

Figure 4-1. The four colored shapes used in this chapter's games

Without getting into too much detail too soon, the following list introduces the three games so you can see how the design of the Tile class might affect them:

Brain Drain Concentration: This is the standard "memory game," where users flip over tiles to find two that match. There are 32 tiles—two of each color/shape combination (four colors and four shapes make 16 possibilities, and two of each possibility makes 32 total). Users can also play a "double game," where there are four possibilities of each, making 64 total tiles.

DeducTile Reasoning: This game creates a puzzle of four tiles. Each shape and each color is represented only once in the puzzle. Clues are then given as to the orientation and position of the four tiles. The player must order the tiles into the correct orientation based on clues.

Lose Your Mind: A variant of Mastermind, this game creates a puzzle of four tiles, each having any shape or color (duplicates allowed). After the player guesses, hints are given as to how many correct shapes and colors appear in the proper locations and how many correct shapes and colors appear in the wrong locations. The variation from traditional Mastermind is that the player is really solving two puzzles at the same time—one for the shapes and one for the colors.

Setting Up the Graphics

Instead of using animated bitmaps for the graphics for these games, this chapter focuses on standard GDI+ drawing routines. GDI+ (which stands for *Graphics Device Interchange, Plus*) is the subset of the .NET Framework that deals with drawing. If you're familiar with pre-.NET drawing in any Windows programming language, you might remember the vast assortment of handles and device contexts and bitblts (oh, my!) and the potential memory problems involved if you forgot to release a handle or failed to recognize a bad return code. Fortunately, .NET has eliminated most of this headache. Like all other .NET Framework classes, the garbage collector manages the memory for all GDI+ classes automatically. This means you often don't have to worry about cleaning up after yourself. Listing 4-1 shows some simple drawing commands that give you most of the backgrounds you need to draw the tiles used in this chapter.

Listing 4-1. Simple GDI+ Example

```
Private Sub DrawTest(ByVal g As Graphics)

    Dim b As SolidBrush
    Dim p As Pen
    Dim r As Rectangle

    b = New SolidBrush(Color.Blue)
    p = Pens.White
    r = New Rectangle(10, 10, 50, 50)

    g.FillRectangle(b, r)
    g.DrawRectangle(p, r)

End Sub
```

Listing 4-1 uses several of the major GDI+ classes. The first of these is the Graphics class, which is passed into the test procedure as a parameter. Think of a Graphics object as a virtual surface onto which the drawing will be done, sort of like a digital sheet of paper.

 NOTE *Old-school Windows programmers might equate a* Graphics *object to a device context. In fact, the* Graphics *class encapsulates all of the device context functionality.*

The next object is a SolidBrush, which is one of several descendants of the Brush class. You use brushes for filling areas with a single color, a color gradient, a pattern, or even a bitmap image. The SolidBrush class fills an area with a solid color. A Pen, on the other hand, draws lines. Listing 4-1 creates a white Pen. Note the difference in how Listing 4-1 creates the Brush instance and the Pen instance. With the Brush instance, a new instance was created by using the standard constructor (which takes a color as a parameter). The Pen instance, on the other hand, was created using a constant Pen object found in the .NET Framework. You can find similar Brush constants, as well; this example uses different methods of creation for illustration purposes.

The third variable used in Listing 4-1 is a Rectangle object—used to define a rectangle, obviously. There are two different constructors for the Rectangle class; this one takes left, top, width, and height parameters that define the location and size of the shape.

NOTE *The second* Rectangle *constructor takes a* Point *structure and a* Size *structure as its two parameters. Both constructors yield similar results—the one you choose depends on what data type you have available at the time you create the rectangle.*

The last two lines of Listing 4-1 do the actual drawing. First, the declared rectangle is filled in with the blue brush. Second, it's outlined with the white Pen. The DrawRectangle and FillRectangle methods both exist on the Graphics object, so this is where the drawing happens.

One final thing to notice about Listing 4-1 is that the Pen and Brush (or the Rectangle, for that matter) are never destroyed, disposed of, freed, released, or any other word you might use to describe removing these objects from memory. As mentioned earlier, the .NET Framework garbage collector handles all of this for you.

Creating the Base Tile Class

You know you're going render the tiles via GDI vs. an animated bitmap/sprite method, so now it's time to decide how to organize the Tile class. At first, it may seem natural to create a base ancestor class and have four descendant classes encapsulate the drawing of each shape, as shown in Figure 4-2.

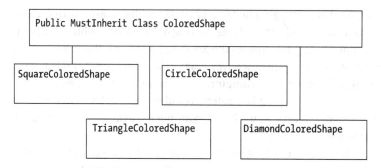

Figure 4-2. First pass at the Tile *class*

CAUTION *You'll see later (unfortunately for me,* much *later) how and why this design for the* Tile *class breaks down. (See the "Developing Lose Your Mind" section.)*

The base class has the name ColoredShape. What's particularly interesting (and happily accidental) about this class once it's completed is that it uses a variety of the object-oriented features available in a .NET Framework language, especially for a relatively small class. Listing 4-2 shows the member interface for this class.

Listing 4-2. The ColoredShape *Base Class Interface*

```
Public MustInherit Class ColoredShape
    Inherits Control
    Implements IComparable

    Public Function CompareTo(ByVal obj As Object) _
      As Integer Implements System.IComparable.CompareTo
    Property Backwards() As Boolean
    Property Border() As Integer
    Property Color() As Color
    ReadOnly Property ColorWord() As String
    MustOverride ReadOnly Property ShapeWord() As String
    Overrides Function ToString() As String
    Protected Overridable Sub Draw(ByVal g As Graphics)
    Protected Overrides Sub OnPaint(ByVal e As _
        System.Windows.Forms.PaintEventArgs)
    Shadows Property Width() As Integer
```

```
Shadows Property Height() As Integer
Public Overloads Function Equals(ByVal s As ColoredShape) As Boolean
Public Shared Function CreateByIndex(ByVal iShape As Integer, _
    ByVal iColor As Integer) As ColoredShape

End Class
```

Just a brief perusal of this class definition should cause you to feel like you're swimming in .NET keywords. `Shared Function`, `MustOverride`, `Overrides`, `Shadows`, `Implements`, `Overloads`...the list is quite impressive for such a relatively small class. This gives you a golden opportunity to learn all about the class while also learning the meaning of these class keywords. Let's study each member individually.

Understanding the Class Definition

The class definition inherits from the base class `Control`, meaning that it acquires all of that class's functionality for free. In other words, properties that define the control's location and size already exist, as well as the inner machinery to maintain a window handle. The second part of the class definition declares that this class implements the `IComparable` interface. An interface is a declared set of properties, events, and methods that provide functionality. However, the author of the interface provides no code implementation for this set of members. Instead, the interface defines a set of functionality that can be obtained by providing the implementation for this subset of members. In the case of the `IComparable` interface, the functionality provided is the ability to compare two classes to determine which one might come before the other when sorting them. You can imagine different requirements for sorting two classes depending on the problem at hand. For example, you might need to sort two customers alphabetically for one report and then sort them by the dollars they've spent at your company for another report. You could do this by implementing separate `IComparable` interfaces for the `Customer` class.

When you declare that a class implements a specific interface, you must implement every member declared in that interface before the program will compile. You'll learn more about interfaces, including how to create and use interfaces that you create yourself, in Chapter 6, "Using Polymorphism via Interfaces."

You might observe that the code in Listing 4-1, which lists the member definitions for the `ColoredShape` class, is a type of code interface in itself. It lists the members for a class without showing their implementation. This code listing as shown isn't 100-percent legal VB .NET code, however. It shows the actual class implementation and hides everything except for the first line that declares each member. Seeing class definitions in this way is a great first way to understand what a class is supposed to do before learning how it actually does those things.

Understanding the CompareTo Method

The CompareTo method implements the CompareTo method of the IComparable interface. As you can see, the code must specify that this member does indeed implement the member for this interface—simply having the same name as the member interface isn't enough:

```
Public Function CompareTo(ByVal obj As Object) _
    As Integer Implements System.IComparable.CompareTo

    Dim o As ColoredShape = CType(obj, ColoredShape)

    Return Me.Top.CompareTo(o.Top)
End Function
```

This CompareTo method compares the tops of the current control instance and the one passed in, meaning that any sort using this method will sort the tile controls in order of their vertical orientation on the form. You'll see why you're using this sorting method in the "Developing DeducTile Reasoning" section later in the chapter.

The CompareTo method is the only member contained in the IComparable interface, meaning that the implementation of this method completes the implementation of this interface for this class. Other interfaces can (and usually do) have multiple members in them.

Understanding the Backwards Property

The Backwards property is a fairly uninteresting Boolean property that determines whether the Tile class is currently displaying its shape (Backwards = False) or whether the tile is "flipped over" and hiding its shape (Backwards = True). You define the property using the standard paired private variable method you've seen in prior examples:

```
Private FBackwards As Boolean
Property Backwards() As Boolean
    Get
        Return FBackwards
    End Get
    Set(ByVal Value As Boolean)
        FBackwards = Value
        Invalidate()
    End Set
End Property
```

The only line of code that might be new to you is the call to the Invalidate method, which forces the control to repaint itself. This method should be called on a control whenever the appearance of the control is changing.

Understanding the Border Property

Another standard property, the Border property specifies how many black pixels are to be drawn around the tile. By drawing the black border between tiles "inside" the tile itself, you save yourself from having to compute a border between tiles when trying to arrange them together. In other words, if you have 32-pixel-wide tiles and want to arrange them horizontally, you can simply set their coordinates at 0, 32, 64, and so on. If the black border wasn't "built into" the control, you'd have to put the tiles at the locations 2, 36, 66, and so on, which is harder to compute. The code for the Border property is as follows:

```
Private FBorder As Integer = 2
Property Border() As Integer
    Get
        Return FBorder
    End Get
    Set(ByVal Value As Integer)
        If Value < 0 Then
            Throw New Exception("Illegal value")
        Else
            FBorder = Value
            Invalidate()
        End If
    End Set
End Property
```

New features in this code include the fact that the private variable initializes to 2 (a value you'll probably rarely change, but you should reserve the right to change it by implementing this property) and the fact that some range validation happens when the property is set to make sure the value is non-negative. If a negative value is attempted, an exception is thrown and the value isn't stored.

Understanding the Color Property

The Color property describes the color of the shape. As mentioned, the shape is always one of four colors, so you can't simply use the existing ForeColor property on the Control class. If you do, nothing prevents a user from setting the color to gray, black, or something that doesn't make sense for the tile games. Instead, you should implement a new property:

```
Private FColor As Color = Color.Red
Property Color() As Color
    Get
        Return FColor
    End Get
    Set(ByVal Value As Color)

        Dim aC() As Color = _
            {Color.Red, Color.Blue, Color.Green, Color.Yellow}

        If Array.IndexOf(aC, Value) = -1 Then
            Throw New Exception(_
                "colors constrained to Red/Blue/Green/Yellow")
        Else
            FColor = Value
            Invalidate()
        End If
    End Set
End Property
```

This property is of type System.Color, but it performs range checking to make sure the color is constrained to one of the four colors necessary for the tile. If the color is invalid, an exception is thrown. The range check itself uses an array of colors and the Array class's IndexOf method to determine if the color is valid. You could just as easily use a series of Or clauses, but I find this code to be more readable.

Understanding the ColorWord Property

The ColorWord property is declared ReadOnly, meaning that the user of the class can't set it. The value of this property is simply the string representation of the color, which is used when a tile needs to be described in text (*Red Square*). You can use this property when testing your games by writing the solution tile sequence to the debug window, for example, to make sure the clue generation or hint code is creating the correct results:

```
ReadOnly Property ColorWord() As String
    Get
        Dim s As String
```

```
    If Color.Equals(Color.Red) Then
        s = "Red"
    ElseIf Color.Equals(Color.Blue) Then
        s = "Blue"
    ElseIf Color.Equals(Color.Green) Then
        s = "Green"
    ElseIf Color.Equals(Color.Yellow) Then
        s = "Yellow"
    Else
        'won't happen, but just in case
        s = Color.ToString
    End If

    Return s
  End Get
End Property
```

Note that because this is a read-only property, it doesn't require a Set clause. In fact, the compiler complains if you attempt to add a Set clause to a read-only property.

Understanding the ShapeWord Property

The ShapeWord property is declared both ReadOnly and MustOverride. A property with the keyword MustOverride has no implementation in the base class; therefore, the only code in the base class related to this property is the declaration line shown in Listing 4-2.

This property returns the shape of the tile as a string, which is used in the same places that the ColorWord property is used—whenever a tile has to be described in text.

Understanding the ToString Method

The ToString method is declared Overrides, meaning that this method exists in an ancestor class and the functionality is being changed in this descendant class. The ToString method is first implemented way up in the Object class—the root, granddaddy class to all other classes in the .NET Framework.

The implementation of the ToString method for this class returns the color and shape of the current Tile object as strings, with a space between them:

```
Overrides Function ToString() As String
    Return Me.ColorWord & " " & Me.ShapeWord
End Function
```

Examples of what this method might return are *Red Circle* and *Blue Triangle*.

Understanding the Draw Method

The Draw method is protected, meaning that it can be called only from within the class and from within descendant classes. In addition, it's defined as Overridable, meaning that descendant classes can extend the functionality of this method by overriding it. The base method handles the drawing of the background part of the tile. The plan is to have the subclasses handle the drawing of the different shapes:

```
Protected Overridable Sub Draw(ByVal g As Graphics)

    Dim b As LinearGradientBrush

    Dim iRad As Integer = Width - (Me.Border * 2)
    Dim r As New Rectangle(Me.Border, Me.Border, iRad, iRad)

    b = New LinearGradientBrush(r, _
        Color.White, Color.DarkGray, LinearGradientMode.Vertical)
    g.FillRectangle(b, r)
    g.DrawRectangle(Pens.White, r)

End Sub
```

This code defines a rectangle within the bounds of the control. The Border property defines the left and top edges of the rectangle, and the rectangle's width and height are defined as the width/height of the control less twice the Border property. This gives you a rectangle that fits inside the control with an even border around it.

 NOTE *This definition doesn't consider the position of the control. That is, you don't have to define the rectangle in relation to where the control might be on its parent form. All drawing within a control happens with the origin in the upper-left corner of the control.*

Drawing the tile happens with a new type of brush. This brush is a LinearGradientBrush, and its function is to draw a color gradient in a specified direction, using two specified colors. The Tile class creates a white-to-gray gradient from top to bottom of the tile, producing a subtle shadow effect. The rectangle is then outlined in white.

Understanding the OnPaint Method

The OnPaint method is part of the Control class; you're overriding it here so you can extend the original functionality of the control. The OnPaint method is called automatically whenever the control is to be redrawn, so this is the "hook," or the proper place, to put the drawing code:

```
Protected Overrides Sub OnPaint(ByVal e As_
    System.Windows.Forms.PaintEventArgs)

    MyBase.OnPaint(e)
    e.Graphics.SmoothingMode = SmoothingMode.AntiAlias
    Draw(e.Graphics)
End Sub
```

The first line calls the OnPaint method in the base class. This ensures that any custom paint event handlers attached to this control by an outside program are called and also that any painting that might be done by the base class actually gets done. For the purposes of this control, the painting is done 100 percent by this class and its subclasses, so this call isn't strictly needed. However, Microsoft recommends your class overrides always call their base class methods whether strictly needed or not. The second line turns anti-aliased drawing on for this control, which makes the shapes appear smoother. The last line calls the Draw method discussed earlier.

Understanding the Width and Height Properties

Yet another member keyword is used for the width and height properties—the Shadows keyword. By indicating these members with Shadows, you're saying that although these members exist in the base class, you want to replace the functionality of those members with your own. This is different from overriding a member because a member must be declared Overridable in a base class or you can't override it in a subclass. You can shadow a member without "permission" from the base class—more like a hostile takeover of a member.

The intended purpose of shadowing the Width and Height members in the ColoredShape class is to constrain the shape of the tile to a square. You do this by

changing the Width and Height to the same value whenever one of these properties changes. The following code shows the shadowed Width property and shows
how it uses the passed-in value to change the width of the control and change
the height at the same time:

```
Shadows Property Width() As Integer
    Get
        Return MyBase.Width
    End Get

    Set(ByVal Value As Integer)
        MyBase.Width = Value
        MyBase.Height = Value
    End Set
End Property
```

Understanding the Equals Method

The Equals method is another one that's defined way up the class tree in the
root class, Object. This method is declared with the keyword Overloads. An overloaded method is where the same method name can be declared multiple times
within a class, differing only in the parameters passed to it. Consider this simple example:

```
Public Overloads Function SumTwoNumbers(_
    ByVal x As Integer, ByVal y As Integer) As Integer

    Return x + y
 End Function

Public Overloads Function SumTwoNumbers(_
    ByVal x As Single, ByVal y As Single) As Single

    Return x + y
End Function
```

You can declare these two functions in the same class even though they have
the same name. When an outsider calls the SumTwoNumbers method, the compiler
determines if any of the overloaded methods have a signature matching the one
that the caller is attempting and allows the call to compile if it finds a match. If it
doesn't find a match, it produces an error.

In the case of the Equals method, it's usually overloaded so that you can pass
in a class of the same type as the class being defined. This allows the method to

directly compare whether the two tiles are the same. In these games, two tiles are defined as being the same if they have the same color and the same shape. Therefore, the Equals function compares these two elements and returns True if they're the same:

```
Public Overloads Function Equals(ByVal s As ColoredShape) As Boolean

    'two tiles equal if color and class equal
    Return Me.Color.Equals(s.Color) _
      And s.GetType.FullName = Me.GetType.FullName

End Function
```

Because the shape of each tile is being implemented as a separate subclass, it's necessary to compare the type of the two classes to determine equality:

```
Public Overloads Function Equals(ByVal s As ColoredShape) As Boolean

    'two tiles equal if color and class equal
    Return Me.Color.Equals(s.Color) _
        And s.GetType.Equals(Me.GetType)

End Function
```

Understanding the CreateByIndex Function

This method is declared as Shared Function, which means you don't actually call this method from an object instance but from the class name itself. The reason you're implementing this method as shared is that its purpose is to return an instance of the ColoredShape class, based on a passed-in integer representing the color and shape to create. You can't implement this method on the ColoredShape class itself because you've already chosen to mark this class as MustOverride, meaning you can't create an instance of this class (you can only create its subclasses). To create a method that was usable from the base class, you have to create it as shared.

Why do you need a method that creates a tile based on an index? The answer to this is so you can create multiple tiles in a loop. The following code creates 16 tiles, one in each shape/color permutation:

```
Dim oShape As ColoredShape
  Dim i, j as Integer

  For i = 0 To 3                          '4 shapes...
      For j = 0 To 3                      '4 colors...
          oShape = ColoredShape.CreatByIndex(i, j)
          oShape.Width = 48

          Me.Controls.Add(oShape)
      Next
  Next
```

You can see where having the ability to create many tiles in an integer-based loop might be useful. In fact, you can use code similar to the previous loop to create the starting board for the Brain Drain Concentration game.

The method itself merely produces the correct subclass based on the two integers and throws exceptions if the passed-in numbers aren't in the range 0–3:

```
Public Shared Function CreateByIndex(ByVal iShape As Integer, _
    ByVal iColor As Integer) As ColoredShape

    Dim o As ColoredShape
    Dim oClr As New Color

    Select Case iShape
        Case 0
          o = New SquareColoredShape
        Case 1
          o = New CircleColoredShape
        Case 2
          o = New DiamondColoredShape
        Case 3
          o = New TriangleColoredShape
        Case Else
          Throw New Exception("iShape index must be 0-3")
        End Select

    Select Case iColor
        Case 0
          o.Color = oClr.Red
        Case 1
          o.Color = oClr.Yellow
        Case 2
          o.Color = oClr.Blue
```

```
        Case 3
          o.Color = oClr.Green
        Case Else
          Throw New Exception("iColor index must be 0-3")
        End Select


      Return o
End Function
```

Subclassing the ColoredShape Class

Learning about the ancestor ColoredShape class is educational for learning object-oriented features, which is why this chapter spends a good deal of time going through each member. However, you still don't have a class you can use in the games. You still need to create descendant classes to implement each shape.

Fortunately, the base class has already done most of the work for the class, and all that remains to implement in the subclasses are two methods—the overridden Draw method and the ShapeWord method. Furthermore, the latter of these two methods is trivial; it merely returns a string corresponding to the name of the shape.

The Draw method on each subclass is pretty interesting, however, and demonstrates some important features in the GDI+ part of the .NET Framework. Listing 4-3 shows the Draw method of the DiamondColoredShape class.

Listing 4-3. Drawing the Diamond-Shaped Tile in a Subclass

```
Protected Overrides Sub Draw(ByVal g As Graphics)

    MyBase.Draw(g)        'draw the background
    If Backwards Then Exit Sub

    Dim b As New SolidBrush(Me.Color)
    Dim iRad As Integer = (Width - Me.Border) \ 2
    Dim ogc As GraphicsContainer

    Dim r As New Rectangle(-iRad \ 2, -iRad \ 2, iRad, iRad)

    ogc = g.BeginContainer
    Try
        With g
            .SmoothingMode = SmoothingMode.AntiAlias
            .TranslateTransform(Width \ 2, Width \ 2)
            .RotateTransform(45)
```

```
                    .ScaleTransform(0.8, 0.8)
                    .FillRectangle(b, r)
                    .DrawRectangle(Pens.Black, r)
                End With
            Finally
                g.EndContainer(ogc)
            End Try
        End Sub
```

The first line of the overridden `Draw` method calls the base class `Draw`, which you've already seen in the code that draws the background of the tile using the cool gradient brush. The next line exits if the tile is backward because the shape on the tile is obscured by design.

Once the method determines that the shape is to be drawn, it creates a new class called `GraphicsContainer`. This object allows you to save the state of a `Graphics` object and return it without having to undo all of the transformations you've done. You accomplish this by calling the `BeginContainer` method on the `Graphics` object, which returns an instance of the `GraphicsContainer` class and then later calls `EndContainer` to restore the `Graphics` object to its exact state when the `BeginContainer` was called. Placing the `EndContainer` inside a `Finally` exception handler guarantees that it gets called regardless of any errors that take place beforehand.

Now that you have a method to save and restore the state of the `Graphics` object, what changes do you intend to make to it? For these shape-drawing routines, the goal is to change the coordinate space of the class so you can draw a diamond. One way to draw the diamond is to manually map out the four coordinates and draw them that way. This method would work perfectly for this case, but consider a second method. What if you could declare a rectangle, move it to the middle of the tile, and rotate it 45 degrees? That would also be a diamond.

The `Graphics` class allows you to perform these transformations on its coordinate system on the fly. Listing 4-3 does exactly this—transforms the graphics coordinate system to the middle of the tile, rotates it 45 degrees, and scales it down so that its size is comparable to the other shapes. Once you've transformed the `Graphics` class in this way, drawing the diamond is as easy as declaring a `Rectangle` object centered on the origin (0, 0) and calling the `DrawRectangle` method. This is much easier than calculating coordinates yourself—why not have the .NET Framework do the calculations for you?

This technique is especially powerful when drawing sprites on the screen. Imagine how easy it'll be to make a square "roll" across the screen by simply translating and rotating the `Graphics` class within a loop calling the same `DrawingRectangle` method over and over. Sounds like the inspiration for a Space Invaders game to me!

Each of the three other tile subclasses performs drawing in a similar way; the difference lies only in which shape is drawn. You can study each as you see fit.

Developing Brain Drain Concentration

You've spent a ton of time creating a game piece—it's finally time to create a game. The first game of the trio is the standard "memory game." It's named *Brain Drain Concentration* because having to memorize the location of colors and shapes gets pretty confusing.

Fortunately, you've already done most of the work in creating the memory game because the Tile class (and its descendants) handles most of the work (following the rule that an object should be responsible for itself). The Tile class draws itself and can be flipped over, which is what's required for a Concentration-style game like this. There are really only a few pieces of logic remaining to get this game working:

- Creating and arranging multiple tiles to make up the board

- Removing tile matches from the board

- Handling when the player wins or loses

The next sections handle each of these tasks individually.

Creating the Game Board

The game board consists of 32 tiles—four possible colors and four possible shapes make 16 total tiles. A pair of each type of tile is required so they can be matched, and this gives you 32. You create the 32 tiles using nested loops, as shown in Listing 4-4.

Listing 4-4. Creating 32 Tiles

```
For i = 0 To 3                    '4 shapes...
   For j = 0 To 3                 '4 colors...
      For k = 0 To 1              '2 copies...
         oShape = ColoredShape.CreateByIndex(i, j)
         oShape.Backwards = True
         oShape.Width = 48
         AddHandler oShape.Click, AddressOf ShapeClick
```

```
'set the location on the form
oShape.Left = (iCtr Mod 8) * oShape.Width
oShape.Top = (iCtr \ 8) * oShape.Height
iCtr += 1

'adding a reference to two places, the form and an arraylist
FTiles.Add(oShape)
Me.Controls.Add(oShape)
        Next
    Next
Next
```

The key to creating the tiles in this way is the CreateByIndex method in the ColoredShape class. If you'll recall, this is a shared method on the base class that returns a tile based on integers to represent both the color and shape that the tile should be.

Once this code creates a tile, it has to do a few other things. First, the code sets the tile's Backwards property to True, meaning that the tile is flipped over so the user can't see the shape. Next, the code sets the size of each tile to 48 (remember that the ColoredShape control forces the tiles to be square), and it sets the location of each tile so that they appear in four rows of eight tiles each. After that, the code attaches a method named ShapeClick to each tile's Click event, meaning that this code will run whenever a user clicks a tile (you'll examine that code later in the section "Removing Tile Matches from the Board"). Finally, the code adds each tile to *two* different collections. The first collection is an ArrayList named FTiles that's declared on the game's form, and the second is the form's Controls collection (you must add all controls explicitly to their parent's Controls collection or they won't render).

You might be asking why each control is added to two collections. The reason is that future routines are going to have to loop through all the tiles and perform some action on them, and it's easier to iterate through a collection containing only ColoredShape class instances than iterating through the form's Controls collection, which may contain other controls besides the ColoredShape classes.

You've now created the 32 tiles, but their arrangement is a problem. Because you created them in a structured loop, all the tiles live in a prearranged pattern on the board. It wouldn't take a player very long to figure out this pattern and use this knowledge to solve the puzzle. Clearly, you need to mix up the arrangement of the tiles on the board. Listing 4-5 handles this.

Listing 4-5. Mixing Up the Tiles

```
Dim oRand As New Random
Dim i, j, k As Integer
Dim p As Point

'swap positions randomly
For k = 0 To 999
    i = oRand.Next(0, FTiles.Count)
    j = oRand.Next(0, FTiles.Count)
    If i <> j Then
        p = CType(FTiles.Item(i), ColoredShape).Location

        CType(FTiles.Item(i), ColoredShape).Location = _
          CType(FTiles.Item(j), ColoredShape).Location

        CType(FTiles.Item(j), ColoredShape).Location = p
    End If
Next
```

The randomizer routine works by looping 1,000 times. In each loop, the program chooses two tiles at random and swaps their positions. This loops gives one example of why the program required a second separate collection containing only ColoredTile instances instead of simply using the form's Controls collection. Having a separate loop allows you to easily choose two tiles randomly in the collection without having to see if the control you chose is actually a Tile instance. In addition, you can typecast the element of the collection back to a ColoredShape (with the CType function) without fear that you've accidentally tried to typecast a MenuItem or a Button into the wrong class, which generates an exception (a runtime error).

Removing Tile Matches from the Board

As mentioned earlier, each tile runs an event handler named ShapeClick whenever it's clicked. Listing 4-6 shows that event handler in its entirety, which runs when a user clicks a tile.

Listing 4-6. The ShapeClick *Method*

```
Private Sub ShapeClick(ByVal sender As Object, _
    ByVal e As System.EventArgs)

    Dim s As ColoredShape = sender
```

```
        s.Backwards = False
        oWav.Play("die1", 100)
        Application.DoEvents()

        If FFirstOneFlipped Is Nothing Then
            FFirstOneFlipped = s
        Else
            If s.Equals(FFirstOneFlipped) Then
                System.Threading.Thread.Sleep(100)
                Me.Controls.Remove(s)
                Me.Controls.Remove(FFirstOneFlipped)

                FTiles.Remove(s)
                FTiles.Remove(FFirstOneFlipped)
                oWav.Play("die1", 100)

                If FTiles.Count = 0 Then
                    oGT.StopTimer()
                    oWav.Play("ovation", 100)
                    MsgBox("you win")
                End If
            Else
                System.Threading.Thread.Sleep(500)
                s.Backwards = True
                FFirstOneFlipped.Backwards = True
                oWav.Play("ouch", 100)
            End If
            FFirstOneFlipped = Nothing
        End If

End Sub
```

The first lines of the ShapeClick routine flip the tile over by simply setting the Backwards property back to False. A sound effect also plays—the same WavLibrary class used in Chapter 3, "Understanding Object-Oriented Programming from the Start." (Code reuse at its finest!)

The next thing to determine is if the tile that was just flipped over is the first tile of a pair or the second. If it's the first tile, then the ShapeClick can end because there's nothing left to do. Only after the second tile is flipped over should you conduct any checks to determine if the user found a match.

You answer the first tile/second tile question by using a form-level variable named FFirstOneFlipped. This variable either holds a ColoredShape instance or is set to Nothing. If the variable is empty, you know that the tile just flipped over is the first one of the pair, and all you need to do is to set the FFirstOneFlipped variable to point to the tile just flipped. If the variable already has a value, then you know that the tile just flipped over is the second of a pair, and you can check to see if the user found a match.

The code after the Else in Listing 4-6 is the code that runs when a user flips over the second tile of a pair. The program first compares the two tiles to see if they're the same color and shape using the Equals method you put on the ColoredShape class. If they're equal, the program then removes the tiles from both collections. If the tiles aren't equal, then both tiles flip back over after a short half-second pause. In either case, whether the tiles are a match or not, the FFirstOneFlipped variable is set back to Nothing, which tells the program after the next tile flip that a new tile pair has begun.

Handling When the Player Wins or Loses

Hidden in Listing 4-6 is the check for whether the player has won the game. You conduct this check by seeing if there are zero tiles left in the FTiles ArrayList (another example of why the game required a separate collection to hold the tile instances). If there are indeed no tiles left, then the player has won the game and is told so.

Losing the game is a bit more complicated because as of yet there's no way to lose the game (the player can simply flip tiles over forever until he clears the board). Because games aren't much of a challenge if there's no way to lose them, you have to introduce some new element so that the player can fail as well as succeed. Let's add a countdown timer to the game so the player loses if the timer reaches zero. The countdown timer is a good candidate for a new class that can count down from a specified time and then fire an event when the clock reaches 0. Listing 4-7 shows the public interface for this new class.

Listing 4-7. The GameTimer *Class Public Interface*

```
Public Class GameTimer
    Inherits Control

    Public Event SecondsChanged(ByVal sender As Object, ByVal t As TimeSpan)
    Public Event TimesUp(ByVal sender As Object)

    Property StartAt() As TimeSpan
    Public Sub StartTimer()
    Public Sub StopTimer()
```

```
Protected Overrides Sub OnPaint(ByVal e As _
    System.Windows.Forms.PaintEventArgs)
Public Sub AddTime(ByVal t As TimeSpan)
Shadows ReadOnly Property Enabled() As Boolean

End Class
```

The GameTimer class doesn't do anything new that needs to be covered on a line-by-line basis. Instead, Table 4-1 summarizes what each member does.

Table 4-1. Members of the GameTimer Class

MEMBER NAME	MEMBER TYPE	DESCRIPTION
StartAt	Property	Defines at which time the clock should begin ("Put three minutes on the clock, Bob"). This property is of type TimeSpan—a .NET Framework type that represents a time interval. This type is different from a DateTime type, which represents a single point in time. See the .NET Framework help documentation for more information on TimeSpan types.
StartTimer	Method	Starts the clock.
StopTime	Method	Stops the clock.
AddTime	Method	Allows time to be added (or taken off) the clock during the game. You could implement a 10-second penalty using this method.
OnPaint	Method	Draws the remaining time onto the control.
SecondsChanged	Event	Fires whenever the seconds tick down by one. Used in this game to change the color of the time remaining to red when less than one minute remains.
TimesUp	Event	Fires when no time remains on the clock.

Listing 4-8 shows a GameTimer being created by the Brain Drain Concentration form during its Load event.

Listing 4-8. Creating a GameTimer *Class and Its Event Handlers*

```
Dim oGT As GameTimer

Private Sub fConcentration_Load(ByVal sender As System.Object, _
    ByVal e As System.EventArgs) Handles MyBase.Load

    oGT = New GameTimer
    With oGT
        .Dock = DockStyle.Bottom
        .Height = 32
        .Font = New Font("Tahoma", 16, _
          FontStyle.Italic Or FontStyle.Bold)
        .ForeColor = Color.LightGray
        AddHandler .TimesUp, AddressOf TimerDone
        AddHandler .SecondsChanged, AddressOf TimerSeconds
    End With
    Me.Controls.Add(oGT)

    StartGame()
End Sub

Private Sub TimerDone(ByVal sender As Object)
    MsgBox("you lose")
End Sub

Private Sub TimerSeconds(ByVal sender As Object, ByVal t As TimeSpan)
    If t.TotalSeconds < 60 Then
        CType(sender, GameTimer).ForeColor = Color.Red
    Else
        CType(sender, GameTimer).ForeColor = Color.LightGray
    End If
End Sub
```

Now that you've implemented a countdown timer opponent, writing the code for the player losing the game is trivial—you simply notify him in the TimesUp event of the GameTimer class.

Wrapping Up Brain Drain Concentration

Brain Drain Concentration is the easiest of the three games in this chapter to implement because the game logic is pretty simple. All you had to do was create two of each tile types, mix them up, and handle the user clicking and removing matches.

The next game, DeducTile Reasoning, is actually the most difficult of the three to implement because the game logic gets pretty difficult. It's a great example of a seemingly simple problem spiraling into a complex logical problem.

Developing DeducTile Reasoning

DeducTile Reasoning is a game where four tiles appear top to bottom, and the player must guess the correct sequence of the tiles based on the clues given. Like Brain Drain Concentration, the user's opponent is the clock—he must solve the puzzle in a set amount of time. Figure 4-3 shows the game.

Figure 4-3. DeducTile Reasoning, guessing the order of tiles by textual clues

In this game, the puzzle is constrained by the fact that each shape and each color is represented only once each. This limits the number of possible puzzle permutations to 576. Where did that number come from? Well, you're dealing with four shapes, which you can represent using the integers 0, 1, 2, and 3. There are 24 ways to order these four integers:

0,1,2,3	2,0,1,3	3,2,0,1
0,1,3,2	2,0,3,1	3,1,0,2
0,2,1,3	3,0,1,2	1,2,3,0
0,2,3,1	3,0,2,1	1,3,2,0
0,3,2,1	1,2,0,3	2,3,1,0
0,3,1,2	1,3,0,2	2,1,3,0
1,0,2,3	2,1,0,3	3,2,1,0
1,0,3,2	2,3,0,1	3,1,2,0

This gives you all the possible arrangements of the four shapes. The same 24 permutations represent the possible arrangements of colors. Multiplying 24 by 24 yields the total possible puzzle permutations of four shapes and four colors, giving a total of 576 puzzle possibilities.

Generating Clues

The difficult part of coding this game is generating the clues. The game must give enough information to solve the puzzle or it'll be impossible to win. Take, for example, a case where you give a single clue:

```
The Red Tile is first.
```

This obviously isn't enough information to solve the puzzle. If this is the only clue you give, the game would devolve into a random guessing game, which isn't fun. Adding a second clue yields a bit more information:

```
The Circle is not Red.
```

This clue tells the player that the circle is green, blue, or yellow. When coupled with the first clue, the player knows that the circle must be in position 2, 3, or 4. This is more information than the player originally had but still not enough information to solve the puzzle.

The game must be sure it generates enough clues so that the player can solve the puzzle. To accomplish this, the program generates all 576 possible solutions and then picks one at random as the puzzle that will be presented to the user. Then, the program generates a clue that pertains to the puzzle, and all the non-solutions that this clue doesn't pertain to are "crossed off the list." Clue generation continues until only one of the 576 puzzles remains—this remaining puzzle is the same as the puzzle presented to the user.

Creating the FourTuple Class

You could spend a ton of time hard-coding the 576 possible puzzles, but you're better off having the computer do the work for you. The first step of generating these puzzles is to store the 24 permutations of the numbers 0–3. Listing 4-9 shows the class to store four integers.

Listing 4-9. The FourTuple *Class, Meant to Store Four Integers Only*

```
Private Class FourTuple
    Public a As Integer
    Public b As Integer
    Public c As Integer
    Public d As Integer

    Public Sub New(ByVal ia As Integer, ByVal ib As Integer, _
        ByVal ic As Integer, ByVal id As Integer)

        a = ia
        b = ib
        c = ic
        d = id
    End Sub
End Class
```

 NOTE *This listing breaks one of my own rules by not even bothering to make "real" properties on this class to store the four integers—instead it uses simple public variables, so you can be pretty sure I'm not going to use this quickie class for anything important.*

Creating the TileCombo Class

The next class, called TileCombo, holds four individual ColoredShape classes. Listing 4-10 shows the public interface for this class.

Listing 4-10. The `TileCombo` *Class, Used During Clue Generation*

```
Public Class TileCombo
    Public Sub New(ByVal a As ColoredShape, ByVal b As ColoredShape, _
        ByVal c As ColoredShape, ByVal d As ColoredShape)
    Public Overloads Function Equals(ByVal t As TileCombo) As Boolean
    ReadOnly Property ColoredShape(ByVal i As Integer) As ColoredShape
    Property Eliminated() As Boolean
    Public Overrides Function ToString() As String
End Class
```

As you can see, the four `ColoredShapes` are passed right into the constructor, and no method exists to change them. The program uses a Boolean property named `Eliminated` when generating clues to determine if this clue has been "crossed off the list" as a possible puzzle solution based on the clues generated to this point.

Creating the TileComboPossiblesList Class

The group of 576 `TileCombo` classes would also benefit from being encapsulated into their own class because it seems natural to think of this "group of tiles" as a separate object with its own responsibilities. I named this class `TileComboPossiblesList`; Listing 4-11 shows its public interface. `TileComboPossiblesList` stores the 576 possible solutions and the one puzzle that will be shown to the user.

Listing 4-11. `TileComboPossiblesList`

```
Public Class TileComboPossiblesList

        Public Sub New()
        Public Function Item(ByVal i As Integer) As TileCombo
        Public Function Solution() As TileCombo
        Public Function SolutionsLeft() As Integer
        Public Function AllNonSolutionsEliminated() As Boolean
        Public Function NumberClueWouldEliminate_
           (ByVal c As TileComboClue) As Integer
        Public Sub EliminateBasedOnClue(ByVal c As TileComboClue)
        Public Sub EnumerateRemaining()
    End Class
```

It's the job of `TileComboPossiblesList` to generate the 576 permutations and then choose one at random as the puzzle to be shown to the player. In addition, clue instances will be passed into this class to eliminate "bad" tile combos from the list until only one remains.

As promised, the design for this seemingly simple game is getting complicated in a hurry. Perhaps seeing some code will help make some sense of how the classes fit together. Listing 4-12 shows a method on `TileComboPossiblesList` named `GeneratePossibles`, which creates the permutations of the solutions. This class is declared as private, which explains why it wasn't listed in the public interface shown in Listing 4-11.

Listing 4-12. The `GeneratePossibles` Method

```
Private Sub GeneratePossibles()

        Dim FTuples As ArrayList
        Dim i, j As Integer

        Dim oTi, oTj As FourTuple

        'these are the 24 ordered possibilities for integers 0,1,2,3
        FTuples = New ArrayList
        With FTuples
            .Add(New FourTuple(0, 1, 2, 3))
            .Add(New FourTuple(0, 1, 3, 2))
            .Add(New FourTuple(0, 2, 1, 3))

            (repeat 24 times for every numeric combination)
        End With

        'we need every permuation of every permutation.
        'this gives us 576 combinations
        FPossibles = New ArrayList
        For Each oTi In FTuples
            For Each oTj In FTuples
                FPossibles.Add(New TileCombo( _
                    ColoredShape.CreateByIndex(oTi.a, oTj.a), _
                    ColoredShape.CreateByIndex(oTi.b, oTj.b), _
                    ColoredShape.CreateByIndex(oTi.c, oTj.c), _
                    ColoredShape.CreateByIndex(oTi.d, oTj.d)))

            Next
        Next

    End Sub
```

Listing 4-12 doesn't show the repetitive code inside the block that starts With FTuples. As you can see, each numeric combination of integers 0–3 is stored in a FourTuple instance, and each instance is in turn stored in an ArrayList named FTuples. From there, a double For Each loop begins and inside a new TileCombo is created based on the integers stored in the FTuples ArrayList.

Creating the TileComboClue Class and Its Subclasses

What's now needed is a class to encapsulate a single textual clue. Listing 4-13 shows the code that serves this purpose, the TileComboClue class.

Listing 4-13. The TileComboClue *Class*

```
Public MustInherit Class TileComboClue

    Public Sub New(ByVal t As TileCombo)
    MustOverride Function ClueText() As String
    MustOverride Function CluePertainsTo(ByVal t As TileCombo) As Boolean
    Function HalfTheTime() As Boolean
    Public Function PositionalText(ByVal iPos As Integer) As String
End Class
```

This class is declared MustInherit, which means you can't create an instance of this class directly. Instead, you must create instances of the subclasses of this class. The subclasses of TileComboClue represent the several different styles of textual clues. For example, one clue type links the color and shape of a tile by stating something such as *The Square is Red* or *The Blue tile is a Circle*. Another type of clue indicates position, such as *The first tile is Green* or *The second tile is the Triangle*. There are eight separate clue subclasses, and you can add more by simply adding subclasses to the program. You'll see a neat trick that allows the program to randomly select which clue subclasses to use a bit later in the section "Creating the PuzzleGenerator Class."

Let's look at one of the clue subclasses in detail to learn how it functions. Listing 4-14 shows the clue class that links the color of one of the tiles to the shape. The ComboClueShapeIsColor class tells the player *The Square is Yellow* or *The Green Tile is a Triangle*.

Listing 4-14. The ComboClueShapeIsColor *Class*

```
Public Class ComboClueTheShapeIsColor
    Inherits TileComboClue

    Private FTile As ColoredShape
```

```
Public Sub New(ByVal t As TileCombo)
    MyBase.New(t)

    Dim oRand As New Random
    FTile = t.ColoredShape(oRand.Next(0, 4))

End Sub

Overrides Function ClueText() As String
    If HalfTheTime() Then
        Return "The " & FTile.ColorWord & _
            " tile is a " & FTile.ShapeWord
    Else
        Return "The " & FTile.ShapeWord & _
            " is " & FTile.ColorWord
    End If
End Function

'return true if the
Overrides Function CluePertainsTo(ByVal t As TileCombo) As Boolean

    Dim ocs As ColoredShape
    Dim i As Integer

    For i = 0 To 3
        ocs = t.ColoredShape(i)
        If ocs.Color.Equals(FTile.Color) Then
            Return ocs.ShapeWord.Equals(FTile.ShapeWord)
        End If
    Next
End Function

End Class
```

The constructor of all the TileComboClue classes receives a TileCombo instance as its parameter. In all cases, this TileCombo instance is the solution to the puzzle that will be displayed to the player. It's the job of the class to take this puzzle and construct a clue based on the puzzle. This class generates clue by simply choosing one of the four tiles randomly and storing it in the local variable FTile for later use.

The method ClueText is the function that returns the text of the clue. As with many of the clues, the clue class can return the same clue in different forms to further vary the appearance of the clues. In this method, a sentence of the form *The <shape> is <color>* displays 50 percent of the time, and a sentence of the form *The <color> tile is <shape>* displays the remainder of the time. Both forms describe the same information, obviously; they just do so slightly differently.

The clue classes use the `CluePertainsTo` method to determine if a passed-in `TileCombo` is correctly described by the clue. This is used when crossing possible tile combinations off the list when whittling the list of 576 possible puzzles down to the final solution. In this subclass, each of the four tiles is scanned until the one matching the clue is found. Once that tile is found, the method returns `True` if that tile is the same shape as the tile in the solution. For example, if one instance of this class generated the clue *The Triangle is Red*, then the `CluePertainsTo` method would return `True` for any `TileCombo` passed into it in which the triangle tile is also red. The method would return `False` for all `TileCombos` passed in where the triangle is some other color.

Creating the PuzzleGenerator Class

The final class to discuss in the clue generation process is the class that links all the other classes together. You can name this class, appropriately enough, `PuzzleGenerator`. One instance of the `PuzzleGenerator` class is created each time the game is played. Listing 4-15 shows the complete `PuzzleGenerator` class so you can study how all these other classes fit together.

Listing 4-15. The PuzzleGenerator *Class*

```
Public Class PuzzleGenerator

    Private oPL As TileComboPossiblesList
    Private FClueClassNames As ArrayList
    Private FClues As ArrayList
    Private FAsm As Reflection.Assembly

    Public Sub New()
        MyBase.New()

        oPL = New TileComboPossiblesList
        GetClueClasses()
        GenerateClues()
    End Sub

    'use reflection to find all the clue subclasses and load them up
    Private Sub GetClueClasses()

        FAsm = System.Reflection.Assembly.GetExecutingAssembly()
        Dim t As Type

        FClueClassNames = New ArrayList
```

```vbnet
        'GetType used when not instantiating
        '(can't instantiate b/c of MustInherit)
        Dim tParent As Type = GetType(TileComboClue)

        For Each t In FAsm.GetTypes
            If t.IsSubclassOf(tParent) Then
                FClueClassNames.Add(t)
            End If
        Next

    End Sub

    Private Sub GenerateClues()

        Dim c As TileComboClue
        Dim oTyp As Type

        Dim oRand As New Random
        Dim oArgs() As Object = {oPL.Solution}

        Debug.WriteLine("---------------------------------------------")
        Debug.WriteLine(oPL.Solution.ToString)
        Debug.WriteLine("---------------------------------------------")

        FClues = New ArrayList
        Do
            oTyp = FClueClassNames.Item(_
              oRand.Next(0, FClueClassNames.Count))
            c = Activator.CreateInstance(oTyp, oArgs)
            If oPL.NumberClueWouldEliminate(c) > 0 Then
                oPL.EliminateBasedOnClue(c)
                FClues.Add(c)
            End If

        Loop Until oPL.AllNonSolutionsEliminated
    End Sub

    Public Sub PopulateListBox(ByVal lb As ListBox)

        Dim c As TileComboClue
```

```
        lb.Items.Clear()
        For Each c In FClues
            lb.Items.Add(c.ClueText)
        Next
    End Sub


    Public Function IsSolution(ByVal a As ColoredShape, _
        ByVal b As ColoredShape, ByVal c As ColoredShape, _
        ByVal d As ColoredShape) As Boolean

        Dim t As New TileCombo(a, b, c, d)

        Return t.Equals(oPL.Solution)

    End Function

End Class
```

As shown in Listing 4-15, the PuzzleGenerator class uses a private instance of the TileComboPossiblesList class to store the 576 puzzle possibilities and remove them in the GenerateClues method. It accomplishes this by generating a random clue that pertains to the solution and then attempting to remove remaining puzzle possibilities whose tile arrangements don't match this clue. If new possibilities are indeed removed, then this clue is added to the list of clues to be shown to the user. If the newly generated clue doesn't remove any new tile combinations, then this clue adds no new information to the puzzle and it's discarded. An example of this might be a new clue being generated that reads *The Triangle is Red* when clues already exist that read *The Triangle is neither Blue nor Yellow* and *The Triangle is not Green*. Because of these two clues, the clue engine has already crossed off all possibilities except those in which the triangle is red, so this latest clue adds no new information.

One other interesting piece of code in the PuzzleGenerator class is how it selects one of the clue classes randomly as the generation process occurs. This happens using a feature of the .NET Framework known as *reflection*. Reflection is the ability to write programs that describe the class structure of other programs. The cliché example is the ability to write a program that can enumerate all of the classes in the .NET Framework for display in a treeview control, similar to the Visual Studio Object Browser (shown in Figure 4-4). You can imagine that in order to write such a program, you'd need the ability to open the .NET Framework assemblies (DLLs) and loop through the classes found within them.

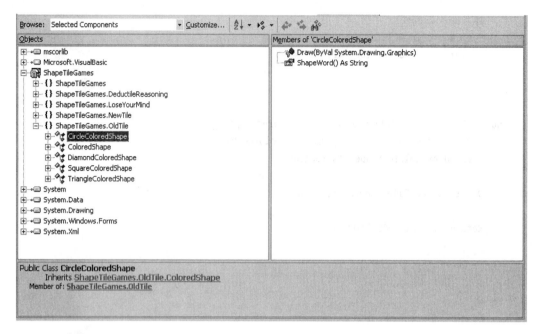

Figure 4-4. You could write a program such as the Object Browser using reflection

In DeducTile Reasoning, you use reflection to loop through the game executable and find all the subclasses of the TileComboClue class. These subclass types are stored in the ever-useful ArrayList, and then this ArrayList is plundered at random when a new clue is required. Listing 4-16 shows the GetClueClasses method.

Listing 4-16. The GetClueClasses Method

```
'use reflection to find all the clue subclasses and load them up
Private Sub GetClueClasses()

    FAsm = System.Reflection.Assembly.GetExecutingAssembly()
    Dim t As Type

    FClueClassNames = New ArrayList

    Dim tParent As Type = GetType(TileComboClue)

    For Each t In FAsm.GetTypes
        If t.IsSubclassOf(tParent) Then
            FClueClassNames.Add(t)
        End If
    Next

End Sub
```

The `Assembly.GetExecutingAssembly` method (a shared class method) is the one that returns the currently executing assembly (a.k.a. this program) as a variable that can be opened and the parts therein studied. In this case, you're interested in looking for all of the classes in your program that inherit from the `TileComboClue` class. You do this using a class named `Type`, a class that represents a type declaration in the assembly.

NOTE *A type declaration can be a class, interface, array, value, or enumeration declaration in an assembly.*

As each `TileComboClue` subclass is discovered, a `Type` variable representing this subclass is stored in the `ArrayList` named `FClueClassNames`. Later, in the `GenerateClues` method, the code that actually selects one of the clues at random is as follows:

```
Dim c As TileComboClue
Dim oTyp As Type

Dim oRand As New Random
Dim oArgs() As Object = {oPL.Solution}

oTyp = FClueClassNames.Item(_
   oRand.Next(0, FClueClassNames.Count))
c = Activator.CreateInstance(oTyp, oArgs)
```

What this code does is select an item out of the `ArrayList`, place that item in a `Type` variable, and then use the `Activator.CreateInstance` method to create an instance variable of this type. The trickiness is that if any parameters are required in the constructor of this variable, then these parameters must be sent to the `Activator.CreateInstance` method enclosed within an array. The array in the previous code is named `oArgs`. Because all the `TileComboClue` classes need a `TileCombo` (the puzzle solution) sent to them in their constructor, you can enclose the `TileCombo` (the `oPL.Solution` property) in the array. When the previous code runs, the variable `c` contains a random clue. The beauty of using reflection in this way is that you can add new subclasses of the `TileComboClue` classes to the program that represent different styles of clues, and you don't have to change any of the clue generation code to "activate" these new clue styles.

The remainder of the `PuzzleGenerator` class is pretty simple. A `PopulateListBox` method fills a listbox with the text of all the generated clues, and an `IsSolution` method determines if four `ColoredShape` tile classes match the generated puzzle.

You now have a complete PuzzleGenerator class, and all that's needed to complete this game is the user interface.

Creating the DeducTile Reasoning Interface

The hard part of this seemingly endless game is done. Completing the game requires creating four tiles on the screen, displaying the clue text, allowing the user to move the tiles around, and determining if the player wins or loses.

You create and display the tiles as you did in the Brain Drain Concentration game. You add four ColoredShape instances both to the game's form and to a private ArrayList so you can get at them exclusively when needed. Listing 4-17 shows the procedure StartGame, in which the tiles are created and added to these collections.

Listing 4-17. The Method StartGame *on the DeducTile Reasoning Form*

```
Private Sub StartGame()

    Dim oShape As ColoredShape
    Dim oRand As New Random
    Dim i As Integer

    Me.Cursor = Cursors.WaitCursor
    oGT.StopTimer()

    If Not FTiles Is Nothing Then
        For Each oShape In FTiles
            Me.Controls.Remove(oShape)
        Next
    End If

    FTiles = New ArrayList

    For i = 0 To 3
        oShape = New ColoredShape(i, i)
        With oShape
            .Backwards = False
            .Width = 64
            .Location = New Point(16, 32 + (i * 64))
            .AllowDrop = True
            AddHandler .MouseDown, AddressOf ShapeMouseDown
            AddHandler .MouseMove, AddressOf ShapeMouseMove
```

```
            AddHandler .MouseUp, AddressOf ShapeMouseUp
            AddHandler .DragOver, AddressOf ShapeDragOver
            AddHandler .DragDrop, AddressOf ShapeDragDrop
        End With

        'adding a reference to two places, the form and an arraylist
        FTiles.Add(oShape)
        Me.Controls.Add(oShape)

    Next

    FPuzGen = New DeductileReasoning.PuzzleGenerator
    FPuzGen.PopulateListBox(lbClues)

    oGT.StartAt = New TimeSpan(0, 3, 0)
    oGT.StartTimer()
    Me.Cursor = Cursors.Default

End Sub
```

In addition to the four user interface tiles being created and attached to a whole slew of event handlers, you can also see the PuzzleGenerator variable (FPuzGen) being instantiated and the PopulateListBox method being called. The puzzle solution and all the clues are generated as part of this class's constructor, so these two lines of code are all that are required by an outside user to create a batch of clues and to fill a listbox with the text of those clues. Finally, you can see another GameTimer class (oGT) created and set up to act as the foil of the player.

Dragging and Dropping

This game has a unique interface in that it allows dragging with both the left and right mouse buttons. Dragging one tile onto the other using the left mouse button switches the positions of the two tiles. Dragging one tile onto another with the right mouse button switches only the color of the two tiles, but the shapes remain in their current places. The user interface code has to handle both types of drag operations.

Listing 4-17 showed five event handlers attached to the four ColoredShape tiles that are displayed on the form, and all five handlers relate to dragging and dropping. Table 4-2 describes these events.

Table 4-2. Drag/Drop Event Handler Code for DeducTile Reasoning

HANDLER NAME	EVENT	PURPOSE
ShapeMouseDown	MouseDown	Defines a rectangle outside of which the dragging should begin
ShapeMouseMove	MouseMove	Begins a drag operation if the mouse moves outside of this rectangle (with the button still down)
ShapeMouseUp	MouseUp	Clears the rectangle
ShapeDragOver	DragOver	Displays the drag icon
ShapeDragDrop	DragDrop	Performs the tile switching

All of the event handlers except for the last one are standard drag/drop code that you can find in the online help, so they won't be defined here. Listing 4-18 shows the DragDrop code.

Listing 4-18. Dropping One Tile onto Another

```
Private Sub ShapeDragDrop(ByVal sender As Object, ByVal e As DragEventArgs)

    Dim oDest As ColoredShape = CType(sender, ColoredShape)

    If oDest.Equals(FDragShape) Then Exit Sub

    If Not FDidRight Then
        'left drag, simply swap positions
        Dim p As Point

        p = FDragShape.Location
        FDragShape.Location = oDest.Location
        oDest.Location = p
    Else
        'right drag, swap colors
        Dim c As Color

        c = FDragShape.Color
        FDragShape.Color = oDest.Color
        oDest.Color = c

        oDest.Invalidate()
        FDragShape.Invalidate()
    End If
End Sub
```

This routine first makes sure that a tile isn't dragged and dropped onto itself. If this happens, then no action is required. If a tile is dragged onto another tile, however, then the code determines whether the right or mouse button was the one doing the dragging (via the Boolean variable FDidRight). If it was a left drag, then the Location variables of the two ColoredShape classes are swapped. If it was a right drag, then the colors are swapped and the two tiles are redrawn.

Ending the Game

The user now has the ability to read the clues and arrange the tiles until he thinks he might have the puzzle solved, at which point he clicks the Guess button at the bottom of the form to see if he's right. Listing 4-19 shows the code that handles the Guess button click.

Listing 4-19. Taking a Guess

```
Private Sub cbGuess_Click(ByVal sender As System.Object, _
    ByVal e As System.EventArgs) Handles cbGuess.Click

    FTiles.Sort()                'calls compareTo

    If FPuzGen.IsSolution(FTiles.Item(0), FTiles.Item(1), _
        FTiles.Item(2), FTiles.Item(3)) Then

        oGT.StopTimer()
        If MsgBox("You win, play again?", _
            MsgBoxStyle.YesNo Or MsgBoxStyle.Question, _
            "Try Again") = MsgBoxResult.Yes Then
            StartGame()
        Else
            Me.Close()
        End If
    Else
        oGT.AddTime(New TimeSpan(0, 0, -5))
    End If
End Sub
```

The first step in the guess routine is to call the Sort method on the ArrayList that holds the tiles. The reason this is required is because the tiles originally went into the array in a certain order, but the user has most likely swapped the physical order of the tiles on the form by dragging and dropping. The IsSolution method on the PuzzleGenerator assumes that the topmost tile is going to be the first parameter passed in, the second tile passed in second, and so on. Before sorting, you really don't know if the first tile in the FTiles ArrayList is really the topmost tile on the form anymore.

The remarkable part of this code is how the Sort method shown in Listing 4-19 "knows" that it needs to sort the tiles according to their positions on the form. Why doesn't it sort them in, say, alphabetical order by color or in descending alphabetical order by the last letter of the name of their shape? These sort criteria seem as arbitrary as the tiles' top-to-bottom arrangement on the form.

The answer to this puzzle is that you *told* the system how you planned to sort the tiles earlier. Do you remember when? If you'll recall, the ColoredShape tile class implemented the IComparable interface, meaning that it contained a CompareTo method. The following code is the implementation of that method:

```
Public Function CompareTo(ByVal obj As Object) _
    As Integer Implements System.IComparable.CompareTo

    Dim o As ColoredShape = CType(obj, ColoredShape)

    Return Me.Top.CompareTo(o.Top)
End Function
```

The result of this CompareTo method is the result of comparing the Top property (an integer) of the two tiles in question. If you were to consult the online help for how CompareTo works on integers, you would find that it returns –1 if the method caller (Me.Top previously) is less than the parameter (o.Top), 0 if they're equal, and 1 if the method caller is greater. This gives you the result you're after—sorting the tiles in their top-to-bottom order on the form.

You might imagine cases where different sorting requirements exist for the same class depending on the circumstance. For example, you might create classes to implement a deck of cards for a card game. In some cases, a pile of cards may have to be sorted according to their position on a form. In other cases, they might have to be sorted by their face value or their suit. In still other cases, a crazy sort value might be required (such as in the game Euchre, where the highest card is one of the Jacks, and the second highest card is the other Jack of the same color).

The .NET Framework can handle classes with multiple sorting requirements by passing an instance of a class that implements the IComparer interface (which is different from IComparable). This isn't covered in detail here except in passing—it's important at this time only to point out that implementing multiple sorting mechanisms within a class is possible.

Once you've sorted the tiles in the Arraylist according to their physical positions on the form, you can pass them to the IsSolution method of the PuzzleGenerator variable. If the solution is indeed correct, the program displays a message and asks if the player wants to play again. If the solution is incorrect, the player is "punished" by having five seconds removed from the available time.

Believe it or not, this finally completes the discussion of the DeducTile Reasoning game! I personally enjoy playing this game as much as any other in the book; it presents a nice little brainteaser for the player.

Developing Lose Your Mind

The third game you'll develop in this chapter is the double-Mastermind-style game, affectionately named *Lose Your Mind*. Like the previous game, it's a four-tile puzzle. Unlike the previous game, however, the game allows repetition in color and/or shapes. The puzzle could theoretically consist of four red squares, for example.

In this game, the user has 10 chances to guess the puzzle. After submitting a guess, a series of black and white pegs display that indicate how close the guess is to the puzzle. A black peg on the top row indicates that one of the shapes is in the correct location. A white peg on the top row indicates that a correct shape exists but isn't in the correct location. The bottom row of pegs indicate the same information but concerning the color of the tiles. Note that no information is given as to which tile is being represented by which peg. Figure 4-5 shows a game in progress.

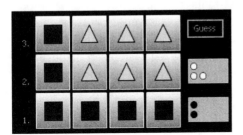

Figure 4-5. A rousing game of Lose Your Mind in progress

In referring to Figure 4-5, you can see that the first guess was four squares (were it a color picture, you could further see four red squares, but you'll have to take my word for it on that one). The indicators to the right of the first guess show one black peg in the bottom row and one in the top row. The top row indicates the accuracy of the *shapes* of the current guess. The single black peg in the top row tells the player that one of the four shapes is correct and in the correct location. Because the first guess is all squares, the player can infer that one of the four tiles is a square. The bottom row of the indicators indicates *color* and also contains one black peg. This indicates that one of the colors is correct and in the correct position. Because all four tiles in the first guess are red, the player can infer that there's one red tile in the solution (he can't tell which of the four tiles are red at this point, though).

Onto the second guess: Knowing that one tile in the solution is a square and one is red, this player changed three of the four tiles to yellow triangles. The top row of indicators now tells the player that he has only one shape correct and that it's in the wrong position. At first, the clues appear to tell the player less than the indicators did in the first guess, but he can infer additional information by these two clues. The player now knows that there's exactly one square in the solution, and that it's not in the first position. Furthermore, the player knows at this time that there are no triangles in the solution. This leaves only diamonds and circles left for the remaining three positions. As for color, the two white indicators tell the player that one of the colors must be red and one yellow. Because both indicators are white, the solution must have a yellow tile in the first position (he doesn't know the red position yet—only that it's not in the first position).

Creating the Interface and Discovering a Problem

The interface of the game involves clicking the currently active row of tiles to change the tiles' shapes and colors. A left-click changes the shape of the tile; a right-click changes the color. The shapes and colors cycle through a preset sequence, so four clicks bring the tile back to its starting point.

Implementing this cycling functionality is difficult given the current design of the ColoredShape class. You might remember that the tiles are implemented as a MustInherit ancestor class with a child subclass to represent each shape. For the game to implement the changing of one shape into another, the program would have to be able to change a tile from one class to a different class on the fly. This is akin to changing a control from a button to a textbox when it's clicked, a task that's not often asked of a .NET program. Objects don't change their classes on the fly. An object instance is created from a class definition, and it remains an instance of that class definition throughout its lifetime.

The only way to change a square tile into a circle tile when clicking it is to remove the shape tile from the form and replace it with an instance of the circle tile. Although this solution works, it seems an odd way to solve the problem. It requires a fair amount of setup code every time a user clicks a tile to make sure the new tile retains the location and color information of the tile that's about to be destroyed. In addition, the program would have to set up event handlers so that the new tile could be clicked again, at which point *it* would be destroyed and replaced with a new class instance.

What's happened here is that the current ColoredShape class has taken on a new requirement—the need to be able to change shapes on the fly, and the current multi-subclass implementation doesn't support this. Note that it's no

Creating the ToggleShape and ToggleColor Methods

These two new public methods represent new functionality required by the Lose Your Mind game. They rotate the shape or the color of the tile in a predetermined pattern so that a user clicking a tile can change the shape or color depending on which mouse button is clicked. The code that follows is for ToggleShape, and the color toggling method is similar:

```
Public Sub ToggleShape()

    Select Case Shape
        Case ShapeType.stCircle
            Shape = ShapeType.stDiamond
        Case ShapeType.stDiamond
            Shape = ShapeType.stSquare
        Case ShapeType.stSquare
            Shape = ShapeType.stTriangle
        Case ShapeType.stTriangle
            Shape = ShapeType.stCircle
    End Select
End Sub
```

Creating a CopyFrom Method

This method loads the color and shape of a passed-in tile to the current tile. The Lose Your Mind game uses it when adding a new row onto the board after the user makes a guess so that the four new tiles have the same color/shape as the previous guess:

```
Public Sub CopyFrom(ByVal c As ColoredShape)
    Me.Color = c.Color
    Me.Shape = c.Shape
End Sub
```

These relatively small changes and few new features have given you the functionality you require—the ability for a tile to change its shape on the fly. Furthermore, you made only one breaking change to the class interface so that almost all of the code in the prior two games remains functional, save for an almost trivial fix in the line that created the tiles.

This isn't the only way you can change the class to support the on-the-fly changing of a tile's shape. In fact, classes such as this—where different functionality is supported through a series of Select Case statements within the class—aren't always considered the best design. Classes designed in this way can be hard to modify or expand upon later. Suppose you want to add new shapes, for example. You'd have to dig through the class looking for all the Case statements that split out the different functionality for each shape and add to it. Although this is a legitimate concern that affects possible future expandability of your game classes, you have to weigh that against using simpler code in the short term. Also, if you have no current plans to expand the class further, this simpler design is adequate for now. If the need does arise to expand the Tile class further, you can refactor the code into a more easily scalable design at that point.

TIP *If you're interested in learning about a more scalable design without using inheritance, look into the Bridge pattern discussed in* Design Patterns Explained: A New Perspective on Object-Oriented Design *by Alan Shalloway and James R. Trott (Addison-Wesley, 2001).*

Implementing Lose Your Mind

With the new functionality of the tile class completed, you have three additional work classes to create in order to complete the Lose Your Mind game. The first of these is TileCollection, and its purpose is to store four tiles. This class stores the puzzle that the player is trying to guess. Listing 4-20 shows the public interface for this class.

Listing 4-20. The TileCollection *Class That Holds Four* ColoredShape *Objects*

```
Public Class TileCollection
    Inherits System.Collections.CollectionBase

    Public Sub Add(ByVal o As ColoredShape)
    Public ReadOnly Property Item _
      (ByVal iIndex As Integer) As ColoredShape

    Public Sub Remove(ByVal o As ColoredShape)
    Public Function Clone() As TileCollection
    Public Overrides Function ToString() As String
End Class
```

This rather small class inherits from a .NET Framework class named CollectionBase. This class has an ArrayList protected within it, meaning your inherited classes can add and remove items to it, but the outside world can't access it directly. Inheriting from CollectionBase allows you to create type-safe collection classes for your programs.

The Add method on this class takes a ColoredShape parameter, meaning that you couldn't add an instance of any other class to this collection. Likewise, the Item property returns a ColoredShape within it, meaning that this collection class can't hold instances of other classes. When using an ArrayList directly, as you did in some of the prior applications, the programmer could inadvertently (or even intentionally) add instances of different classes to a single ArrayList, which could make for buggy (or, at the least, confusing) code.

The second class required to finish the game is TileCollectionGuess, which inherits from TileCollection. This class not only stores four tiles but also provides support for deciding how close this group of four tiles is to the puzzle that the player is trying to determine. Listing 4-21 shows the public interface for this class.

Listing 4-21. TileCollectionGuess, *Inherits Off of* TileCollection

```
Public Class TileCollectionGuess
    Inherits TileCollection

    Public Sub CheckAgainst(ByVal oSolution As TileCollection)

    ReadOnly Property NumShapeCorrect() As Integer
    ReadOnly Property NumShapeWrongSpot() As Integer
    ReadOnly Property NumColorCorrect() As Integer
    ReadOnly Property NumColorWrongSpot() As Integer

    Public Overrides Function ToString() As String
    Public Function Wins() As Boolean
End Class
```

The workhorse of this class is the CheckAgainst method. This method counts the number of shapes and colors both in correct and incorrect spots in this tile set against a passed-in solution. The function Wins returns True if all the colors and shapes are in the correct spots.

The last worker class, GuessHintRenderer, is a control to render the black and white pegs. This class has almost no public implementation at all:

```
Public Class GuessHintRenderer
    Inherits Control

    Public Sub New(ByVal oTC As TileCollectionGuess)
End Class
```

The only public method is a constructor that takes a `TileCollectionGuess` as its parameter, which it uses to determine how many black and white indicator pegs to draw. The drawing code uses standard GDI+ calls to render black and white circles on the control surface.

With all the worker classes completed, all that remains is putting them together on a form to create the game. The method `StartGame`, shown in Listing 4-22, sets up the game controls.

Listing 4-22. The `StartGame` *Method*

```
Private Sub StartGame()

    Dim oRand As New Random
    Dim oShape As ColoredShape
    Dim i, iTop As Integer

    DeleteOldGameControls()

    FGuesses = New ArrayList
    cbGuess.Visible = True

    FSolution = New LoseYourMind.TileCollection
    i = 0
    Do
        oShape = New ColoredShape(oRand.Next(0, 4), oRand.Next(0, 4))
        oShape.Backwards = True
        oShape.Width = TILESIZE
        oShape.Left = 32 + (i * oShape.Width)

        FSolution.Add(oShape)
        pnTop.Controls.Add(oShape)
        i += 1
    Loop Until FSolution.Count = NUMTILES

    iTop = HeightFromTurnNumber(0)
    cbGuess.Location = New Point((TILESIZE * NUMTILES) + 40, iTop + 8)

    Call SetupGuess()
End Sub
```

This procedure executes whenever a new game begins. The first thing called is a procedure named `DeleteOldGameControls`, which simply loops through all the controls on the form and removes any old tiles that might exist from a prior game. Then, an `ArrayList` named `FGuesses` initializes (which holds the guesses the player makes), as well as a variable named `FSolution` (which is an instance of the class `TileCollection`). Four `ColoredShape` instances (of random shape and color) are then created and added to both `FSolution` and to the form (in truth, they're added to a `Panel` named `pnTop`, which is a member of the form). These four tiles represent the puzzle that the user is trying to guess. Finally, a procedure named `SetupGuess` is called, which is shown in Listing 4-23.

Listing 4-23. The `SetupGuess` *Method, Called Whenever a New Turn Begins*

```
Private Sub SetupGuess()

    Dim oShape As ColoredShape
    Dim oTC As New LoseYourMind.TileCollectionGuess
    Dim o As Control
    Dim i, iTop As Integer

    'create 4 tiles for guessing, put in a guess object.

    'remove clicking ability on all shapes
    For Each o In Me.Controls
        If TypeOf o Is ColoredShape Then
            RemoveHandler o.MouseDown, AddressOf ShapeMouseDown
        End If
    Next

    FCurrentGuess = New LoseYourMind.TileCollectionGuess

    iTop = HeightFromTurnNumber(FGuesses.Count)
    Do
        oShape = New ColoredShape(i, i)
        With oShape
            .Location = New Point(32 + (i * TILESIZE), iTop)
            .Width = TILESIZE
            .Backwards = False

            'copy from guess before
            If FGuesses.Count > 0 Then
                oTC = FGuesses.Item(FGuesses.Count - 1)
                .CopyFrom(oTC.Item(i))            'copies shape and color
            End If
            AddHandler .MouseDown, AddressOf ShapeMouseDown
        End With
```

```
        Me.Controls.Add(oShape)
        FCurrentGuess.Add(oShape)


        i += 1
    Loop Until i >= NUMTILES

End Sub
```

The purpose of this method is to create four clickable tiles on the form and add these tiles to a `TileCollectionGuess` class so that they can be compared against the puzzle when the user hits the Guess button. Each tile is created as a copy of the tile immediately below it (from the guess before, unless of course this is the first guess in the game). Also, each of the four tiles has an event handler named `ShapeMouseDown` added to it (shown in Listing 4-24) so that it can respond when the player clicks it. (Actually, at the top of this method, all previous tiles on the form don't contain this same handler so that previous guesses no longer respond to mouse clicks.)

Listing 4-24. The `ShapeMouseDown` Event

```
Private Sub ShapeMouseDown(ByVal sender As _
    System.Object, ByVal e As _
    System.Windows.Forms.MouseEventArgs)

    Dim oShape As ColoredShape = sender

    If ((e.Button And MouseButtons.Left) = MouseButtons.Left) Then
        oShape.ToggleShape()
        oWav.Play("die1", 100)
    End If

    If ((e.Button And MouseButtons.Right) = MouseButtons.Right) Then
        oShape.ToggleColor()
        oWav.Play("die1", 100)
    End If
End Sub
```

The event handler calls the `ToggleShape` or `ToggleColor` method on the tile that's clicked, which changes the shape or color of the tile in a repeating pattern. If you'll recall, the need to change the shape of a tile on the fly was the primary reason that you needed to rework the `ColoredShape` class from an inherited scheme into a single class scheme.

The final major piece of code to implement is the code that runs when a user clicks the Guess button. This code, shown in Listing 4-25, renders the white and black pegs and determines if the player has won or lost the game.

Listing 4-25. Guess Button Event Handler

```vb
Private Sub cbGuess_Click(ByVal sender As System.Object, _
    ByVal e As System.EventArgs) Handles cbGuess.Click

    Dim oGH As LoseYourMind.GuessHintRenderer
    Dim cMsg As String

    FGuesses.Add(FCurrentGuess)
    FCurrentGuess.CheckAgainst(FSolution)

    oGH = New LoseYourMind.GuessHintRenderer(FCurrentGuess)
    oGH.Location = cbGuess.Location
    oGH.Size = New Size(54, 32)
    Me.Controls.Add(oGH)

    If FCurrentGuess.Wins Then
        oWav.Play("ovation", 100)
        ShowSolution()

        cMsg = "Winnah, Winnah, Chicken Dinnah!" & Environment.NewLine
        cMsg &= "Play again?"
        If MsgBox(cMsg, MsgBoxStyle.Question Or _
          MsgBoxStyle.YesNo, "You win") = MsgBoxResult.Yes Then
            Call StartGame()
            Exit Sub
        Else
            Me.Close()
        End If

    Else
        If FGuesses.Count = 10 Then
            oWav.Play("ouch", 100)
            ShowSolution()
            cMsg = "You Lose!" & Environment.NewLine
            cMsg &= "Play again?"
            If MsgBox(cMsg, MsgBoxStyle.Question Or _
              MsgBoxStyle.YesNo, "You lose") = MsgBoxResult.Yes Then
                Call StartGame()
                Exit Sub
            Else
                Me.Close()
            End If
```

```
        Else
            oWav.Play("8ping", 100)
        End If
        cbGuess.Top -= TILESIZE
        Call SetupGuess()
    End If

End Sub
```

The guess code creates an instance of GuessHintRenderer and adds it to the form so that the white and black pegs can be drawn. This object takes as its parameter the current guess that the player has just made, currently stored in the variable FCurrentGuess. If the player has indeed won the game, he is told so and asked if he wants to play again. The game action is performed if the player has lost the game, which happens if he hasn't correctly guessed the solution in 10 tries.

Summary

This chapter took a basic game element, a colored tile with a shape on it, and reused it in three different games. The basic Tile class required some refactoring along the way to support new functionality that wasn't required of it in earlier games. As you've seen, the trick to refactoring a class is to avoid changes to the public interface of the class. If you can do this, then you can refactor without negatively impacting the rest of the project.

CHAPTER 5

Understanding Polymorphism

THE PREVIOUS CHAPTERS COVERED two of the three features of object-oriented programming languages. In review, *encapsulation* is the hiding of functionality (implementation details) inside classes. This allows the developer to separate distinct parts of code so those parts can't interact with each other at all (or can interact with each other only in ways the developer can control via the public interface of the class). By achieving this separation, the developer assures that changes to one part of the code won't produce undesired side effects in another part.

The second object-oriented feature is *inheritance*, which is the ability to create a class by basing it on some other class. This allows the developer to extend or change the functionality of an existing class without having to duplicate the code for all the existing functionality.

This chapter discusses the third feature of object-oriented programming: *polymorphism*. This rather imposing word means that different classes can provide similar functionality to the outside world but through different (possibly very different) implementations.

For example, real-world objects behave in a polymorphic manner. Suppose you're throwing a party and five people at your workplace ask you for directions to your house. You give the same directions to all five people: "From the office, go south on Main Street for three blocks. Turn right on Maple. At the first stop sign, turn right again on Evergreen. My house is the fifth on the left, 1234 Evergreen."

If you think of the five people as instances of some imaginary `Person` class (or some subclass of `Person`), you can consider that you've invoked each person's `Travel` method, which takes as a parameter a `TravelDirections` object. This object is the object-oriented version of the directions given (ignore how one might implement such an object for the moment).

What you haven't considered in calling each person's `Travel` method is exactly *how* each person plans to travel to your party using the directions given. The following items represent how each person might come to your party:

- Person 1 drives her car from work to your house.

- Person 2 drives home first to change, then takes a cab to your party so he doesn't have to worry about driving home if he has a few drinks.

- Person 3 hitches a ride with Person 1.

- Person 4 walks to your house from work and plans to have her roommate, who is also coming to the party, drive her home.

- Person 5 takes his nifty new Segway personal transport device from work to your house.

Even though you're the host of the party, it isn't your responsibility to understand how each person is going to get to your house. Instead, you merely invoke each person's Travel method with the proper parameters (the directions and perhaps the time to show up), and each person decides on the best way to perform the task asked of them (to show up to the party).

Polymorphism in an object-oriented programming language works the same way. You can invoke a method on a class without knowing (or caring) *how* the class gets the job done so long as the job does indeed get done.

Seeing Polymorphism in Action

Let's look at a simple example of polymorphism before getting into some game code. The little project PolymorphismExample comes with the source code for this book. This do-nothing project contains a single form. On this form are one textbox, one button, one label, one radio button, and one checkbox control. The name for each control is the default name given to it by Visual Studio when it was placed on the form. The Click event for all five controls is the same event handler:

```
Private Sub SomethingClick(ByVal sender As Object, _
    ByVal e As System.EventArgs) Handles RadioButton1.Click, _
    Button1.Click, CheckBox1.Click, Label1.Click, TextBox1.Click

    Debug.WriteLine(sender.ToString)
End Sub
```

As with most event handlers, the object being acted upon is passed in as the first parameter in the variable named sender, which is of type Object. This is the root ancestor class for every other class in the .NET Framework and every class you create yourself (in other words, *every* class is a descendant of the Object class).

The lone line of code in this event handler calls the ToString method on the passed-in sender variable, and the result of this method is written to the Visual Studio .NET debugger window. If you were to run this program and click each of the five controls one time, you would see the following output in the debugger window:

```
System.Windows.Forms.Button, Text: Button1
System.Windows.Forms.Label, Text: Label1
System.Windows.Forms.TextBox, Text: TextBox1
System.Windows.Forms.CheckBox, CheckState: 1
System.Windows.Forms.RadioButton, Checked: True
```

As you can see, the job of the ToString method is to output the class name of the control and a little piece of information about the control itself. In the case of the button, label, and textbox, the Text property of the control outputs. In the case of the checkbox, the CheckState property displays, and in the case of the radio button, the Checked property displays.

The polymorphic behavior is that the sender variable can point to any one of the five controls attached to this event handler, but it doesn't need to know which control it points to in order to call the ToString method on each of them, even though the implementation of the ToString method might be totally different. You could, for example, create some crazy control that opens an Internet connection and downloads a string from across the globe to use as the output of its ToString method, but you could invoke this method using the same Click event handler that the other controls use.

Understanding Life and Something Like It

You can find the polymorphic game example in the solution CellularAutomata, which contains the three programs you'll develop in this chapter. A *cellular automaton* is a type of program that produces a lattice of *cells*. Each cell exists in one of a finite number of states at a given time. With each tick of some dictatorial time clock, the state of each cell updates by using some local logic or rule set. This rule set often depends on the state of the cell's neighbors. Figure 5-1 shows the cellular automaton displayer in action.

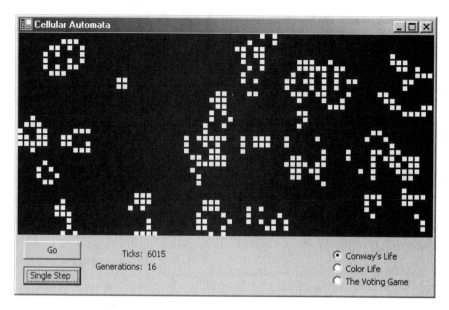

Figure 5-1. The Cellular Automata program

The most well known of all the cellular automaton programs is Conway's Game of Life. It's so well known, in fact, that most student programmers learn these concepts in the reverse order presented in this chapter—first they learn about Conway's Game of Life, and then they learn that this program is but one example of a group of programs named *cellular automaton programs*. Presenting these concepts in the reverse order emphasizes that all the instances of this type of program are to be treated equally, at least from the standpoint of this example program. The main point is that the cellular automaton display program treats all cellular automaton programs equally and can run each through the concept of polymorphism without having to know details about what each program is doing. You'll see the details of how each type of cellular automaton program works in due time.

Creating the CellularAutomataGame Class

One of the most common ways a program can achieve polymorphism is through inheritance, as demonstrated in the PolymorphismExample program. All five of the objects on the sample form are descendants of the Object class (as is every object), so the program accesses the ToString method of each object without having to know which object it is. In fact, the code within that Click event can access any member defined in the Object class directly without having to know what specific class it is.

The solution CellularAutomata, found in the source code that accompanies this book, contains several other examples of polymorphic behavior through inheritance hierarchy.

Creating the Public Members of the CellularAutomataGame Class

The CellularAutomata solution contains three different cellular automaton examples. All three games inherit off of the ancestor class CellularAutomataGame. This class handles the storage of the cell lattice and the user interface requirements for all of the game types. Listing 5-1 shows the public interface for that class.

Listing 5-1. The CellularAutomataGame *Class Public Interface*

```
Public MustInherit Class CellularAutomataGame
    Public Sub New(ByVal oCtl As Control)
    Property CellRadius() As Integer
    ReadOnly Property GenerationCount() As Integer
    ReadOnly Property TimerTicksElapsed() As Long
    Public Sub Tick()
End Class
```

There certainly isn't a whole lot going on here, right? First, notice that this class is declared MustInherit, meaning that you can't create an instance of it directly. Second, there's a constructor that takes some type of Control as a parameter. This Control serves as the drawing surface for the game. There's also a CellRadius property to define how big each cell will be, a Tick method that increments the all-seeing clock by one unit, and some read-only properties to describe how many generations have been run and how many timer ticks it took for the last generation to run. As you can see, the public interface for this program remains small, so it should be quite easy to create an instance of this class and execute the Tick method repeatedly to watch the patterns created by the cellular automaton programs.

Creating the Protected Members of the CellularAutomataGame Class

Although the public interface for the CellularAutomataGame is quite small, there's quite a bit going on in this class under the hood. Listing 5-2 shows the protected interface for the same class.

Listing 5-2. The Protected Interface for the `CellularAutomataGame` *Class*

```
Public MustInherit Class CellularAutomataGame

        Protected FCtl As Control
        Protected FCells As ArrayList
        Protected oRand As Random
        Protected FRows As Integer = 16
        Protected FCols As Integer = 16

        Protected Function HalfTheTime() As Boolean
        Protected Sub IndexToRowCol(ByVal i As Integer, _
           ByRef iRow As Integer, ByRef iCol As Integer)
        Protected Function RowColToCell(ByVal iRow As Integer, _
           ByVal iCol As Integer, _
           Optional ByVal bWrap As Boolean = False) As CellularAutomataCell
        Protected MustOverride Function _
           CreateOneCell(ByVal FPos As Point) As CellularAutomataCell
        Protected MustOverride Sub RunAGeneration()
    End Class
```

Now you can start to see some of the work this class does. A number of protected variables are declared inside this ancestor class, including a holding place for the passed-in `Control` that will serve as the painting surface, an `ArrayList` to hold all of the cell objects, a random number generator, and integers to store the number of rows and columns that will make up the lattice. As for protected methods, there's a `HalfTheTime` method (something that simply returns `True` half the time and `False` the other half—kind of a "coin flipping" method) and two translation methods that convert a row/column pair into a straight integer index and vice versa. The integer index serves as the index into the `ArrayList` variable, but much of the logic of the program is easier to think of in terms of row/column indexes in the cell lattice, especially when considering neighbor cells.

The last two protected methods on the `CellularAutomataGame` class are the most interesting. The first is the `CreateOneCell` method. This method is responsible for creating one cell in the lattice and initializing that cell's state. Each cellular automaton game can have different possible cell states, and therefore the initialization of each cell needs to take place in the individual game classes. This explains why this method is declared `MustOverride`. The last method is `RunAGeneration`. This method is responsible for updating the state of each cell during a timer tick. Again, because the rules of each cellular automaton game are different, this method is declared `MustOverride`.

Creating the CreateData Member of the CellularAutomataGame Class

Between the public and protected interfaces of the CellularAutomataGame class, you can pretty much discern how this class works. However, let's look at a few private methods. The first of these is CreateData, shown in Listing 5-3. This method is responsible for creating and initializing all of the individual cell objects.

Listing 5-3. The CreateData *Member of the* CellularAutomataGame *Class*

```
Private Sub CreateData()

    Dim oC As CellularAutomataCell
    Dim iRow As Integer = 0
    Dim iCol As Integer
    Dim oPt As Point

    FCells = New ArrayList
    Do
        iCol = 0
        Do
            oPt = New Point(iCol * CellRadius, iRow * CellRadius)
            oC = Me.CreateOneCell(oPt)
            FCells.Add(oC)

            iCol += 1
        Loop Until iCol * CellRadius > FCtl.Width
        iRow += 1

    Loop Until (iRow * CellRadius) > FCtl.Height

    FRows = iRow
    FCols = iCol
    FGenerationCount = 0

    Debug.Assert(FRows * FCols = FCells.Count)
End Sub
```

The CreateData method is called when the class is first created or whenever the surface control FCtl is resized. This ensures that the array of cells completely covers the surface area of the form. In this method, one loop is nested inside a second, and these loops terminate based on cells covering the current width and height. Within the loop, the CreateOneCell method is called to create an instance of the CellularAutomataCell class, and then this cell is added to the Arraylist FCells. When the loops are completed, the protected variables FRows and FCols are set to the number of cells that make up a row and column of the cell lattice. Also, the variable that holds the generation count is reset back to 0.

Other than the loops and a bit of math to determine how many cells to create across and down, there isn't much to notice about the CreateData method, with one important exception. Review the line of code that creates an individual cell:

```
oC = Me.CreateOneCell(oPt)
```

Do you remember discussing the CreateOneCell method? (You should—it was only one page ago!) This method is defined on the game class, but it's declared as MustOverride, meaning there's no implementation in the current class. Each subclass must create its own CreateOneCell method, and then the line of code calls it, without having to know the details of what that method is doing. Sound familiar? It should. This is a perfect example of polymorphism in action. You've got a class calling a member that provides the same functionality (creating an instance of a different CellularAutomataCell class) but through different implementations (the code for the CreateOneCell method in each subclass can do many different things as long as it finally returns the requested class instance back to the caller).

Creating the User Interface Methods of the CellularAutomataGame Class

The last functionality that the ancestor CellularAutomataGame class implements is the basic user interface functions. To do this, it takes the passed-in Control variable and attaches some event handlers to it. Listing 5-4 shows the full code for the constructor of the class as well as these event handlers.

Listing 5-4. Event Handlers Attached to the Passed-in Control *Class*

```
Public Sub New(ByVal oCtl As Control)
    MyBase.New()
    FCtl = oCtl

    AddHandler FCtl.Paint, AddressOf ControlPaint
    AddHandler FCtl.Resize, AddressOf ControlResize
    AddHandler FCtl.MouseDown, AddressOf ControlMouseDown

    oRand = New Random
    oHRT = New HighResTimer
```

```
        CreateData()
        FCtl.Invalidate()
End Sub


Private Sub ControlPaint(ByVal sender As Object, _
        ByVal e As System.Windows.Forms.PaintEventArgs)

        Dim oC As CellularAutomataCell
        For Each oC In FCells
            oC.Draw(e.Graphics)
        Next
End Sub


Private Sub ControlMouseDown(ByVal sender As Object, _
        ByVal e As System.Windows.Forms.MouseEventArgs)

        Dim oC As CellularAutomataCell

        For Each oC In FCells
            If oC.ClientRectangle.Contains(e.X, e.Y) Then
                If e.Button = MouseButtons.Left Then
                    oC.OnMouseDown(e)
                    FCtl.Invalidate()
                    Exit Sub
                End If
            End If
        Next
End Sub


Private Sub ControlResize(ByVal sender As Object, _
        ByVal eventargs As System.EventArgs)

        CreateData()
        FCtl.Invalidate()
End Sub
```

This code sets up event handlers for the control's Paint event, the MouseDown event, and the Resize event. As mentioned earlier, the cell lattice is re-created via a call to the CreateData method whenever the source control is resized, which you can see in the simple ControlResize event in Listing 5-4. The only other line of code in this event handler invalidates the control, which forces it to repaint itself.

The other two event handlers contain some further examples of polymorphism. The ControlPaint event handler loops through all of the cell objects in the

FCells ArrayList and calls the Draw method on each. The call to this method works no matter what subclass of CellularAutomataCell is stored in the ArrayList, even though different classes may implement the drawing in different ways. The ControlMouseDown event also acts polymorphically—it first determines which cell was clicked by the left mouse button, and then it calls the OnMouseDown method on that cell class. Each subclass of the CellularAutomataCell class can do whatever it likes in this method—the job of this code is to simply notify the cell that it has been clicked.

Creating the CellularAutomataCell Class

The CellularAutomataCell class serves as the ancestor class to each cell type for the different types of cellular automaton games. Each type of game has a descendant of the CellularAutomataGame class and a corresponding CellularAutomataCell class descendant to go with it. This class is much simpler than the game class; Listing 5-5 shows its public interface (along with the implementation of one method, the Draw method).

Listing 5-5. The CellularAutomataCell *Class*

```
Public MustInherit Class CellularAutomataCell
    Public Sub New(ByVal oPos As Point, ByVal r As Integer)
    ReadOnly Property Position() As Point
    ReadOnly Property Radius() As Integer

    ReadOnly Property ClientRectangle() As Rectangle
    Public MustOverride Function GetColor() As Color
    Public MustOverride Sub OnMouseDown(_
      ByVal e As System.Windows.Forms.MouseEventArgs)

    Public Sub Draw(ByVal g As Graphics)
      Dim r As Rectangle
      Dim b As Brush

      r = New Rectangle(FPos.X, FPos.Y, FDrawRad, FDrawRad)
      b = New SolidBrush(Me.GetColor)
      g.FillRectangle(b, r)

    End Sub
End Class
```

This little class does nothing out of the ordinary, so this chapter won't cover all of the implementation details on a line-by-line basis. The constructor takes a point instance and a radius as parameters. All that the constructor does with these parameters is store them in private variables, which are both exposed through the read-only properties Position and Radius, respectively.

The Draw method is nothing you haven't seen in previous chapters; it uses the FillRectangle method on the passed-in Graphics class to draw the cell at the appropriate position on the control's surface. You'll notice that it uses the GetColor method to determine what color to draw the rectangle. The GetColor method is declared on this class but is declared MustOverride, meaning that its functionality is implemented entirely in the subclasses. If you've perceived that the call to the GetColor method from Draw is another example of polymorphic behavior, you're correct. Note that the Draw method has no idea how the subclass determines what color will be returned—it cares only that a color is returned so it knows how to draw the cell.

The ClientRectangle property returns a .NET Framework Rectangle object that represents the location and radius of this cell (it's used in the ControlMouseDown event handler of the game class, shown in Listing 5-4). The last method, OnMouseDown, instructs the cell how to behave when the cell is clicked. You saw that this method is called polymorphically in Listing 5-4. It's declared MustOverride, meaning that no implementation exists in this ancestor class.

Developing Conway's Game of Life

As mentioned earlier, the most common cellular automaton game (by far) is Conway's Game of Life. In fact, I had to program a Conway's Game of Life (heretofore called simply *Life*) program in my assembly language class back in 1987 (egads, I'm old). The cells in this automaton contain only two states, dead and alive. The fate of each cell in a turn depends on its eight neighbors—three above, three below, and one each to the immediate left and right. If a cell is alive and has two or three alive neighbors in turn x, then that cell will remain alive in turn x+1. A living cell with fewer than two alive neighbors dies of starvation; a cell with more than three living neighbors dies of overcrowding. Furthermore, cells that are dead will suddenly spring to life in turn x+1 if they contain exactly three living neighbors in turn x. Figure 5-2 shows a block of cells on the left and how that same area looks one turn later.

Figure 5-2. Life cell state in turn x (left) and turn x+1 (right)

Describing the rules of Life does the process no justice whatsoever. The only way to understand and learn about the patterns and complexity formed out of these seemingly simple rules is to watch a Life program run through multiple clock ticks in succession. If you're new to the Life scene, compile the source code for this project and play with it for a while before studying the code so you can better understand the intent of the classes described. Discovering all of the rule variations and amazing patterns in Life can be (and often is) the subject of entire books, so this one makes no attempt to cover such a complex topic with any depth.

Creating the Life Game Class

To implement a cellular automaton variant in the program, you must create subclasses of the CellularAutomataGame and CellularAutomataCell classes.

Creating the CreateOneCell Method

In the game class, you must override two methods minimally. The first of these methods is CreateOneCell, and its job is to return an initialized instance of the game-specific cell class to the caller. If you'll recall, the caller is the CellularAutomataGame class itself—specifically, the CreateData method shown in Listing 5-3. This method calls CreateOneCell, which can vary widely from subclass to subclass. Listing 5-6 shows this method for the Life class.

Listing 5-6. The CreateOneCell *Method in the Life Class*

```
Protected Overrides Function CreateOneCell(_
    ByVal oPos As Point) As CellularAutomataCell

    Dim oC As ConwaysLifeCell

    fSetupNeighbors = False
    oC = New ConwaysLifeCell(oPos, Me.CellRadius)
    oC.Alive = oRand.Next(0, Int32.MaxValue) Mod 5 = 0
    Return oC

End Function
```

Given a point parameter, this method creates a single instance of the ConwaysLifeCell class, initializes the Alive property to True about 20 percent of the time, and returns this instance to the caller. It also sets a class-level variable named fSetupNeighbors to False. This variable indicates that a process that defines each cell's eight neighbors needs to execute before the next clock iteration occurs. The idea is that if a new cell is being created via a call to this method, then the lattice has changed enough so that all of the cells need their neighbors set up again before a clock cycle can happen.

TIP *How does the* CreateOneCell *code create a 20-percent chance of something occurring? To obtain a result 20 percent of the time, you can take a random integer, divide it by 5, and then look at the remainder using the* Mod *operator. The remainder of dividing a number by 5 will be 0, 1, 2, 3, or 4. Because each of the five possible remainders of a random integer divided by 5 is equally likely, you have a 20-percent chance of getting any one of them. In the* CreateOneCell *method, you can test that the remainder is 0, and if it is, you set the* Alive *property to* True.

Setting Up the Neighbors

The cell neighbor setup process is fairly slow, so it isn't beneficial to perform it more often than required (certainly you wouldn't need or want to perform this neighbor setup on every clock tick, for example). Listing 5-7 shows the code for the neighbor setup process.

Listing 5-7. Defining the Neighbors of Each Cell

```
Private Sub SetupNeighbors()

    Dim i As Integer
    Dim iRow, iCol As Integer       'loop variables
    Dim iLRow, iLCol As Integer     'loop variables
    Dim oCn As ConwaysLifeCell

    Dim oC As ConwaysLifeCell
    For i = 0 To FCells.Count - 1
        oC = FCells.Item(i)
        oC.ClearNeighbors()
        IndexToRowCol(i, iRow, iCol)

        For iLRow = -1 To 1
            For iLCol = -1 To 1
                If iLRow = 0 And iLCol = 0 Then
```

```
                        'nothing, same cell
               Else
                   oCn = RowColToCell(iRow + iLRow, iCol + iLCol)
                   If Not (oCn Is Nothing) Then
                       oC.AddNeighbor(oCn)
                   End If
               End If
           Next
       Next
   Next

   fSetupNeighbors = True

End Sub
```

The neighbor setup process iterates through each cell in the FCells ArrayList. You can use an integer-based For loop as opposed to a For..Each construct so the index of each cell is needed to determine the cell's row and column position within the lattice. You find the row/column position using the IndextoRowCol method, which is declared as protected in the base class and therefore available to call. Once you find the row/column position, create a nested loop pair to loop between all cells –1 and +1 away from the current cell. Figure 5-3 shows the cell indexes for a cell. The center cell is at position iRow, iCol.

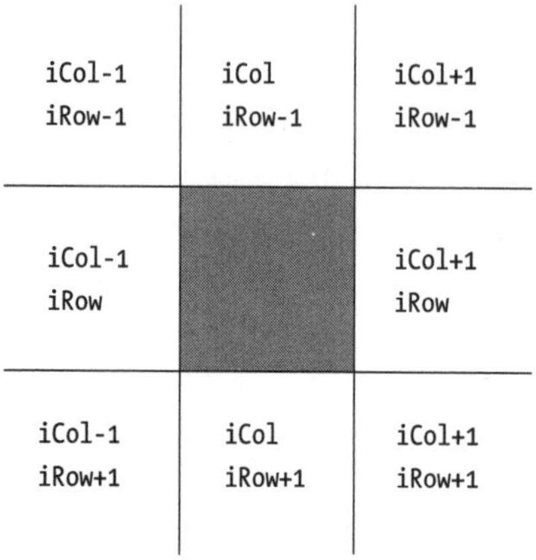

iCol-1 iRow-1	iCol iRow-1	iCol+1 iRow-1
iCol-1 iRow		iCol+1 iRow
iCol-1 iRow+1	iCol iRow+1	iCol+1 iRow+1

Figure 5-3. The center cell's eight neighbors and their indexes

Within this nested loop, the eight neighbor cells are determined using the starting row/column added to the loop indexes, and the protected method RowColToCell method is called to translate this row/column pair back to a cell in the lattice. This method returns nothing if the passed-in indexes are out of range (the cells on the left edge have no left neighbor, for example). Each cell that's successfully returned is set to be a neighbor of the original cell using the AddNeighbor method. The last line sets the neighbor setup Boolean flag to True. This prevents this code from running again, unless of course more cells are added to the lattice later—say, when the game form is resized.

Creating the RunAGeneration Method

The final method for the ConwaysLifeGame class is the overridden RunAGeneration method, shown in Listing 5-8.

Listing 5-8. Running One Tick of Conway's Game of Life

```
Protected Overrides Sub RunAGeneration()

    Dim oC As ConwaysLifeCell

    If Not fSetupNeighbors Then
        SetupNeighbors()
    End If

    'clear neighbor count
    For Each oC In FCells
        oC.PreCountReset()
    Next

    'if I'm alive, updated neighbor count on all 8 neighbors
    For Each oC In FCells
        oC.UpdateNeighborsBasedOnMe()
    Next

    For Each oC In FCells
        oC.UpdateAliveBasedonNeighbors()
    Next
End Sub
```

As hinted at earlier, the beginning of the RunAGeneration method sets up the neighbor cells but only if the Boolean flag is False. If the flag is True, then the neighbors of each cell have already been defined and this call is skipped.

To determine what happens to each cell in this generation, one must loop through all the cells and count neighbors. Then, according to the rules of the game, each cell will live or die based on these neighbor counts. The algorithm that most Life programmers first attempt loops through every cell, living or dead. For each cell, the code checks all eight neighbors and sums them if living to create a total. This neighbor count is then stored until all the cells have been counted (you can't change the state of this cell now or else its new state would incorrectly affect the neighbor count of the cells bordering this one). Once all the cells have had their neighbors counted, each cell is iterated again to have its state changed if required by the rules and its neighbor count.

This algorithm works but turns out to be inefficient because every cell in the lattice is accessed multiple times. A given cell is passed through in the main loop and then checked for its life/death state up to eight times because it serves as the neighbor to eight other cells.

A much more efficient algorithm is to first initialize all cell neighbor counts to 0. Then the main cell loop begins. If a cell is alive, the program adds 1 to the neighbor count of all eight neighbors of that cell. If a cell is dead, the program takes no action. At the end of the loop, the neighbor counts will all equal the number of living neighbors as desired, and the rules can then be applied to determine the state of each cell. This algorithm is faster because no action is taken when a cell is dead, so the process accesses the total lattice far fewer times.

The code in Listing 5-8 carries out this algorithm. Three For..Each loops are iterated upon the lattice. The first merely resets the neighbor cell count of each cell to 0. The second calls the UpdateNeighborsBasedOnMe method of each cell, which adds 1 to the neighbor count of the eight neighboring cells if the given cell is alive. The third loop calls UpdateNeighborsBasedOnMe, which changes the living/dead state of each cell based on its neighbor count.

Creating the Life Cell Class

The ConwaysLifeCell class descends from the CellularAutomataCell class. The ancestor class handles the location information for a cell and most of the drawing functionality. One thing the ancestor class doesn't handle, however, is determining the color of the cell to be drawn. That method, called GetColor, is declared on the ancestor as MustOverride and must be implemented in the subclasses. That method is quite simple in the ConwaysLifeCell class:

```
Overrides Function GetColor() As Color
    Return IIf(Not Alive, Color.Black, Color.Yellow)
End Function
```

A Life cell can only display one of two colors, which are yellow for a living cell and black for a dead cell in this example.

The other required MustOverride member in the ancestor cell class is the OnMouseDown method, which describes what's to happen when a user clicks a cell.

That too is quite simple in this variation—you merely want to toggle the alive/dead state of the cell when it's clicked:

```
Public Overrides Sub OnMouseDown(ByVal e As _
  System.Windows.Forms.MouseEventArgs)
    Me.Alive = Not Me.Alive
End Sub
```

The remainder of the cell class handles the neighbor storage and the functionality of updating neighbor counts and state. Listing 5-9 displays the remainder of the cell class (omitting a few trivial members such as the Alive and NeighborCount properties).

Listing 5-9. The Remainder of the ConwaysLifeCell *Class*

```
Public Class ConwaysLifeCell
    Inherits CellularAutomataCell

    Protected FNeighbors As ArrayList
    Public Sub AddNeighbor(ByVal oC As ConwaysLifeCell)
        If FNeighbors Is Nothing Then
            FNeighbors = New ArrayList
        End If

        FNeighbors.Add(oC)
    End Sub

    Public Overridable Sub PreCountReset()
        NeighborCount = 0
    End Sub

    Public Overridable Sub UpdateNeighborsBasedOnMe()

        Dim oC As ConwaysLifeCell

        If Me.Alive Then
            For Each oC In FNeighbors
                oC.NeighborCount += 1
            Next
        End If
    End Sub
```

```
Public Overridable Sub UpdateAliveBasedonNeighbors()
    If Not Alive Then
        'not alive now, comes to life if 3 neighbors
        Alive = (NeighborCount = 3)
    Else
        'alive now, stays alive w/ 2 or 3 neighbors
        Alive = (NeighborCount = 2 Or NeighborCount = 3)
    End If
End Sub
End Class
```

The neighbors of each cell are stored in an ArrayList named FNeighbors. The implementation of the AddNeighbor method is pretty straightforward—all that's required is to initialize this ArrayList if it hasn't already been done and then add the passed-in neighbor to it. The method UpdateNeighborsBasedOnMe is also quite simple. This method increments the alive neighbor count of all the neighbors of this cell, but only if this cell is currently alive (dead cells don't affect neighbor counts, remember). Finally, the method UpdateAliveBasedOnNeighbors implements the living/dead rules for a cell—alive cells with two or three neighbors stay alive, and dead cells with exactly three neighbors spring to life. I particularly like how the code in this method resembles English: "If not Alive, Alive is true if NeighborCount equals three...."

Note that the methods PreCountReset, UpdateNeighborsBasedOnMe and UpdateAliveBasedOnNeighbors are defined as Overridable, meaning that their functionality can be changed in any subclasses created from the ConwaysLifeCell class. But do you really intend to create a subclass from this cell class, which is already itself a subclass?

Developing Rainbow Life

Conway's Game of Life is popular enough that people have come up with variations of it. Some variations tinker with the neighbor counts that determine a cell's state. Others take the two-dimensional lattice of cells into the third dimension and create a three-dimensional version of life with cubes representing the cells. One particularly interesting Life variation is a multicolored version, called *Color Life* or *Rainbow Life.* In this version, each living cell contains a color property, and the cell is rendered in that color. When a new cell is born, the color of that cell is determined by the average color of the three living neighbor cells that made its birth possible. This lends a sort of parent-child relationship to the game because the three "parent" cells give birth to a new "child" that inherits a trait from all three of them—the trait of color.

An example will shed some further light on the issue. Figure 5-4 shows a grid of cells. In the next clock tick, the center cell will spring to life because it has three living neighbors. Suppose that neighbor 1 is pure red, neighbor 2 is pure blue, and neighbor 3 is white. The center cell's color will inherit from its three parents by averaging their colors together. Table 5-1 shows the red/green/blue components of these cells.

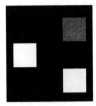

Figure 5-4. The Rainbow Life game

Table 5-1. Cell Color Averaging in Rainbow Life

NEIGHBOR	COLOR	RED	GREEN	BLUE
1	Red	255	0	0
2	Blue	0	0	255
3	White	255	255	255
Result	--	170	85	170

You obtain the result by adding the three color components and dividing by 3. RGB color 170, 85, 85 is a medium brown. This is the color that the newborn cell will have. Like its one-color cousin, watching Rainbow Life in action gives you far more insight into how it works than reading an explanation of it. Have fun exploring the sample program by simply running it before studying the code.

Creating the RainbowLifeGame Class

Because Rainbow Life is so similar to its monochromatic cousin, the best way to implement this game is to inherit directly off of the two Life classes discussed previously. The game class is the easier of the two because you need to change only one method to achieve the rainbow functionality. That member is the CreateOneCell method, which you'll recall is the method that's called polymorphically on the base class to return an instance of the game-specific cell descendant. Listing 5-10 shows the new code for the Rainbow Life variation of this method.

Listing 5-10. Rainbow Life CreateOneCell *Method*

```
Protected Overrides Function _
   CreateOneCell(ByVal oPos As Point) As CellularAutomataCell

   Dim oC As RainbowLifeCell

   oC = New RainbowLifeCell(oPos, Me.CellRadius)
   If oRand.Next(0, Int32.MaxValue) Mod 5 = 0 Then
      oC.Alive = True
      oC.SetRandomColor()
   End If

   Return oC

End Function
```

Like the single-color version, Rainbow Life creates a living cell 20 percent of the time. This newly born cell is also given a random color using the SetRandomColor method on the cell class.

What's cool about inheriting the rainbow version of the Life game class from the standard Life game class is that you don't have to change the functionality of anything except the method you've just seen. The RunAGeneration method, for instance, needs no changing because you want the same actions to occur. Those actions (to give you a refresher) are to reset all the cells' neighbor counts to 0, then to rip through all the living cells and update their neighbor counts, and finally to change the state of each cell according to its neighbors.

What *does* change in the rainbow version is what's going on in some of these subparts. For example, when updating neighbor counts, the program also needs to keep track of the colors of all the neighbors so that a newly born cell can determine what its new color should be. The cell class declares all of this new functionality, however.

Creating the RainbowLifeCell Class

The cell class for the rainbow version of Life also inherits from the "standard" Conway version of the CellularAutomataCell class, but there are quite a few more changes. The first change was already hinted at earlier—a method named SetRandomColor that picks a starting color for each cell. Listing 5-11 displays that method, which chooses the color of each cell at the start of the game, along with some other members.

Listing 5-11. The Method SetRandomColor

```vb
Private FColor As Color
Private FNeighborRTot As Integer
Private FNeighborGTot As Integer
Private FNeighborBTot As Integer

Public Sub SetRandomColor()

    Dim c As Color

    Select Case oRand.Next(0, Int32.MaxValue) Mod 10
        Case 0 : c = Color.Yellow
        Case 1 : c = Color.Green
        Case 2 : c = Color.Blue
        Case 3 : c = Color.Red
        Case 4, 5 : c = Color.White
        Case 6 : c = Color.Orange
        Case 7 : c = Color.Violet
        Case 8 : c = Color.DarkBlue
        Case 9 : c = Color.Magenta
    End Select
    Me.SetColor(c)
End Sub

Overrides Function GetColor() As Color
    Return IIf(Not Alive, Color.Black, FColor)
End Function

Private Sub SetColor(ByVal c As Color)
    FColor = c
End Sub
```

This method doesn't implement a *truly* random color (selecting random
numbers from 0–255 for red, green, and blue and constructing a color from these
components). The technique in this method, which is to choose from nine
"base" colors (including white), gives a much more interesting starting state and
much prettier results once the cells start on their life cycles.

Also shown in Listing 5-11 is the GetColor method, which overrides the original member found in the CellularAutomataCell class (this method is declared
MustOverride in the ancestor). This method returns the private FColor variable if
the current cell is alive and black if the cell is dead. You've also implemented
a SetColor method to set the private color variable. The more common way of

implementing code to get and set a private variable is to declare a property, but you can't do that in this case because you were already forced to implement a GetColor method by the ancestor class. Implementing a Color property would be redundant to this existing method.

The remaining private variables, named FNeighborRTot, FNeighborGTot, and FBeighborBTot, store the color components of living neighbor cells for the purpose of creating a new offspring with the arithmetic mean of the new cell's parents.

Listing 5-12 shows how the program uses these color-counting variables. First, it resets them to the value 0 in the overridden PreCountReset method. This method is called before neighbor counting begins in each clock tick iteration of the game. Note how the method calls the ancestor method using the keyword MyBase, meaning that this method is extending the functionality defined in the ancestor class.

The actual neighbor counting happens in the method UpdateNeighborsBasedOnMe, which is also overridden from the ancestor class. Because no MyBase call exists here, this method totally replaces the functionality in the base class. If the cell is currently alive, then the neighbor count of all neighbor cells is incremented by 1 (like the standard Life class), and the color component's counting variables are also incremented by the red, green, and blue components of this cell's current color.

Listing 5-12. Overridden Neighbor-Counting Classes

```
Public Overrides Sub PreCountReset()
    MyBase.PreCountReset()
    FNeighborRTot = 0
    FNeighborGTot = 0
    FNeighborBTot = 0
End Sub


Public Overrides Sub UpdateNeighborsBasedOnMe()

    Dim oC As RainbowLifeCell

    If Me.Alive Then
        For Each oC In FNeighbors
            oC.NeighborCount += 1

            oC.FNeighborRTot += Me.GetColor.R
            oC.FNeighborGTot += Me.GetColor.G
            oC.FNeighborBTot += Me.GetColor.B
        Next
    End If
End Sub
```

```
Public Overrides Sub UpdateAliveBasedonNeighbors()

   Dim oC As ConwaysLifeCell

   If Not Alive Then
      If NeighborCount = 3 Then
         Alive = True
         Me.SetColor(Color.FromArgb(_
            FNeighborRTot \ 3, _
            FNeighborGTot \ 3, _
            FNeighborBTot \ 3))
      End If
   Else
      'alive now, stays alive w/ 2 or 3 neighbors
      Alive = (NeighborCount = 2 Or NeighborCount = 3)
   End If
End Sub
```

The final method, `UpdateAliveBasedOnNeighbors`, runs after all the neighbor counting. This method is similar to the version it overrides in the standard Life game. If a living cell has two or three neighbors, it remains alive. If a dead cell has exactly three neighbors, it springs to live and its starting color is set to the average color of the three neighbor cells. (The summed value of the three red, green, and blue components of the three neighbors are calculated during the counting process—all you need to do here is to divide those values by 3.)

That wraps it up for the Rainbow Life variant. By inheriting off of the base Life class, you were able to change the functionality enough to create a whole new game.

Developing the Voting Game

The final cellular automaton game is a bit subtler in its complexities than the Life variants. It's called the *Voting Game*, and I read about it for the first time in the book *The Armchair Universe: An Exploration of Computer Worlds* by A. K. Dewdney (W .H. Freeman and Company, 1988). This book contained a compilation of excerpts of articles from *Scientific American* magazine from 1984 and 1987 (there I go dating myself again).

The lattice in the Voting Game contains cells of two colors. Each color represents a political party affiliation (Democrat and Republican if you want to assign an American slant to the game). At the start of the game, each cell is randomly assigned one party or the other. Within each tick of the clock, the game chooses a single cell at random, as well as a single neighbor of that cell. The political party of the chosen cell changes to that of the neighbor cell, regardless of the party of either cell at the start of the process. Figure 5-5 shows a VB .NET representation of the Voting Game.

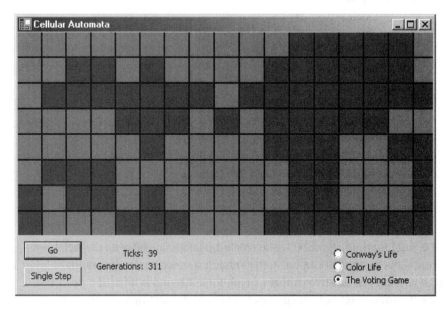

Figure 5-5. The Voting Game

Like in Conway's Game of Life and its variants, you can find patterns in the Voting Game, though you often have to wait a bit longer to see them form. After a time, blocks of same-partied cells group themselves together. Usually, one of the two parties becomes dominant, leaving only a small island or two of the minority party. These small blocks sometimes migrate around the lattice over time. Finally, the dominant party often completely eliminates the minority party, leaving the entire population voting with a unanimous voice.

Creating TheVotingGame Class

The game class, which is unimaginatively named TheVotingGame, contains functionality that differs little from the game classes you've already seen. As required, the class implements the CreateOneCell method to return an instance of the cell class associated with this game, as shown in Listing 5-13.

Listing 5-13. The CreateOneCell *Method of the* TheVotingGame *Class*

```
Protected Overrides Function _
  CreateOneCell(ByVal oPos As Point) As CellularAutomataCell

  Dim oC As VotingCell

  fSetupNeighbors = False

  oC = New VotingCell(oPos, Me.CellRadius)
  oC.IsDemocrat = HalfTheTime()
  Return oC

End Function
```

The only setup required for a voting cell class is its party affiliation. You implement this as a Boolean property named IsDemocrat, which is set to true 50 percent of the time, using the HalfTheTime method defined in the ancestor game class. Once the party affiliation is set, the cell class is returned.

The other required method for all descendant game classes is the RunAGeneration method, which is simpler in the Voting Game than it was in the Life games. Listing 5-14 shows this method.

Listing 5-14. The RunAGeneration *Method of* TheVotingGame *Class*

```
Protected Overrides Sub RunAGeneration()

  Dim oC As VotingCell

  If Not fSetupNeighbors Then
     SetupNeighbors()
  End If

  'choose a random neighbor
  oC = fCells.Item(oRand.Next(0, fcells.Count))
  oC.ChangePartyAffiliation()

End Sub
```

Like the Life games, you need to set up the cell neighbors before the first generation runs. After that, however, each tick of the clock selects a random cell in the FCells Arraylist (declared protected in the ancestor class and thus available here) and calls the ChangePartyAffiliation method of this cell.

The only other code of note in TheVotingGame class is the neighbor setup method SetupNeighbors. This method is almost identical to the same-named method in the Life game classes (shown in Listing 5-7 and thus not repeated here)—with one notable exception. When looking for the neighbor cells of a given cell, the RowColToCell method declared in the ancestor class is sent an additional parameter bWrap, which is set to True:

```
oCn = RowColToCell(iRow + iLRow, iCol + iLCol, bWrap:=True)
```

The bWrap parameter tells the RowColToCell method to wrap around the edges of the lattice when looking for neighbors. Therefore, cells along the top row and bottom row are considered adjacent, as are the far-left and far-right columns. This gives every cell in the lattice exactly eight neighbors.

Creating the VotingCell Class

The VotingCell class contains the same neighbor handling code as the Life games did. As required, it implements the GetColor method, which returns blue or red depending on the party affiliation of the cell. As shown in Listing 5-13, the VotingCell class contains a property named IsDemocrat to denote the party affiliation of the cell. Listing 5-15 shows that property definition and the GetColor method.

Listing 5-15. The Overridden GetColor *Method, the* IsDemocrat *Property, and the* ChangePartyAffiliation *Method of the* VotingCell *Class*

```
Overrides Function GetColor() As Color
    Return IIf(Not FDemocrat, Color.Blue, Color.Red)
End Function

Private FDemocrat As Boolean = False
Property IsDemocrat() As Boolean
    Get
        Return FDemocrat
    End Get
    Set(ByVal Value As Boolean)
        FDemocrat = Value
    End Set
End Property
```

```
Public Sub ChangePartyAffiliation()

    Dim oC As VotingCell

    oC = FNeighbors.Item(oRand.Next(0, FNeighbors.Count))
    Me.IsDemocrat = oC.IsDemocrat

End Sub
```

The last important member in the VotingCell class is the ChangePartyAffiliation method, also shown in Listing 5-15. This function selects a random neighbor to the current cell and copies that neighbor cell's party affiliation to the current cell. It's quite possible (50-percent possible, in fact) that the current cell and the neighbor cell already have the same party affiliation. When this happens, there's no change to the lattice during that timer tick.

Building the Main Cellular Automaton Program

Polymorphism is all about shielding parts of the program from each other. In this case, the ancestor class called CellularAutomataGame declares the base functionality required to display the cells in a type of cellular automaton and to tick the giant clock. During each tick, it's up to the inner workings of the individual descendant class to determine the new state of each cell, based on whatever rules that class defines. Because of this design, the main program doesn't need to know about what each game class is doing during each timer tick. It only has to instantiate the game class, pass it a control upon which drawing should be done, and tell it when to run a clock tick. The ancestor class handles all of these actions.

The form for the program contains a panel on the bottom that serves as the parent for a few controls. Two buttons will allow the cellular automaton to run a single clock tick or to start and stop a timer that runs the clock ticks in succession. Two labels report the number of total clock ticks that have occurred, as well as the time elapsed during the previous clock tick. Finally, a series of radio buttons on the lower right allow users to change which automaton game they're playing. Figure 5-6 shows the design-time version of the form.

All of the game drawing happens in a class used earlier in the book—the FlickerFreePanel (called the PaintPanel back in Chapter 1, "Developing Your First Game"). Now, you can give it a more descriptive name and place it into a common folder so that you can share it between programs. There are two ways to use a visual control on a form. The first way is to add the control to the Toolbox (demonstrated in Chapter 2, "Writing Your First Game, Again") and then drag it onto the form. The second method is to instantiate the control and add it to the form in code, as in this example. Listing 5-16 shows two private variables declared on the form, the Form_Load event and an important method called CreateGame.

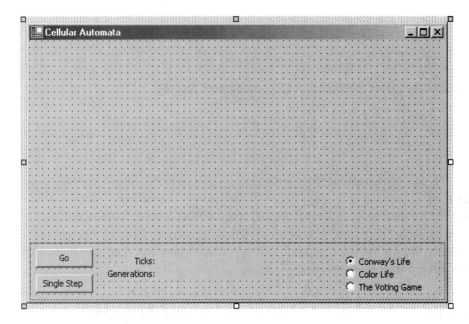

Figure 5-6. Design-time view of the cellular automaton executor

Listing 5-16. Setting Up the Cellular Automaton Executor

```
Public Class fLife
    Inherits System.Windows.Forms.Form

    Private oP As FlickerFreePanel
    Private oCell As CellularAutomata.CellularAutomataGame

    Private Sub Form1_Load(ByVal sender As System.Object, _
      ByVal e As System.EventArgs) Handles MyBase.Load

        oP = New FlickerFreePanel
        oP.Dock = DockStyle.Fill
        Me.Controls.Add(oP)

        CreateGame()

    End Sub

    Private Sub CreateGame()

        If rbGame0.Checked Then
            oCell = New CellularAutomata.ConwaysLife(oP)
```

```
        oCell.CellRadius = 8
    ElseIf rbGame1.Checked Then
        oCell = New CellularAutomata.RainbowLife(oP)
        oCell.CellRadius = 8
    Else
        oCell = New CellularAutomata.TheVotingGame(oP)
        oCell.CellRadius = 32
    End If


End Sub
```

The form-level `FlickerFreePanel` control is declared private and attached to the form in the form's `Load` event. To make sure it conforms to the size of the parent form (less the size of the lower panel that houses the buttons and other controls), set the `Dock` property to `Fill` on this panel. The last line in the form's `Load` event is to call a method named `CreateGame`. This method is responsible for creating the correct `CellularAutomataGame` descendant based on which radio button the user clicks. The variable holding the current game is named `oCell`. The only difference between the game classes from this level of the program is the cell size. Set the cell size much larger for the Voting Game than for the Life games (32 pixels instead of 8 pixels), which makes it easier to see the patterns emerge for this particular game. The larger cell size also makes it possible to see one party or the other completely take over the board after several thousand generations.

 NOTE *A cooler way to create the individual cellular automaton game descendants is to use a form of reflection to iterate through the program assembly, look for all subclasses of the `CellularAutomata` game class, and create a radio button dynamically for each game type found. Chapter 4, "More OOPing Around," used a similar approach when generating random clues for the DeducTile Reasoning game.*

The only remaining functionality left to code is the event handlers for the two buttons, a timer control, and the radio buttons that control the game. Listing 5-17 shows all of these event handlers.

Listing 5-17. Event Handlers for the Cellular Automaton Executor Form

```
Private Sub rbGame_CheckedChanged(ByVal sender As System.Object, _
    ByVal e As System.EventArgs) Handles rbGame0.CheckedChanged, _
    rbGame1.CheckedChanged, rbGame2.CheckedChanged
```

```
        If oP Is Nothing Then Exit Sub

    CreateGame()
End Sub


Private Sub RunOne(ByVal sender As System.Object, _
  ByVal e As System.EventArgs) Handles aTimer.Tick, _
  cbSingle.Click

    oCell.Tick()
    lbTime.Text = oCell.TimerTicksElapsed
    lbGen.Text = oCell.GenerationCount

End Sub


Private Sub cbGo_Click(ByVal sender As System.Object, _
  ByVal e As System.EventArgs) Handles cbGo.Click

    If aTimer.Enabled Then
        aTimer.Enabled = False
        cbGo.Text = "Go"
        rbGame0.Enabled = True
        rbGame1.Enabled = True
        rbGame2.Enabled = True
    Else
        aTimer.Enabled = True
        cbGo.Text = "Stop"
        rbGame0.Enabled = False
        rbGame1.Enabled = False
        rbGame2.Enabled = False
    End If

End Sub
```

The event handler for the radio buttons, named rbGame_CheckedChanged, is trivial—they simply call the CreateGame method that loads one of the game classes based on the value of those same radio buttons. The program first checks to make sure the FlickerFreePanel variable oP has already been created. This is necessary because a radio button CheckChanged event fires as the form is being constructed by the .NET Framework, but you don't want to start the cellular automaton game at this early stage (without the FlickerFreePanel, there would be nowhere to render the cell lattice).

The method RunOne serves a dual purpose. It runs when the user clicks the Single Step button, and it serves as the Tick event of a timer control named aTimer. You've seen demonstrations of a single method serving as the event handler for more than one control (the event handler for the radio buttons just discussed is one such example), but this is the first example you've seen where a single event handler is attached to different events on different types of controls. This is allowable as long as the event handler signature is the same for both events. For example, you couldn't use the same event handler to handle a Click event and a Paint event because one event expects a System.EventArgs variable as a parameter and the other expects a System.Windows.Forms.PaintEventArgs as a parameter.

The final event handler runs when the user clicks the Go button. This code turns the Go button into a toggle. The first time the user clicks this button, the timer starts ticking, the radio buttons are disabled (so a game can't be changed midtick), and the button itself changes its text to *Stop*. When the user clicks the button again, this process is reversed—the timer is disabled, the radio buttons enabled, and the text changes once again to *Go*.

Expanding the Cellular Automaton Games

As mentioned, cellular automaton programs serve as a popular topic in computer science discussions. There are dozens of variations of cellular automaton programs that you could create and add to this program by creating more subclasses of the CellularAutomataGame and CellularAutomataCell classes and adding a bit of "wireup" code to make the main program aware of the new class (or you could go to the reflection-based self-discovery mechanism hinted at earlier).

One popular topic within the study of cellular automaton programs is optimizing them for speed so that a single tick executes as quickly as possible. I introduced one such optimization in the neighbor counting algorithm of the Life games—it turns out to be much more efficient to update neighbor counts of all living cells by 1 than it is to iterate through every cell counting living neighbors. Other algorithmic optimizations have been discovered, such as ones that identify blank regions of the lattice and skip the processing of those regions. You can find more information on such topics online. (Do a Google.com search on *cellular automata* to get started.)

The design of this chapter's example program certainly warrants some refactoring if speed becomes your priority. This program redraws the entire lattice after each tick, for example. This isn't always necessary depending on the type of game running. For example, it's possible in the Voting Game for a turn to yield no change to the lattice. Why waste time redrawing it? You might also consider a region-based redrawing algorithm, where only cells that actually change state are redrawn. This may or may not speed up the process. Others might argue that the entire class-based design of this example program would never be as fast as a more low-level data structure, such as a 2×2 array of integers, paired with some highly optimized functions for reading/writing this array. This structure of course defeats the purpose of the example—to demonstrate the object-oriented concept of polymorphism.

This cellular automaton program demonstrates polymorphism through inheritance. The subclasses of the `CellularAutomataGame` class can implement their functionality in many different ways, but the users of this class need to understand only the interface of the base class to use all of the subclasses effectively. Another major means of achieving polymorphism exists in the .NET Framework besides inheritance; it's discussed in the next chapter.

CHAPTER 6

Using Polymorphism via Interfaces

CHAPTER 5, "UNDERSTANDING POLYMORPHISM," introduced the concept of *polymorphism*, a fundamental concept underlying object-oriented programming. Polymorphism is when objects implement similar functionality in different ways, and the user of the objects doesn't necessarily know about these different implementations.

All of the examples in the previous chapter demonstrated polymorphism though class inheritance. An ancestor class defined the baseline functionality, and one or more subclasses augmented or changed that functionality. You can achieve polymorphism by declaring a variable of the ancestor type. This variable can refer to any of the subclasses, yet the code at the scope of this variable declaration doesn't need to know to which subclass it's pointing.

Class inheritance isn't the only way to achieve polymorphism. A second technique is through the use of a class *interface*. An interface declares properties, events, and methods just like a class does, but an interface doesn't implement any of these members through code. Instead, the interface simply lists the members that comprise it.

Previous chapters unofficially introduced the concept of interfaces while describing key classes in the game examples. Chapter 2, "Writing Your First Game, Again," described the Die class in terms of its public interface. Chapter 4, "More OOPing Around," did the same thing for the TileData and WavFile classes. To reiterate, discussing a class in terms of its public interface is a good way to learn *what* a class does without having to pay attention to *how* it does it. And learning what a class does is the important part because the user of a class needs to learn only the tasks that it accomplishes to use it. He doesn't need to know about the implementation details (the "how") of that class.

I'm not the only one who thinks that separating class interfaces from implementation is a useful learning tool. Most object-oriented languages have the concept of class interfaces built into them. Chapter 4, "More OOPing Around," introduced a class interface built into the .NET Framework—the IComparable interface. You'd usually use this interface on an object that needs to be sorted in a specific sort order. If you'll recall back that far, you'll remember that you needed to sort the four tile classes used in the DeducTile Reasoning game in top-to-bottom order on the screen so that they could be properly compared against the solution that the player was trying to guess.

In this chapter, you'll write two games, Tic-Tac-Toe and Reversi, to practice implementing polymorphism via interfaces.

Seeing an Example Interface in Action

The .NET Framework contains dozens of built-in class interfaces, but these don't represent the entire universe of interfaces you can use in your programs. Just as you can create your own class definitions, you can also create your own interface definitions. This concept is important, so this section provides a simple example before getting into a more complex, game-related example. You'll find this program in the folder InterfaceExample in the source code that comes with this book.

NOTE *You can download the source code from the Downloads section of the Apress Web site (*http://www.apress.com*) if you haven't done so already.*

The InterfaceExample project is a different project style than you've seen thus far in the book. You'll implement this program as a console application because it doesn't require any user input. A console application runs in a command prompt (called a *DOS prompt* back in the day), and all input and output happens via the console, or the command line. You select the project type on the same dialog box where you first name the project, shown in Figure 6-1.

The interface you'll create and then implement is IIntegerSequencer. Any class that implements the IIntegerSequencer interface is expected to spit out a sequence of integers. The interface itself consists of a single member definition, a method named GetNext:

```
Interface IIntegerSequencer
    Function GetNext() As Integer
End Interface
```

Remember, an interface by itself is simply a declaration of functionality. It doesn't provide any implementation of that functionality. To use the interface, you need to declare a class and state that the class implements the desired interface:

```
Public Class IntegerCounter
    Implements IIntegerSequencer
```

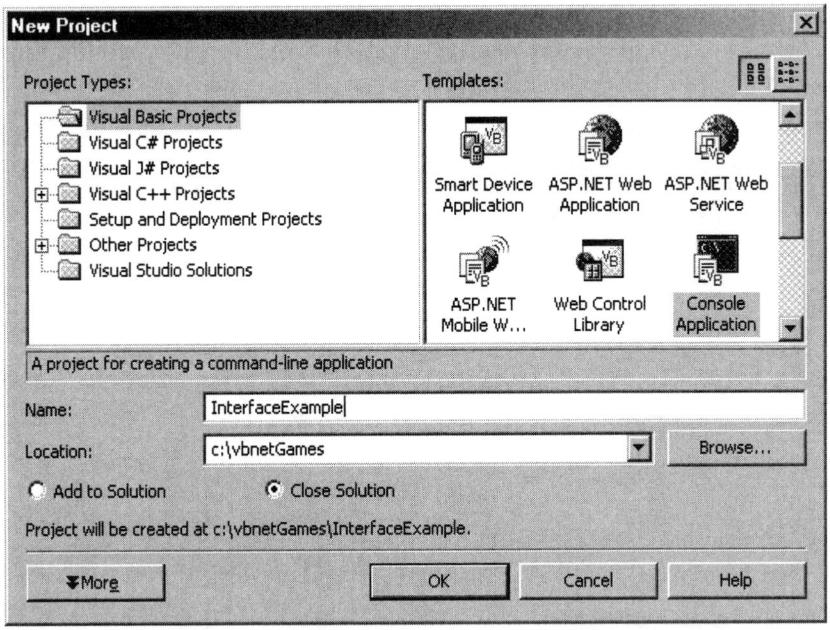

Figure 6-1. Creating a console application

Something pretty cool happens in Visual Studio .NET as soon as you declare a class and then complete the Implements line as shown. Visual Studio "stubs out" all of the members of that interface for you, as shown in Listing 6-1.

Listing 6-1. Stubbing Out Interface Members

```
Public Class IntegerCounter
    Implements IIntegerSequencer

    Public Function GetNext() As Integer _
        Implements IIntegerSequencer.GetNext

    End Function
End Class
```

Creating the IntegerCounter Class

Visual Studio created the function template for the GetNext method on the IntegerCounter class as soon as you hit Enter on the line that reads Implements IIntegerSequencer. If IIntegerSequencer had more members besides the lone GetNext method, these members would also have been stubbed out in the new class declaration.

All that remains is to write the code that implements the GetNext interface for this class. The intention of the IntegerCounter class is to simply count upward each time the GetNext method is called, so this class is pretty trivial to implement (see Listing 6-2).

Listing 6-2. A Counter Class That Implements the IIntegerSequencer Interface

```
Public Class IntegerCounter
    Implements IIntegerSequencer

    Private FLast As Integer = 1

    Public Function GetNext() As Integer _
        Implements IIntegerSequencer.GetNext

        FLast += 1
        Return FLast
    End Function
End Class
```

All this class has to do is keep track of the last integer returned via a private variable named FLast. When the GetNext method is called, the program adds 1 to the variable and returns it. Instant counting class!

Creating the FibonacciCounter Class

Proving you can move beyond the trivial to the merely simple, the second implementation of the IIntegerSequencer class returns the Fibonacci sequence. For the math-impaired, the Fibonacci sequence starts with the integers 1, 1 and then obtains each subsequent number by adding the two numbers before it. The beginning of the sequence is as follows: 1, 1, 2, 3, 5, 8, 13, 21, 34.... Listing 6-3 shows the FibonacciCounter class, which returns the next value in the Fibonacci sequence each time the GetNext method is called.

Listing 6-3. The FibonacciCounter Class

```
Public Class FibonacciCounter
    Implements IIntegerSequencer

    Dim iTurn As Integer = 0
    Private FLast1 As Integer = 1
    Private FLast2 As Integer = 1
```

```
    Public Function GetNext() As Integer _
        Implements IIntegerSequencer.GetNext

        Dim iTemp As Integer

        iTurn += 1
        If iTurn < 3 Then
            Return 1
        Else

            iTemp = FLast1 + FLast2

            FLast1 = FLast2
            FLast2 = iTemp
            Return iTemp
        End If
    End Function
End Class
```

This class returns a 1 for the first two turns (as the rules of the Fibonacci sequence state). After the second turn, the program returns the sum of the variables FLast1 and FLast2 and then "slides" the values over—placing the value of FLast2 into FLast1 and placing the new sum into FLast2.

Achieving Polymorphism Using the Sequencer Classes

You've now got two classes that implement the IIntegerSequencer interface, and neither of these classes inherits from the other. Can a program access either one of the classes polymorphically without knowing which one it's calling? This would be a short chapter if the answer was "no," wouldn't it? Listing 6-4 demonstrates how the program selects one of the two classes randomly and then displays the beginning of that class's sequence.

Listing 6-4. Accessing a Class Interface Polymorphically

```
Sub Main()
    Dim oInt As IIntegerSequencer
    Dim oRand As New Random
    Dim i As Integer
```

```
        If oRand.Next(0, 1000) Mod 2 = 0 Then
            oInt = New IntegerCounter
        Else
            oInt = New FibonacciCounter
        End If

        Console.WriteLine("couting started ")
        Do
            i = oInt.GetNext
            Console.Write(i & ",")
        Loop Until i > 100
        Console.ReadLine()
    End Sub
```

The most important line of this listing, and perhaps of the chapter, is the first line after the Sub Main declaration. A variable named oInt is declared, but it's not declared to be an instance of a certain class. Instead, *it's declared to be an instance of a certain interface.* You might read this declaration in English as "The variable oInt will hold an instance of some class that implements the IIntegerSequencer interface." And, this, my friends, is how you achieve polymorphism using interfaces. With this capability, the sample program can now point to either an IntegerCounter instance or a FibonacciCounter instance with the variable oInt because each of these classes implements the IIntegerSequencer interface. Furthermore, the program can call the GetNext method on the variable oInt polymorphically because you've declared that variable as implementing the IIntegerSequencer interface.

Why Use Interfaces and Not Class Inheritance?

You might be having some trouble distinguishing between writing two classes that implement the same interface and creating classes that inherit from the same ancestor. Admittedly, the difference is subtle, and you can solve a given problem either way. For example, you could've easily created a base class named IntegerSequencer and then created two descendant classes from the base class. The previous sample program would change very little and would still provide polymorphic behavior.

You should think about inheritance when you want to *extend* functionality in some way. For example, you may have some type of problem space that you can solve within a class and then some new variation of that problem space, or an extension of it, makes a descendant class seem like the natural way to go. Interfaces, on the other hand, often solve problems where two classes need to provide similar functionality, but the implementation of that functionality may share little or nothing in common. Even the small integer sequencer gives a good example of this. The problem called for creating classes that generate an infinite sequence of integers, but the two classes you ended up creating didn't use any common code to do this. That is, there's no baseline functionality that you could've extracted out of each class and placed into an ancestor class. Because no baseline implementation details could be shared, the best solution is to remove all thought of implementation details at the higher level and describe the classes only by a common, newly defined interface, which of course is what you did.

Using More Complex Interfaces

All of the interfaces discussed to this point have contained a single member, but of course more complicated interfaces are possible. The game sample in this chapter consists of two-player games where the computer controls one of the players.

How would you declare the functionality for an interface that controls a two-player game? Such an interface would need to select a legal move and make it. It would also need to know if a move that the human opponent attempted was illegal so that it could thusly notify the player. It would need to be able to draw itself. Furthermore, it would probably need to be able to notify the outside caller if the game was over. It may also need to be able to relate the current score of the game, if it were the type of game where a running score was useful.

In coming up with the design for the two-player game interface, I stumbled across a second need for an interface. The game pieces for each game could probably be expressed via an interface. Each piece, for example, would probably need to have a location on the game board. In addition, it should be able to draw itself. Game pieces often have some sort of value (cards have face values and suits, Tic-Tac-Toe pieces are Xs or Os, and chess pieces are one of a finite type of piece).

Creating the Base IPCOpponent Interfaces

Without further delay, Listing 6-5 shows the two interfaces that you'll use to create the two-player games in the sample program. You can find this code in the PCOpponent folder as part of the source code that accompanies this book.

Listing 6-5. Game Interfaces

```
Public Interface IPCOpponentGame

    Property pForm() As Form

    Event BadMove()
    Event PlayerWon()
    Event ComputerWon()
    Event NobodyWon()
    Event CurrentScore(ByVal iPlayer As Integer, _
        ByVal iComputer As Integer)

    Sub StartGame()
    Sub DrawBoard(ByVal sender As Object, _
        ByVal e As System.Windows.Forms.PaintEventArgs)
    Sub MouseDown(ByVal sender As Object, _
        ByVal e As System.Windows.Forms.MouseEventArgs)
    Sub MakeMove()

End Interface

Public Interface IPCOpponentGamePiece
    Property Value() As Integer
    Property Location() As Point
    Property Size() As Size
    Function MouseIn(ByVal x As Integer, _
        ByVal y As Integer) As Boolean
    Sub Draw(ByVal g As Graphics)
End Interface
```

As promised earlier, these two interfaces each contain more than one member in them. Not only that, but the IPCOpponentGame interface contains at least one of each type of member—one property, five events, and four methods. The IPCOpponentGamePiece interface contains properties and methods but no events.

One of the first things you might notice about the interface members is that no access modifiers are listed for any of them. In other words, none of the members are declared as private, protected, friend, or public. In fact, if you try and put any of these access modifiers on one of the members, Visual Studio barks at you with a somewhat vague error:

```
C:\vbNetGames\PCOpponent\PCOpponent.vb(20): 'Protected' is not valid
on an interface method declaration.
```

The reason you can't put access modifiers on interface member declarations is because interfaces describe *only public functionality*. It makes no sense to declare a private member as part of an interface because that member wouldn't be visible to an outside user of the class implementing the interface anyway. If it's not visible, then why make it part of an interface to the outside world? The same goes for any protected members of a class—these members aren't available to the outside world anyway, so it doesn't make sense to include them in an interface that's meant to describe class functionality to the outside world.

One distinction, though: An interface may *itself* be declared as public, private, protected, or friend. The interface access modified describes what parts of the program may use that interface to declare new classes. However, all members of all interfaces are assumed public, so access modifiers on these members are redundant (not only that, they're superfluous and unnecessary, too).

Creating the IPCOpponentGame Interface

Table 6-1 describes what each member of the IPCOpponentGame interface should accomplish once it's implemented in a class.

Table 6-1. Members of the IPCOpponentGame *Class*

MEMBER NAME	TYPE	FUNCTION
pForm	Property	Acts as the "parent" for the game and its drawing surface
BadMove	Event	Fires when the player makes an illegal move
PlayerWon	Event	Fires when the human player wins the game
ComputerWon	Event	Fires when the computer player wins the game
NobodyWon	Event	Fires in the case of a tie
CurrentScore	Event	Fires to display score of each player
StartGame	Method	Clears the board to starting state and initializes pieces
DrawBoard	Method	Renders the board and all the pieces
OnMouseDown	Method	Called when the user clicks the parent form
MakeMove	Method	Causes the computer player to take a turn

All games that implement this interface require a form to act as the game's drawing surface. The property pForm references this form. The various events return status information to the program that instantiates the game class. This allows the program to display scores or act appropriately in a game-ending condition.

The methods on the game class handle the bulk of the game functionality. The method StartGame sets up all of the board and piece information that the game requires. It may also be responsible for clearing any board and piece information from the last game played. The method DrawBoard renders the current board onto the form. The method MakeMove is what the class calls when it's time for the computer player to make a move. Finally, the OnMouseDown method serves as the event handler that executes when the player clicks onto the game surface.

Using Private Methods in a Public Interface

Technically, I didn't have to include the DrawBoard, OnMouseDown, and MakeMove methods in the IPCOpponentGame interface because the outside program in this chapter doesn't access any of them directly. Each of these methods is called privately in the two game implementations that implement the interface.

I finally chose to include them in the interface for two reasons. The first was that I thought certain situations might benefit from having these methods callable from outside the class. For example, each of the games I'm about to explain waits for the human player to make the first move and then calls the MakeMove method internally after recording the player's move. A useful extension might be to allow the computer opponent to move first, which may be implemented by exposing the MakeMove method to the outside world. The second reason I decided to include these methods in the interface was to complete the game functionality. I've decided that any two-player game written against this interface is going to need to implement a MakeMove method, whether that method ends up being public or not. By including it in the interface, I gain the benefit of Visual Studio's design-time errors if I forget to implement the method.

Creating the IPCOpponentGamePiece Interface

The second interface describes the game piece that you must implement to write a two-player game. Table 6-2 describes the members of that interface.

Table 6-2. Members of the IPCOpponentGamePiece *Class*

MEMBER NAME	TYPE	FUNCTION
Value	Property	Represents the value of the piece (the player color, the suit, and so on).
Location()	Property	Represents the coordinates where the piece lives on the board.
Size()	Property	Represents the size of the piece when drawn (most pieces are all the same size in one game).
MouseIn	Method	Returns True if passed-in coordinates lie within the boundary of the piece. This determines if this piece was clicked.
Draw	Method	Renders this piece.

The IPCOpponentGamePiece class contains just enough information to render itself onto a surface and determine if a player has clicked it. Notice that there's no information about how a piece is rendered onto the game surface—using bitmaps such as the dice game used in previous chapters or using Graphics Device Interchange, Plus (GDI+) calls such as the tile games used in Chapter 3, "Understanding Object-Oriented Programming from the Start." The word *how* refers to implementation, and of course interfaces are devoid of implementation. Thus, the *how* doesn't get answered until the classes are written that implement the interface in question. The next section describes the first implementation.

Creating the Tic-Tac-Toe Implementation

You've now defined the interfaces—it's time to implement them and create a working two-player game. You'll develop a simple Tic-Tac-Toe implementation for the first game, mainly so the second, more complicated game becomes a point of comparison on how you can implement quite different games using the same interface. Figure 6-2 shows the Tic-Tac-Toe game in action.

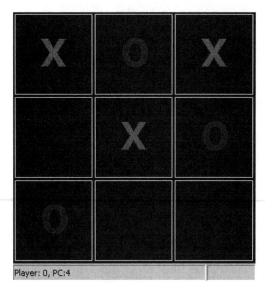

Figure 6-2. Tic-Tac-Toe

Creating the TicTacToePiece Class

Listing 6-6 shows the TicTacToePiece class, the first to be discussed. This class implements the IPCOpponentGamePiece class, as you can see from the first lines of the listing.

Listing 6-6. The TicTacToePiece *Class*

```
Public Class TicTacToePiece
    Implements IPCOpponentGamePiece

    Private FLocation As Point
    Public Property Location() As System.Drawing.Point _
        Implements IPCOpponentGamePiece.Location

        Get
            Return FLocation
        End Get
        Set(ByVal Value As System.Drawing.Point)
            FLocation = Value
        End Set
    End Property
```

```
Private FSize As Size
Public Property Size() As System.Drawing.Size _
    Implements IPCOpponentGamePiece.Size

    Get
        Return FSize
    End Get
    Set(ByVal Value As System.Drawing.Size)
        FSize = Value
    End Set
End Property


Private FValue As Integer
Public Property Value() As Integer _
    Implements IPCOpponentGamePiece.Value

    Get
        Return FValue
    End Get
    Set(ByVal i As Integer)
        If i < -1 Or i > 1 Then
            Throw New Exception("Invalid Piece Value")
        Else
            FValue = i
        End If
    End Set
End Property


Public Function MouseIn(ByVal x As Integer, _
    ByVal y As Integer) As Boolean _
    Implements IPCOpponentGamePiece.MouseIn

    Dim r As New Rectangle(Location, Size)
    Return r.Contains(x, y)

End Function


Public Sub Draw(ByVal g As System.Drawing.Graphics) _
    Implements IPCOpponentGamePiece.Draw

    Dim r As New Rectangle(Location, Size)
    Dim p As New PointF(Location.X, Location.Y)
    Dim f As New Font("Tahoma", 36, FontStyle.Bold)
```

```
        r.Inflate(-2, -2)
        g.DrawRectangle(Pens.White, r)

        p.X += 28
        p.Y += 20

        Select Case Value
            Case -1
                g.DrawString("O", f, Brushes.Blue, p)
            Case 1
                g.DrawString("X", f, Brushes.Red, p)
            Case Else
                Exit Sub
        End Select

    End Sub
End Class
```

The first thing you should notice about Listing 6-6 is that every member in this class contains the keyword Implements IPCOpponentGamePiece.<member> in its declaration. It's not enough to name your members the same as the members in the interface declaration; you must also add the Implements verbiage to each member that's implementing part of the interface, or the compiler will yell at you.

The TicTacToePiece class contains Location, Size, and Value properties, and each of these properties use the standard "hidden private field exposed by a VB .NET property" trick discussed previously (see Chapter 2, "Writing Your First Game, Again," if you're feeling forgetful). The only tidbit of note in these three properties is the error checking logic in the Value property, which makes sure the passed-in value is in the range of –1 to 1 or else an exception is thrown. The game uses the value –1 to represent an O, 0 to represent a blank square, and 1 to represent an X. The reason you're using these values will become apparent when the next section explains the game logic.

The MouseIn routine is interesting because you get to use some great .NET Framework class functionality to determine if a passed-in coordinate falls within the boundaries of this piece. The trick is to take the Location property (which is of type Point) and the Size property (of type Size), and construct a .NET Framework Rectangle class from this information. The Rectangle class has a constructor that accepts Point and Size parameters and returns a rectangle at that position and size. With such a rectangle constructed, you can then call the Contains method on the Rectangle class, which accepts an x and y coordinate as parameters and returns True if that coordinate is within the bounds of the rectangle. Two short, sweet lines of code to implement a hit test on the game piece!

The last method on the TicTacToePiece class is the Draw method. This method also uses a Rectangle class created from the location and size of this piece as specified by the two similarly named properties. This time, however, a method named Inflate is called to shrink the rectangle by two pixels along both the height and width, and then the rectangle is drawn in white pen on the drawing surface.

TIP   *The method* Inflate *enlarges a rectangle when called with positive integer coordinates and shrinks the rectangle when called with negative coordinates, as in this example.*

After the program draws the rectangle around the border of the piece, it draws the X or O in place using the DrawString method on the Graphics class (an instance of the Graphics class is passed into the Draw method). The DrawString method requires as parameters the string to draw (an X or O in this case), font information (encapsulated in the .NET Framework Font class), a Brush instance (which determines the color or pattern of the string), and a location in the form of a PointF class instance. The PointF class differs from the Point class in that it holds floating-point values. For some reason, the DrawString method can't accept an integer-based Point class, so this program constructs a PointF class using the piece's location information and passes this as the last parameter of the DrawString method.

Creating the TicTacToeGame Class

The class that implements the Tic-Tac-Toe game is a bit more complex than the TicTacToePiece class, so the following sections cover it on a member-by-member basis. The game class consists of both members to implement the IPCOpponentGame interface, as well as some additional private members to provide support functionality to the game.

Investigating the Declaration and Private Stuff

The game class implements a number of private members to handle piece storage and score evaluation. The following code shows these members:

```
Public Class TicTacToeGame
    Implements IPCOpponentGame

    Private aPieces As ArrayList
    Private FComputerWon As Integer
    Private FPlayerWon As Integer

    Private Function RowScore(ByVal i As Integer, _
      ByVal j As Integer, ByVal k As Integer) As Integer
```

```
            Dim aPi, aPj, aPk As TicTacToePiece

            aPi = aPieces.Item(i)
            aPj = aPieces.Item(j)
            aPk = aPieces.Item(k)

            Return aPi.Value + aPj.Value + aPk.Value
        End Function


Public Function RowScoreExists(ByVal iScore) As Boolean

            Return RowScore(0, 1, 2) = iScore OrElse _
                    RowScore(3, 4, 5) = iScore OrElse _
                    RowScore(6, 7, 8) = iScore OrElse _
                    RowScore(0, 3, 6) = iScore OrElse _
                    RowScore(1, 4, 7) = iScore OrElse _
                    RowScore(2, 5, 8) = iScore OrElse _
                    RowScore(0, 4, 8) = iScore OrElse _
                    RowScore(2, 4, 6) = iScore

End Function


Private Function HasPlayerWon() As Boolean
            Return RowScoreExists(3)
End Function


Private Function HasComputerWon() As Boolean
            Return RowScoreExists(-3)
End Function


Private Function EmptySpots() As Integer

            Dim aP As TicTacToePiece
            Dim r As Integer = 0

            For Each aP In aPieces
                If aP.Value = 0 Then
                    r += 1
                End If
            Next

            Return r
End Function
```

The first part of the class declares a few private variables. The class defines the often-used Arraylist to hold the nine instances of the TicTacToePiece objects that the game will require. Additionally, the class declares integer variables named FComputerWon and FPlayerWon to hold the number of times each player wins a game. These variables will be passed back to the declarer of the class in the form of an event so that the score can be recorded.

The remaining private functions are all related to determining the state of the board. The function RowScore returns the summed values of three pieces on the board. For example, if all three locations are empty, this method returns 0. If all three passed-in locations contain an X, this function returns a 3. (X is represented by the value 1 in this game.) A row with one X, one O, and one empty spot returns 0 (1 + –1 + 0 = 0). The method RowScoreExists determines if any one of the eight possible places on the board that one can achieve three in a row contain a passed-in score. In other words, if the program wants to see if the board contains a situation where X has two in a row and the third location is empty (meaning X could win on the next turn), the program could call RowScoreExists(2) and look for a True result.

The methods HasComputerWon and HasPlayerWon are simple extensions of the RowScoreExists method, looking for the score that indicates the X player (3) or the O player (–3) has won the game.

The last private method is EmptySpots, which merely returns the number of blank squares on the board. This method determines if the game has ended in a tie. If EmptySpots returns 0, if HasComputerWon is False, and if HasPlayerWon is False, then the game has ended in a draw.

Investigating the Interface Events

The following code shows the interface events of the game class:

```
Public Event BadMove() Implements IPCOpponentGame.BadMove
Public Event PlayerWon() Implements IPCOpponentGame.PlayerWon
Public Event ComputerWon() Implements IPCOpponentGame.ComputerWon
Public Event NobodyWon() Implements IPCOpponentGame.NobodyWon
Public Event CurrentScore(ByVal iPlayer As Integer, _
  ByVal iComputer As Integer) _
  Implements IPCOpponentGame.CurrentScore
```

You implement the events in a desired interface simply by declaring them. Once you've declared them, you can raise them using the RaiseEvent keyword. You'll see each of the events being raised in the implemented members that follow.

Investigating the StartGame Method

The following code shows the StartGame method of the game class:

```
Public Sub StartGame() Implements IPCOpponentGame.StartGame

    Const WID = 104

    Dim i As Integer
    Dim aP As TicTacToePiece

    aPieces = New ArrayList

    For i = 0 To 8
        aP = New TicTacToePiece
        aP.Location = New Point((i Mod 3) * WID, (i \ 3) * WID)
        aP.Size = New Size(WID, WID)
        aP.Value = 0
        aPieces.Add(aP)
    Next

End Sub
```

A new Tic-Tac-Toe game starts using the StartGame method. This method instantiates nine game piece classes and stores them in the private ArrayList named aPieces. Each piece has the same size and is placed into its proper spot in the 3×3 game grid. Also, each piece's Value is set to 0, representing blank in this game.

Investigating the Drawing Code

The following code shows the drawing of the game class:

```
Public Sub DrawBoard(ByVal sender As Object, _
  ByVal e As System.windows.forms.PaintEventArgs) _
  Implements IPCOpponentGame.DrawBoard

    Dim aP As TicTacToePiece

    e.Graphics.SmoothingMode = SmoothingMode.AntiAlias
    e.Graphics.FillRectangle(Brushes.Black, pForm.ClientRectangle)

    For Each aP In aPieces
        aP.Draw(e.Graphics)
    Next
End Sub
```

Because you've followed the maxim that an object should remain responsible for itself, drawing the board becomes a simple matter of asking each game piece to draw itself. The DrawBoard method, which is the implementation of the game interface, sets up the Graphics class to draw in an anti-aliased mode, fills the surface in black, and then calls the Draw method on each TicTacToePiece class found in the ArrayList.

Investigating the Method MakeMove

The following code shows the MakeMove method of the game class:

```
Public Sub MakeMove() Implements IPCOpponentGame.MakeMove

    Dim i As Integer
    Dim aP As TicTacToePiece

    'try every blank spot with me. See if I would win there
    For Each aP In aPieces
        If aP.Value = 0 Then
            aP.Value = -1
            If HasComputerWon() Then         'i win
                Exit Sub
            End If
            aP.Value = 0
        End If
    Next

    'try every blank spot with him. See if HE would win there
    For Each aP In aPieces
        If aP.Value = 0 Then
            aP.Value = 1
            If HasPlayerWon() Then           'player would win here. move there
                aP.Value = -1
                Exit Sub
            End If
            aP.Value = 0
        End If
    Next

    'try every blank spot with him. See if he would win there in 2 moves
    'try the center first (spot 4), though
```

```
For i = 4 To aPieces.Count - 1
    aP = aPieces.Item(i)
    If aP.Value = 0 Then
        aP.Value = 1
        If RowScoreExists(2) Then        'player wins in 2 moves. move there
            aP.Value = -1
            Exit Sub
        End If
        aP.Value = 0
    End If
Next

For i = 0 To 3
    aP = aPieces.Item(i)
    If aP.Value = 0 Then
        aP.Value = 1
        If RowScoreExists(2) Then        'player wins in 2 moves. move there
            aP.Value = -1
            Exit Sub
        End If
        aP.Value = 0
    End If
Next

Debug.Assert(False, "Beep")

End Sub
```

The MakeMove method is where the logic exists so that the computer finds the best move available and puts his piece there. Granted, this isn't the world's greatest Tic-Tac-Toe computer opponent ever written. It uses the following simple algorithm to choose where to move:

- If an empty spot exists that would result in winning the game by moving there, then move there.

- If an empty spot exists that would result in the opponent winning by moving there, then move there to block the opponent.

- If an empty spot exists that would result in the opponent having two in a row with the third space being empty, then move there (and give preference to the center square over others).

Each of the three subcomponents of the described algorithm are implemented as a For..Each loop in the MakeMove algorithm. Each loop works by checking for an empty spot. When it finds one, the algorithm temporarily puts an X or O (1 or –1) into the spot, checks the state of the board, and then removes that temporary piece if it doesn't find the desired result.

The last part of the algorithm (looking for rows with one opponent piece and two blanks) comes in two For..Each loops so the fourth location (the center square) can be checked first. This makes the algorithm favor the center square when blocking because of that square's strategic importance.

The last line in the MakeMove method is a Debug.Assert that will stop the program if the code ever reaches this line. The algorithm is arranged in such a way that the program will always find a move using the three previous cases, and an Exit Sub ensures that the code leaves the method as soon as the program finds a proper move. If execution ever reaches the end of the method without finding a proper move, then the algorithm isn't working properly, and Debug.Assert(false) will halt execution.

Investigating the OnMouseDown Method

The following code shows the OnMouseDown method of the game class:

```
Public Sub OnMouseDown(ByVal sender As Object, _
    ByVal e As System.Windows.Forms.MouseEventArgs) _
    Implements IPCOpponentGame.OnMouseDown

    Dim aP As TicTacToePiece

    Try
        'don't let him click again
        RemoveHandler fForm.MouseDown, AddressOf OnMouseDown

        For Each aP In aPieces
            If aP.MouseIn(e.X, e.Y) Then

                If aP.Value = 0 Then

                    aP.Value = 1
                    pForm.Invalidate()
```

```
                    If HasPlayerWon() Then
                        FPlayerWon += 1
                        RaiseEvent PlayerWon()
                        RaiseEvent CurrentScore(FPlayerWon, FComputerWon)
                        Exit For
                    Else
                        If EmptySpots() = 0 Then
                            RaiseEvent NobodyWon()
                            RaiseEvent CurrentScore(FPlayerWon, FComputerWon)
                            Exit For
                        Else

                            MakeMove()
                            pForm.Invalidate()
                            If HasComputerWon() Then
                                FComputerWon += 1
                                RaiseEvent ComputerWon()
                                RaiseEvent CurrentScore(FPlayerWon, FComputerWon)
                            End If
                            Exit For
                        End If
                    End If

                Else
                    RaiseEvent BadMove()
                    Exit For
                End If

            End If
        Next

        Finally
            AddHandler fForm.MouseDown, AddressOf OnMouseDown
        End Try

    End Sub
```

The method OnMouseDown runs when the player clicks somewhere on the form. The first action is to temporarily remove the OnMouseDown handler from the form so that additional clicks don't happen until the processing of this click is complete. Next, a loop starts to locate which piece within the game was clicked. When the MouseIn method locates that piece, the program first checks the piece to see if it's empty (one can't move onto a spot that's already taken). If this piece isn't empty, then the program raises the BadMove event. If the spot is empty, however, then the work begins.

The empty, clicked-on spot has its value changed from 0 to 1. If this results in the player winning, the program adds 1 to the variable that tracks player wins and then fires two methods. The first method indicates that the player has won, and the second relays the current score to the calling program. If the player doesn't win with this move, then the computer player can make a move. This happens with the already-discussed MakeMove method. After the computer player makes a move, the program checks the board to see if the computer player has won. If it has, the program updates the score and calls the two proper methods.

The Finally block makes sure this procedure is reattached to the MoveDown event of the form no matter what has happened in the code beforehand.

Investigating the pForm Property and Constructor

The following code shows the pForm property and constructor of the game class:

```
Public Sub New(ByVal f As System.Windows.Forms.Form)
    MyBase.New()
    pForm = f
End Sub

Private fForm As Form
Property pForm() As Form _
    Implements IPCOpponentGame.pForm

    Get
        Return fForm
    End Get
    Set(ByVal Value As Form)

        fForm = Value
        fForm.Width = 324
        fForm.Height = 384
        AddHandler fForm.Paint, AddressOf DrawBoard
        AddHandler fForm.MouseDown, AddressOf OnMouseDown

    End Set
End Property
```

The last member to discuss is the pForm member, which references some form in the calling program. The pForm variable is set as in the class constructor (it could also be set outside the class). Once set, the width and height of the form are coded to set values, and the Paint and MouseDown events are linked to event handlers declared as part of this class. This is the thing that makes sure the OnMouseDown code runs when the outside form is clicked.

Creating the Reversi Implementation

The interface example contains two games, the Tic-Tac-Toe implementation just discussed and an implementation of Reversi (or Othello). You can see the Reversi game in action in Figure 6-3. Before looking at any of the code for this game, though, you should already have a pretty good idea of how this game will be structured. Because the game will contain implementations of the PCOpponentGame and PCOpponentGamePiece interfaces, you already have a good idea of what the classes that implement those interfaces look like from the first example.

This isn't anything revolutionary, of course, but the fact that you can obtain a good mental picture about the structure of a class that you've never seen is what interfaces are all about. Interfaces create expectations. In particular, they create expectations about exactly what members need to be implemented by a class. In a more abstract way, they create an expectation of a certain set of functionality. You now know that if this book presents a program that implements the PCOpponentGame and PCOpponentGamePiece interfaces, then you'll have a two-player game program, with one human and one computer-controlled player. You can assume all of that just by learning that a class is an implementation of an interface.

The nice thing about the Reversi implementation is that much of the code is similar (or even identical) to the Tic-Tac-Toe game, so this section won't repeat it. Of course, hearing that two classes have identical code should start the warning bells flashing in your head. If two classes share the same code, why not go with an inheritance scheme and put the shared code in a base class? Furthermore, if you're going to go with inheritance, then do you really need the interface at all?

The answer in the short term is "probably not," but the developer often has to look beyond the current project and into the future. Even if the first two implementations of the interface end up sharing code, this won't necessarily hold true for future implementations of the game. Say you write a game that uses DirectX, for example—you certainly won't be able to share any drawing code with the drawing code found in these simple GDI+ games.

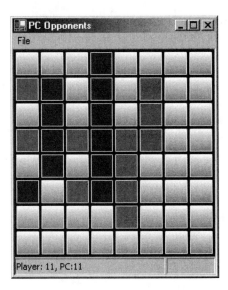

Figure 6-3. A rousing game of Reversi

NOTE *Still, I can't say for certainty that the interface solution is better than a class hierarchy, just as I can't say that the walls in my bedroom are better in beige than they are in red or that my living room arrangement is better with the couch against the far wall than with it on a diagonal. These are all design issues, and there often isn't a "right" or "best" solution. You say* to-may-to, *I say* to-mah-to; *you say inheritance, I say interfaces.*

Creating the ReversiPiece Implementation

Most of the interface members of the ReversiPiece class are identical to the TicTacToePiece class, so this section won't duplicate the effort of explaining those members again. The Draw method is a bit different because the Reversi pieces are simply colored squares, but this code is all stuff you've seen before. The first place that the Reversi piece differs from its Tac-Tac-Toe counterpart is in some functionality to tell where on the board an instance of this class is located. You can see this functionality in Listing 6-7.

Listing 6-7. Location-Specific Code in the ReversiPiece *Class*

```
ReadOnly Property xElt() As Integer
    Get
        Return Location.X \ Size.Width
    End Get
End Property


ReadOnly Property yElt() As Integer
    Get
        Return Location.Y \ Size.Height
    End Get
End Property


Public Function IsEdge() As Boolean
    Return xElt = 0 OrElse yElt = 0 _
      OrElse xElt = 7 OrElse yElt = 7
End Function


Public Function IsCorner() As Boolean

    Return (xElt = 0 And yElt = 0) OrElse _
           (xElt = 0 And yElt = 7) OrElse _
           (xElt = 7 And yElt = 0) OrElse _
           (xElt = 7 And yElt = 7)

End Function
```

The properties xElt and yElt define the location of this piece on the board, with location 0,0 being the upper-left corner. The IsEdge and IsCorner methods use these coordinates to determine if a piece is along the edge of a board or in one of the four corners. Edge and corner pieces are more valuable in Reversi, so it's important that you can find these pieces on the board when trying to make the best move.

The IsEdge and IsCorner methods both use the OrElse operator, which is new to Visual Basic .NET. OrElse is a Boolean operator that usually provides the same functionality as the standard Or operator, but it uses a short-circuiting logic to do so. What this means is that if the left side of an OrElse statement is True, then the right-side evaluation is skipped altogether. Skipping the evaluation of part of an expression might result in a faster program, especially if this expression is evaluated many times in a loop.

The second new functionality provided by the ReversiPiece class is the ability to "save" the value of the piece and to then restore it. It accomplishes this using simple push and pop routines, shown in Listing 6-8.

Listing 6-8. State-Saving Code in the `ReversiPiece` *Class*

```
Private FSaveValue As Integer

'store prior value
Public Sub PushValue()
    FSaveValue = Value
End Sub

Public Sub PopValue()
    Value = FSaveValue
End Sub
```

There's nothing fancy here, just a private variable to store the value of this piece and routines to save the current value into the private spot and restore it from that same spot. This functionality becomes important when evaluating potential moves because the program actually makes each available move to determine how good that move is, restoring the board back to its current state between each attempt.

There's one final point about the game piece to make here—you might have noticed that this new functionality doesn't have anything to do with the original interface. Is this legal? That is, can a class implement an interface and provide functionality beyond that interface? The answer is an unqualified "yes." An interface is meant to provide some subset of functionality, but the classes implementing that functionality may do much more than what the interface suggests. Think back to the tile games in Chapter 4, "More OOPing Around." You might recall that you had to implement the `IComparable` interface so that you could sort the tiles in top-top-bottom location order on the screen for the DeducTile Reasoning game. And of course the tile class provided much more functionality than that found in this one interface.

Creating the ReversiGame Implementation

The Reversi game is obviously more complex than Tic-Tac-Toe, so of course the implementation of that game will be more complex as well. Not every member of the class needs to be discussed because once again some functionality is similar to the TicTacToeGame implementation. The more complex elements of the class warrant some dialogue, though.

Creating the Piece Storage Implementation

The first change to discuss is that this game stores the board in an actual two-dimensional array instead of an `ArrayList`. The entire algorithm refers to rows, columns, and traveling along straight lines, and it's simply much easier to think in terms of a square matrix of piece objects. The declaration for the array looks like this:

```
Private aPieces(7, 7) As ReversiPiece
```

and the board is filled as shown in Listing 6-9, which is the implementation of the IPCOpponentGame.StartGame member.

Listing 6-9. Initializing the Board in the ReversiGame *Class*

```
Public Sub StartGame() Implements IPCOpponentGame.StartGame

    Dim x, y As Integer

    For x = 0 To 7
        For y = 0 To 7

            aPieces(x, y) = New ReversiPiece
            With aPieces(x, y)
                .Location = New Point(x * 32, y * 32)
                .Size = New Size(32, 32)

                Select Case (y * 8) + x
                    Case 27, 36
                        .Value = 1
                    Case 28, 35
                        .Value = -1
                    Case Else
                        .Value = 0
                End Select
            End With
        Next
    Next

    Call CalcScores()
End Sub
```

This method fills the 8×8 array with instances of the ReversiPiece class, sets up the location and size of each, and then initializes the four center pieces to their starting colors, as shown in Figure 6-4.

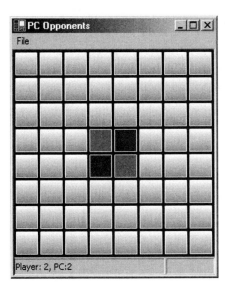

Figure 6-4. The starting board in a Reversi game

Looking at Similar Stuff

The following members are similar to the TicTacToeGame class:

Event declarations: The events declared in the IPCOpponentGame require only declaration in the game class. You declare these events in the same way as in the TicTacToeGame class.

DrawBoard method: This method is almost identical to the same-named method in the TicTacToeGame class. It loops through each piece in the array and calls that class's Draw method.

Class constructor: The constructor is also identical—it sets the pForm variable to the passed-in Form parameter.

pForm property: The pForm property differs only in the hard-coded size that it makes the form in order to hold the board.

OnMouseDown method: This method controls what happens when the user clicks the form. The flow of this method is similar to the same-named method in the prior game. The class first determines if the user has clicked a board location that represents a valid move. If this is a legal move, then the class makes the move. After the player moves, the code checks to see if anyone has won the game. If not, then the computer moves, and the program checks the winning conditions again.

Making a Move

A player placing a piece on the board in Reversi flips over the pieces of the opponent in all eight directions, only if these pieces are "bounded" by a piece of that player. Much of the game algorithm consists of implementing the basic piece movement and takeover rule. Listing 6-10 shows the three routines used when a player makes a move on the board.

Listing 6-10. Placing a Piece in Reversi

```
Private Sub MoveHere(ByVal aP As ReversiPiece, ByVal Player As Integer)

    Dim x, y As Integer

    aP.Value = Player

    For x = -1 To 1
        For y = -1 To 1
            If Not (x = 0 And y = 0) Then
                If CanMoveOnThisLine(aP, Player, x, y) Then
                    MoveGuysOnThisLine(aP, Player, x, y)
                End If
            End If
        Next
    Next

    Call CalcScores()
End Sub

Private Function CanMoveOnThisLine(_
    ByVal aP As ReversiPiece, _
    ByVal Player As Integer, ByVal iX As Integer, _
    ByVal iY As Integer) As Boolean

    Dim x, y As Integer
    Dim bDone As Boolean
    Dim bFound As Boolean = False

    'travel 1 piece away in the proper direction
    x = aP.xElt + iX
    y = aP.yElt + iY

    'if off board, exit
    If x < 0 Or x > 7 Then Exit Function
    If y < 0 Or y > 7 Then Exit Function
```

```
'make sure piece one away is opposite color
If aPieces(x, y).Value <> -Player Then Exit Function

'now, start looping. Looking for one of
'our pieces before the edge of the board or a blank
x += iX
y += iY
bDone = (x < 0 Or x > 7 Or y < 0 Or y > 7)
Do While Not (bDone Or bFound)
    If aPieces(x, y).Value = Player Then
        bFound = True
    ElseIf aPieces(x, y).Value = 0 Then
        bDone = True
    Else
        x += iX
        y += iY
        bDone = (x < 0 Or x > 7 Or y < 0 Or y > 7)
    End If
Loop

Return bFound
End Function

Private Sub MoveGuysOnThisLine(_
  ByVal aP As ReversiPiece, _
  ByVal Player As Integer, ByVal iX As Integer, _
  ByVal iY As Integer)

  Dim x, y As Integer
  Dim bDone As Boolean

  'travel 1 piece away in the proper direction
  'don't have to check that piece is right color
  'or off board, already determined
  x = aP.xElt + iX
  y = aP.yElt + iY

  bDone = False
  Do While Not bDone
      If aPieces(x, y).Value = Player Then
          bDone = True
      ElseIf aPieces(x, y).Value = 0 Then
          bDone = True
```

```
        Else
          aPieces(x, y).Value = Player
          x += iX
          y += iY
          bDone = (x < 0 Or x > 7 Or y < 0 Or y > 7)
        End If
    Loop

End Sub
```

The procedure MoveHere is where the desired piece, passed in as a parameter, is set to be one player's color. Then the fun starts. A double loop is set up from –1 to +1 in both the x and y directions. The effect of this loop is to travel in eight directions outward from the given piece. (The case where both x=0 and y=0 is ignored because this would result in moving in *no* direction.)

For each direction, the program determines if the opponent has one or more pieces directly adjacent to the piece just moved, with an eventual "bound" of the player's piece. This happens in the function CanMoveOnThisLine. This method takes a piece, a player value (–1 or 1), and an x and y direction. It travels on the board along this direction, starting at the passed-in piece, and looks for opponent pieces. If it finds one, it continues along the line until it finds a blank square, until it reaches the edge of the board, or until it finds a piece of the player's own color. In the case of a blank square or the edge, the function must return False—no bounding piece was found. In the case that it finds the bounding piece, the function can return True.

The Searching Loop

The structure of the loop in the CanMoveOnThisLine method is one I use frequently. I call it the "searching" loop. In searching loops, I always declare Boolean variables named bDone and bFound and then start this loop with the following code:

```
Do While not (bDone or bFound)
```

I like this line of code because it reads like English. Within the loop, I set bFound to True if I find the thing I'm searching for (in this case, a bounding piece), and I set bDone to True if I reach the end (an empty piece or the edge of the board). At the end of the loop, the variable bFound tells me if I found the element for which I was looking.

The method MoveGuysOnThisLine is similar in structure to the method CanMoveOnThisLine. It differs in that its job is to actually change the color of pieces in a certain direction until it reaches the bounding piece. This method assumes that the row in question has already been verified to have a bounding piece somewhere down the line, so it doesn't do any searching.

Finding a Move to Make

You've seen how to make a move, but the program needs to determine *which* move is the best. The procedure MakeMove, along with a few support routines, handles this task. Listing 6-11 shows this functionality.

Listing 6-11. The Method MakeMove *and Related Methods*

```
Public Sub MakeMove() Implements IPCOpponentGame.MakeMove

    Dim aP As ReversiPiece

    Dim iScore As Integer
    Dim iHigh As Integer = -1
    Dim aPHigh As ReversiPiece

    PushBoard()
    For Each aP In aPieces
        If aP.Value = 0 Then
            If CanMoveHere(aP, -1) Then
                MoveHere(aP, -1)
                 iScore = BoardScore(-1)
                 If iScore > iHigh Then
                     iHigh = iScore
                     aPHigh = aP
                 End If
                 PopBoard()
            End If
        End If
    Next

    If iHigh > 1 Then
        MoveHere(aPHigh, -1)
        pForm.Invalidate()
    Else
        MsgBox("computer has to pass")
    End If
End Sub
```

```
Private Function BoardScore(ByVal Player As Integer) As Integer

    Dim aP As ReversiPiece
    Dim r As Integer

    For Each aP In aPieces
        If aP.Value = Player Then
            If aP.IsCorner Then
                r += 20
            ElseIf aP.IsEdge Then
                r += 5
            Else
                r += 1
            End If
        End If
    Next
    Return r

End Function

Private Function CanMoveHere(ByVal aP As ReversiPiece, _
    ByVal Player As Integer) As Boolean

    Dim x, y As Integer

    For x = -1 To 1
        For y = -1 To 1
            If Not (x = 0 And y = 0) Then
                If CanMoveOnThisLine(aP, Player, x, y) Then Return True
            End If
        Next
    Next

    Return False

End Function

Private Sub PushBoard()

    Dim aP As ReversiPiece

    For Each aP In aPieces
        aP.PushValue()
    Next
End Sub
```

```
Private Sub PopBoard()

    Dim aP As ReversiPiece

    For Each aP In aPieces
        aP.PopValue()
    Next
End Sub
```

The basic flow of the method MakeMove is as follows: The method checks each empty board space. If it determines that a computer piece could be placed here (remember, not every free space is eligible to receive a given piece—at least one opponent piece must be "trapped" and its color flipped, or the move is invalid), then it saves the current board and makes that move. Then, it determines the "score" of that board. The score is a simple ranking system that adds up all of the pieces of the computer's color, giving bonus points for edge and corner squares. Of all the legal moves, the algorithm chooses the one that results in the highest score after that move is made.

It's possible that no legal move is available. In this case, that player has to pass his turn and allow the other player to go again. Board configurations are possible that cause one player or the other to have to pass several turns in a row (this usually happens when one player is crushing the other, and there are so few of the opponents pieces that there's no empty space adjacent to those pieces).

The MakeMove method uses the PushBoard and PopBoard routines to save and restore the state of the board.

NOTE *Even though I used the terminology of a computer "stack,"
my push and pop routines don't work like a traditional stack from
the standpoint that I push the state of the board a single time, but
I pop it back to this state several times within a loop. The traditional stack allows only one pop for each push operation.*

Finally, Seeing the Polymorphism in Action

The chapter has taken the long way and demonstrated two implementations of a game class and a piece class. Listing 6-12 shows the code in the main form of the PCOpponent solution, which you can find in the source code that accompanies the book.

Listing 6-12. Calling an Implementation of an Interface Polymorphically

```
Private aGame As IPCOpponentGame

Private Sub mTic_Click(ByVal sender As System.Object, _
    ByVal e As System.EventArgs) Handles mTic.Click

    aGame = New TicTacToeGame(Me)
    SetupGame()
End Sub

Private Sub mReversi_Click(ByVal sender As System.Object, _
    ByVal e As System.EventArgs) Handles mReversi.Click

    aGame = New ReversiGame(Me)
    SetupGame()
End Sub

Private Sub SetupGame()

    With aGame
        AddHandler .PlayerWon, AddressOf PlayerWon
        AddHandler .ComputerWon, AddressOf ComputerWon
        AddHandler .NobodyWon, AddressOf NobodyWon
        AddHandler .BadMove, AddressOf BadMove
        AddHandler .CurrentScore, AddressOf UpdateScores

        .StartGame()
    End With
    Me.Invalidate()

End Sub
```

In this code, the variable aGame is declared as being of the game interface
type. If you'll recall, this isn't really saying "The variable aGame is an instance of
class x." Instead, it's really saying "The variable aGame is an instance of *some class
that implements interface* x." Once declared in this way, the program can use this
variable to store either an instance of the ReversiGame class or the TicTacToe game
class, and it can access any of the members of these classes polymorphically (as
long as these members are part of the interface).

Additional Interface Topics

Interfaces are a deep topic within Visual Basic .NET. You've now seen how to declare your own interfaces and then to program classes to implement those interfaces. This section covers a few additional interface topics so that you know they exist; you can read about them further when you think they might help you solve a particular problem.

First, a single class can implement more than one interface. Perhaps you've deduced this fact already because you learned that a class that implements a single interface can declare additional members outside the interface to provide further functionality. Why not, then, have a class that implements multiple interfaces? A class definition might look like the following:

```
Public Class ISpaceInvadersGuy
    Implements IPCOpponentGamePiece, IEnumerable, IComparable
    <lots of code removed>
End Class
```

This class implements three different interfaces—the game piece interface discussed in this chapter and the two .NET Framework interfaces IEnumerable and IComparable.

Second, interfaces can inherit from each other just like classes can. Consider the legal interface definitions shown in Listing 6-13.

Listing 6-13. Inheriting Interfaces

```
Interface ITwoDimensionalObject
    Property Width() As Integer
    Property Length() As Integer

    Property xCoord() As Integer
    Property yCoord() As Integer

    Sub MoveLeft(ByVal iHowFar As Integer)
    Sub MoveRight(ByVal iHowFar As Integer)
    Sub MoveForward(ByVal iHowFar As Integer)
    Sub MoveBackward(ByVal iHowFar As Integer)
End Interface

Interface IThreeDimensionalObject
    Inherits ITwoDimensionalObject
```

```
    Property Height() As Integer
    Property zCoord() As Integer

    Sub MoveUp(ByVal iHowFar As Integer)
    Sub MoveDown(ByVal iHowFar As Integer)
End Interface
```

The first interface declares some properties for a two-dimensional object and some simple methods to move that object. The second interface extends the first one and adds properties and methods that help describe a three-dimensional object. You could use the first interface to implement classes for your two-dimensional game and then use the three-dimensional interface when it comes time to define classes for your first Quake clone or similar first-person shooter.

Defining interfaces in this way gives you all the benefits of inheritance. If you add a member to the two-dimensional interface, all of the classes that implement this interface as well as the three-dimensional interface will be required to implement this member before these classes will compile.

This chapter has shown you the power and structure that developing to interfaces gives you.

CHAPTER 7

Creating
Multiplayer Games

CHAPTER 6, "USING POLYMORPHISM VIA INTERFACES," discussed a basic framework for the creation of two-player games, but it did so with the assumption that one player would be human controlled and the other computer controlled. This chapter introduces a two-player game in which the first player is always human and the second player is either a human or a computer. Furthermore, the second human player can be sitting at the same computer as the first player, or she can be on another computer connected to the first one via a network.

If you put your object-oriented-design hat on, you might quickly conclude that the concept of a "player" in this a two-player game might be a useful construct to abstract through one or more classes. After all, a player is a thing with responsibilities. A computer-controlled player must select the best move to make. A human-controlled player object needs to determine what piece a player clicked on and move a piece there. It should also disallow movement if it's currently not that player's turn. With two human players, the player object might be responsible for telling the other computer what move was made. Clearly, many of these responsibilities are simply not present when designing two-player games for one human player and one computer player. I smell a refactor!

Understanding Network Communication

The .NET language has a number of features that allow program components to communicate over a network (in fact, the name *.NET* implies some type of intranet-based software). Many of these features imply some form of server that acts as a data source to which programs can connect. An Extensible Markup Language (XML) Web Service, for example, is a .NET class that resides on a server; a remote program can access it over a regular Hypertext Transfer Protocol (HTTP) channel. Another feature known as *remoting* allows programs to use objects on the other side of a network that's being served by another program.

Much of the .NET method of program communication is new; if you'd like to study remoting in an in-depth way, pick up *Advanced .NET Remoting* (C# Edition) by Ingo Rammer (Apress, 2002). For this chapter, you'll explore the VB .NET version of a C# example program written by student Nguyen Kinh Luan that contains a good example of peer-to-peer communication. By coincidence, this example was also a two-player game—the game of Gomoku (kind of a Connect Four without the gravity for you Americans). After looking at this game, I was impressed with the way Kinh Luan organized his classes within the game program. With his permission, this chapter uses his basic class layout and a similar method of his program-to-program communication in a two-player version of Reversi.

Creating the Player Class and Subclasses

Kinh Luan's two-player game example abstracted the responsibilities of a game player into a series of interfaces and then implemented those interfaces in a series of classes. The game uses different classes for a human player, a computer-controlled player, and a local version of a network player.

Creating the Base Class

For this program, instead of using interfaces to define functionality, you'll instead create a base class and then create subclasses from it. This enables you to put some commonly used code inside the base class without duplicating it. Listing 7-1 shows the base player class for the network Reversi game.

Listing 7-1. The ReversiPlayer *Class, the Base Class for All Reversi Players*

```
Public MustInherit Class ReversiPlayer

    Private FName As String
    Private FColor As Color
    Private FScore As Integer
    Private FMyTurn As Boolean

    Public Event IsMyTurn(ByVal oPlayer As ReversiPlayer)

    Sub New(ByVal cNm As String, ByVal cClr As Color)
        MyBase.New()

        FName = cNm

        'only two colors allowed
        Debug.Assert(cClr.Equals(Color.Red) Or cClr.Equals(Color.Blue))
        FColor = cClr
    End Sub
```

```
ReadOnly Property Name() As String
    Get
        Return FName
    End Get
End Property


ReadOnly Property Color() As Color
    Get
        Return FColor
    End Get
End Property


ReadOnly Property OpponentColor() As Color
    Get
        Return IIf(FColor.Equals(Color.Red), _
            Color.Blue, Color.Red)
    End Get
End Property


Overridable Property MyTurn() As Boolean
    Get
        Return FMyTurn
    End Get
    Set(ByVal Value As Boolean)
        FMyTurn = Value
        If Value Then
            RaiseEvent IsMyTurn(Me)
        End If
    End Set
End Property


Property Score() As Integer
    Get
        Return FScore
    End Get
    Set(ByVal Value As Integer)
        FScore = Value
    End Set
End Property

End Class
```

The Reversi player class contains properties for the player name, the color of the player's pieces on the board (currently constrained to blue or red), the color of the opponent's pieces on the board (if this player is red, then the opponent is blue, and vice versa), the player's score (how many pieces of her color are on the board), and a Boolean property named MyTurn that represents if it's currently her turn. There's also an event raised whenever the MyTurn property is set to True. The Name and Color properties are defined as ReadOnly, and they're set in the constructor for this class. This structure makes sure that an instance of this class can't change its name or color after it has been initially created.

Creating the Human Player Class

The first variant of the player class to discuss is the player controlled by a human. There's only a small amount of specialized code beyond the base player class; Listing 7-2 shows that code.

Listing 7-2. The HumanReversiPlayer *Class*

```
Public Class HumanReversiPlayer
    Inherits ReversiPlayer

    Private FForm As Form
    Public Event MyMoveLoc As MoveToLocationDef

    Sub New(ByVal cNm As String, ByVal cClr As Color, ByVal f As Form)
        MyBase.New(cNm, cClr)
        FForm = f
    End Sub

    Overrides Property MyTurn() As Boolean
        Get
            Return MyBase.MyTurn
        End Get
        Set(ByVal Value As Boolean)
            If Value Then
                AddHandler FForm.MouseDown, AddressOf OnMouseDown
            Else
                RemoveHandler FForm.MouseDown, AddressOf OnMouseDown
            End If

            MyBase.MyTurn = Value
        End Set
    End Property

    Private Sub OnMouseDown(ByVal sender As Object, _
        ByVal e As System.Windows.Forms.MouseEventArgs)
```

```
        If Not MyTurn Then Exit Sub
        If Not e.Button = MouseButtons.Left Then Exit Sub

        RaiseEvent MyMoveLoc(Me, e.X, e.Y)
    End Sub
End Class
```

The first thing that differs in the human-specific version of the player class is the constructor. This constructor takes a form variable as well as a `Color` property and a `Name` property. This passed-in form variable is equal to a private variable, so the class can access it later.

The next extension to the human player class is an overridden version of the `MyTurn` property. Some interesting syntax exists here. Your intent is to store the `MyTurn` variable data in the same way but to selectively attach or detach a `MouseDown` event handler to the form variable depending on whether it's currently the human player's turn. By doing this, you can disable the ability for the human player to click the form when it's not her turn.

The property `Get` function returns the value of `MyBase.MyTurn`, which is another way of saying "The value of `MyTurn` in the ancestor class `ReversiPlayer`." Likewise, the last line of the `Set` statement for this property writes the intended value to `MyBase.MyTurn`, meaning that the underlying property is still being used to hold the `MyTurn` variable data.

The remainder of the `MyTurn` property's `Set` statement adds or removes the `MouseDown` handler of the private form variable, depending on the new value of the property. If `MyTurn` is `True`, then the `MouseDown` event handler becomes active. If `MyTurn` is `False`, then the `MouseDown` event handler is unattached.

The `MouseDown` event itself, named `OnMouseDown`, raises an event named `MyMoveLoc` when it's called. Look at the definition of the `MyMoveLoc` event earlier in the `HumanReversiPlayer` class definition:

```
Public Event MyMoveLoc As MoveToLocationDef
```

This event declaration looks just like a variable declaration, doesn't it? It contains an access specifier (`Public`), a name (`MyMoveLoc`), and a type (`MoveToLocationDef`). So exactly what type is `MoveToLocationDef`? Is it an integer, a string, or a class?

In truth, `MoveToLocationDef` describes a *type of function*. Think about that statement for a second. Can a function be of a certain type? Or, perhaps more clearly put, can two functions be of different types? The answer is obviously "yes"; a function is of a specific type, and that type is described by the parameters sent to the function. So, if function A accepts a single integer parameter, then you could say that the function is of type A, and if function B accepts an integer and a string parameter, then that function is of type B.

The description of a function type happens in Visual Basic .NET through a *delegate*. A delegate is a function type declaration. It describes a class of functions that are related from the standpoint that they all pass the same parameter lists. You can declare the delegate declaration for the MoveToLocationDef event as follows:

```
Public Delegate Sub MoveToLocationDef(ByVal sender As ReversiPlayer, _
    ByVal x As Integer, ByVal y As Integer)
```

This declaration declares a type of function (actually, a Sub in this case) that takes a ReversiPlayer parameter and two integer parameters named x and y. Once you make this declaration, you can declare an event as having this type:

```
Public Event MyMoveLoc As MoveToLocationDef
```

What this means is that the MyMoveLoc event will pass back the same three parameters as specified in the delegate declaration—a ReversiPiece variable and two integers. Looking back at the MyTurn property declaration in Listing 7-2, you can see that this is indeed the parameter list when the program raises the event:

```
RaiseEvent MyMoveLoc(Me, e.X, e.Y)
```

Creating the Computer Player Class

The class that controls the computer player is similarly simple. It changes little from the base class, as shown in Listing 7-3.

Listing 7-3. The ComputerReversiPlayer *Class*

```
Public Delegate Sub MakeBestMoveDef(ByVal sender As ReversiPlayer)

Public Class ComputerReversiPlayer
    Inherits ReversiPlayer

    Public Event MyMakeBestMove As MakeBestMoveDef

    Sub New(ByVal cNm As String, ByVal cClr As Color)
        MyBase.New(cNm, cClr)
    End Sub
```

```
Overrides Property MyTurn() As Boolean
    Get
        Return MyBase.MyTurn
    End Get
    Set(ByVal Value As Boolean)

        MyBase.MyTurn = Value
        If Value Then
            RaiseEvent MyMakeBestMove(Me)
        End If
    End Set
End Property


End Class
```

This class declares a second delegate for use by the computer player class. This delegate, named MakeBestMoveDef, describes a function that takes a single parameter of type ReversiPlayer. It also declares an event within the ComputerReversiPlayer class as being of this type, and it raises this event whenever the MyTurn property of this class is set to True. In other words, the event executes whenever it becomes the computer's turn.

Creating the Network Player Class

The player class that represents a network player is sort of a "proxy" class. Imagine two people who are going to play the game over a network, player A and player B. On the machine being used by player A, a HumanReversiPlayer class instance will be created to represent and handle the responsibilities of player A, and NetworkReversiPlayer will be created to send and receive the move information over the network to the computer of player B. On player B's machine, the opposite is true. Player B will have a HumanReversiPlayer instance to control her own moves and a NetworkReversiPlayer instance to send and receive move data from player A. Listing 7-4 shows the NetworkReversiPlayer class, which contains the send and receive move code.

Listing 7-4. The NetworkReversiPlayer *Class*

```
Public Class NetworkReversiPlayer
    Inherits ReversiPlayer

    Private FStream As NetworkStream
    Public Event MyMoveLoc As MoveToLocationDef

    Sub New(ByVal cNm As String, ByVal cClr As Color, _
      ByVal oStream As NetworkStream)
        MyBase.New(cNm, cClr)
        FStream = oStream
    End Sub

    Public Sub LookForTurn()

        Do
            If FStream.DataAvailable Then

                Dim cPiece As String
                Dim oPiece As New ReversiPiece
                Dim oSer As New XmlSerializer(oPiece.GetType)
                Dim oRead As StreamReader

                oRead = New StreamReader(FStream)
                cPiece = oRead.ReadLine
                oPiece = oSer.Deserialize(New StringReader(cPiece))

                RaiseEvent MyMoveLoc(Me, _
                    oPiece.Location.X, oPiece.Location.Y)
            End If
            System.Threading.Thread.Sleep(250)
        Loop Until False

    End Sub

    Public Sub SendMyTurnToOpponent(ByVal aP As ReversiPiece)

        Dim oSer As New XmlSerializer(aP.GetType)
        Dim oSW As New StringWriter
        Dim oWriter As New XmlTextWriter(oSW)

        Dim oByte() As Byte
        Dim cSend As String
```

```
    oSer.Serialize(oSW, aP)
    oWriter.Close()
    cSend = oSW.ToString
    cSend = cSend.Replace(Chr(10), "")
    cSend = cSend.Replace(Chr(13), "")
    'add crlf so READLINE works
    cSend &= Microsoft.VisualBasic.vbCrLf
    Try
        oByte = System.Text.Encoding.ASCII.GetBytes(cSend.ToCharArray())
        FStream.Write(oByte, 0, oByte.Length)
    Catch oEX As SocketException
        MsgBox(oEX.Message)
    End Try

End Sub

End Class
```

There's no overridden functionality in the network player class, only new functionality. It declares an event named MyMoveLoc, which is raised within the LookForTurn method once it's determined that this network player has moved somewhere. This LookForTurn method is an endless loop that polls for data on an object called NetworkStream. This class sends data over a network from one program to another. The section "Sending Game Data" discusses the format of the data; let's focus on the class structure of the program for the time being. The new SendMyTurnToOpponent method also uses this NetworkStream object instance to send the information of a move over the wire to the other player.

Creating "Thin" Player Classes?

You might be asking yourself "Where's the beef?" after studying the player classes. In other words, the player classes don't seem to do much in the way of game playing, do they? They contain no information about the board, for instance, or any logic to decide what move might be the best to make. In fact, all they seem to do is store some player-specific information and raise some events.

This design choice was made, uh, by design. The player classes were kept "thin" purposefully so that they know as little as possible about the specific game being played. Take a second look at the player classes, and you'll probably agree that you could use these same classes for a number of different games, not only for the Reversi game being discussed here.

This is what's known as keeping the *coupling* between classes *loose*. Coupling (apart from a hilarious sitcom on the BBC) describes how "linked" classes are to one another. Listing 7-5 shows a sample definition of a more tightly coupled player class.

Listing 7-5. A Tight Coupling of a Player and Game Class

```
Public Class TightlyCoupledComputerReversiPlayer
    Inherits ReversiPlayer

    Private FReversiGame as ReversiGame
    Sub New(ByVal cNm As String, ByVal cClr As Color, g as ReversiGame)
        MyBase.New(cNm, cClr)
        FreversiGame = g
    End Sub
<more stuff here>
End Class
```

This version of the class passes in an instance of a ReversiGame class, probably so that the code that determines the best move to make resides inside the computer player class. Although this makes sense from a "responsibilities" standpoint, it doesn't make sense from a "loose coupling" standpoint because the player class and the game class are now forever linked to one another. Such linkage is bad because it prevents the reuse of the player class in another game without modification.

Developing the ReversiPiece Class

The class that contains information for a single piece is almost identical to the Reversi class described in Chapter 6, "Using Polymorphism via Interfaces," so this section won't cover it in depth. As a refresher, Table 7-1 shows the members of the piece class and describes their functions.

Table 7-1. `ReversiPiece` *Members*

MEMBER NAME	TYPE	DESCRIPTION
Draw	Method	Draws the piece on the passed-in Graphics instance
Location	Property	Point where the piece resides on the board
Size	Property	Size of the piece on the board
MouseIn	Function	Returns True if a passed-in x, y coordinate is within the boundary of this piece
Value	Property	The color of this piece (red or blue)
UnOccupied	Function	True if cell is empty
xElt	Property (ReadOnly)	Column coordinate of this piece within the array (0–7)
yElt	Property (ReadOnly)	Row coordinate of this piece within the array (0–7)
PushValue	Sub	Saves the current value to a holding place, used in the "which move is best" algorithm
PopValue	Sub	Restores the holding place value, used in the "which move is best" algorithm
IsEdge	Function	True if this piece is along an edge (top, bottom, right, left)
IsCorner	Function	True if this piece in one of the four corners

Developing the ReversiGame Class

The game class contains all of the logic for the game, including all of the data storage for the pieces, the drawing code, the algorithm for the computer to choose the next move, and the logic that determines whose turn is next. Much of this code is similar, if not identical, to the Reversi implementation described in Chapter 6, "Using Polymorphism via Interfaces." Some functionality differs enough that it needs explanation, though.

Creating the Constructor

The constructor for the game class takes a form variable and two ReversiPlayer variables as parameters, and it immediately assigns these to private variables so they can be accessed throughout the game:

```
Public Class ReversiGame
    Private aPieces(7, 7) As ReversiPiece

    Private FPlayer1 As ReversiPlayer
    Private FPlayer2 As ReversiPlayer

    Public Sub New(ByVal f As System.Windows.Forms.Form, _
        ByVal p1 As ReversiPlayer, ByVal p2 As ReversiPlayer)

        MyBase.New()
        pForm = f

        FPlayer1 = p1
        FPlayer2 = p2

        If TypeOf FPlayer1 Is HumanReversiPlayer Then
            AddHandler CType(FPlayer1, HumanReversiPlayer).MyMoveLoc, _
                AddressOf MoveToLocation

        ElseIf TypeOf FPlayer1 Is NetworkReversiPlayer Then
            AddHandler CType(FPlayer1, NetworkReversiPlayer).MyMoveLoc, _
                AddressOf MoveToLocation

        ElseIf TypeOf FPlayer1 Is ComputerReversiPlayer Then
            AddHandler CType(FPlayer1, _
                ComputerReversiPlayer).MyMakeBestMove, _
                AddressOf MakeBestMove

        End If

        If TypeOf FPlayer2 Is HumanReversiPlayer Then
            AddHandler CType(FPlayer2, HumanReversiPlayer).MyMoveLoc, _
                AddressOf MoveToLocation

        ElseIf TypeOf FPlayer2 Is NetworkReversiPlayer Then
            AddHandler CType(FPlayer2, NetworkReversiPlayer).MyMoveLoc, _
                AddressOf MoveToLocation

        ElseIf TypeOf FPlayer2 Is ComputerReversiPlayer Then
            AddHandler CType(FPlayer2, _
                ComputerReversiPlayer).MyMakeBestMove, _
                AddressOf MakeBestMove

        End If
        StartGame()
    End Sub
```

You might notice that I'm not worried about coupling in the game class like I was in the player class. I've made the game class dependent on the player classes by passing them into the constructor. You should understand that coupling isn't really a two-way street; I've kept the player class decoupled from the game class even though the game class is coupled to the player class.

Given the choice, the player class is better left independent because the potential for reuse is greater than it is for the game class. The game class seems to be much more specific to implementing a specific type of game, with its two-dimensional array of piece classes and so forth. Of course, you could employ some other design strategies to improve on the design even more. You could go back to abstracting the game and piece classes using an interface as in Chapter 6, "Using Polymorphism via Interfaces," and then coupling the interfaces together rather than the specific classes. This might allow for better extensibility in future projects.

The large If..Then block that makes up the remainder of the constructor determines what types of players are playing this game and then attaches appropriate event handlers to these players based on their classes. For example, if either player is a computer player, then the MyMakeBestMove event is attached to a method within the game class called MakeBestMove. Human and network players have their MyMoveLoc events attached to a method named MoveToLocation, which handles placing a piece on the board, given an x, y coordinate.

Attaching event handlers between the player and game classes is how you achieve communication between them without having them tightly coupled. An instance of the player class doesn't know that its event handlers are being attached to methods in a game class. All the player class is instructed to do at the appropriate time is to raise the event. Whatever has attached itself to this event will receive the information and do with it what it chooses.

Creating the MoveToLocation Methods

The human and network players raise an event when it's time to place a piece on the board. This event handler is attached to a method in the game class named MoveToLocation:

```
Private Overloads Sub MoveToLocation( _
    ByVal oPlayer As ReversiPlayer, _
    ByVal x As Integer, ByVal y As Integer)

    Dim aP As ReversiPiece

    aP = PieceLandedOn(x, y)
    If aP Is Nothing Then Exit Sub 'didn't land on a square
```

```
            MoveToLocation(oPlayer, aP)
    End Sub


    Private Overloads Sub MoveToLocation( _
    ByVal oPlayer As ReversiPlayer, _
    ByVal aP As ReversiPiece)

        If aP.UnOccupied Then

            If CanMoveHere(aP, oPlayer) Then
                MoveHere(aP, oPlayer)

                If TypeOf OtherPlayer(oPlayer) Is NetworkReversiPlayer Then
                    CType(OtherPlayer(oPlayer), _
                        NetworkReversiPlayer).SendMyTurnToOpponent(aP)
                End If

                pForm.Invalidate()
                Application.DoEvents()
                Call CalcScores()
            Else
                RaiseEvent BadMove()
                Exit Sub
            End If

            If Not CheckIfGameOver() Then
                If PlayerCantMoveAnywhere(OtherPlayer(oPlayer)) Then
                    RaiseEvent RepeatingTurn(oPlayer)
                    oPlayer.MyTurn = True                're-fires event
                Else
                    oPlayer.MyTurn = False
                    OtherPlayer(oPlayer).MyTurn = True
                End If
            Else
                oPlayer.MyTurn = False
                OtherPlayer(oPlayer).MyTurn = False
            End If

        Else
            RaiseEvent BadMove()
        End If

    End Sub
```

There are actually two MoveToLocation methods in the game class, which is legal in a "real" object-oriented language as long as each like-named method has a different parameter list so the compiler can differentiate them. Having like-named methods on a class is known as *overloading* the method. Visual Basic .NET requires the Overloads keyword on each overloaded method, as you can see in the code.

The first, shorter MoveToLocation method merely determines which piece was clicked on based on the passed-in x, y coordinate pair by using a private method named PieceLandedOn. This method returns a ReversiPiece object instance. Once it finds out which piece was clicked, the first MoveToLocation method calls the second one, passing in that ReversiPiece instance.

The second, longer MoveToLocation method determines first if the passed-in piece instance represents a valid move for the passed-in player instance. For a piece to represent a valid move, it must first be unoccupied, and of course at least one opponent tile must be "flipped over" using the rules of the game. These rules are defined in the CanMoveHere method, which was shown in Chapter 6, "Using Polymorphism via Interfaces" (specifically, see Listing 6-11).

If the move is indeed valid, then the program makes the move. At this point, the program checks to see if the other player (the one *not* making this current move) is a network player. If so, then the program must notify that player of this current move so that instance of the game can update its board. A function named OtherPlayer is called often in this code and other code in the class. This method takes a player instance as a parameter and simply returns the player instance (stored in the private variables FPlayer1 and FPlayer2) that *isn't* equal to that parameter.

After the program makes the move, it checks to see if the game is over. If not, then the program determines who gets to move next. Most of the time, player 2 will get to move next if player 1 just moved. However, if player 2 doesn't have a valid move, then player 1 gets to move again. If neither player has a valid move, then the game is over.

Setting Up the Computer Moves

The computer player class has an event wired up to a method named MakeBestMove to determine where to move next:

```
Private Sub MakeBestMove(ByVal oPlayer As ReversiPlayer)

    Dim aP As ReversiPiece

    Dim iScore As Integer
    Dim iHigh As Integer = -1
    Dim aPHigh As ReversiPiece
```

```
        PushBoard()

    For Each aP In aPieces
        If aP.UnOccupied Then
            If CanMoveHere(aP, oPlayer) Then
                MoveHere(aP, oPlayer)
                iScore = BoardValue(oPlayer)
                If iScore > iHigh Then
                    iHigh = iScore
                    aPHigh = aP
                End If
                PopBoard()
            End If
        End If
    Next

    System.Threading.Thread.Sleep(1000) 'wait a sec

    If iHigh > 1 Then
        MoveToLocation(oPlayer, aPHigh)
    End If
End Sub
```

This code works by checking every unoccupied location on the board and then moving there to see what the "board score" would be after flipping over all the opponent pieces. This code then selects the move resulting in the best board score as the place to move.

Before trying out moves, the state of the board is saved (*pushed*) into place, and after each move is attempted, the board is restored (*popped*) back to its original state. Finally, once the code determines the best move, it makes that move by calling the friendly old MoveToLocation method.

 NOTE   *A "smarter" move selection algorithm would travel more moves into the future. For example, the computer could determine which move would result in the* worst *possible board score for the human player on her next turn, even if that player selected her best possible move. This algorithm is called the* minimax *algorithm.*

Setting Up the Game

The player classes, piece class, and game class are all complete. All that remains is a way to set up the game in its various modes (one player vs. a computer, two humans at the same computer, two players at different computers). A form named fNewGame, shown in Figure 7-1, does all this.

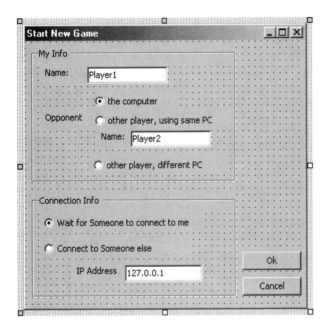

Figure 7-1. This form starts a new game

The form allows for all options of the game to begin. The player's first task is to give herself a name to be used in the game. Then the player selects her opponent. If the player selects a computer opponent, the game can begin immediately by instantiating a ReversiGame class and two player classes—one of the HumanReversiPlayer subclass and the other of the ComputerReversiPlayer subclass. This is also true if the choice is two human players playing on the same computer. The game then begins by creating the HumanReversiPlayer instances and passing those into a game class.

If the player is setting up a network game, the game must do some further work before starting. The two machines that want to play the game must make initial contact and exchange names. There are two options for a player when setting up a network game—she can either act as player 1 (the "server") or player 2 (the "client"). The server machine begins by waiting in a loop for the client machine to contact it. Once the client makes the contact, the computers exchange player names, and the game can begin.

Listing 7-6 shows the code that displays the Start New Game dialog box and then sets up the new game according to the game options displayed.

Listing 7-6. Setting Up a New Game

```
Private Sub mNew_Click(ByVal sender As System.Object, _
  ByVal e As System.EventArgs) Handles mNew.Click

    ShutStuffDown()        'shut down old stuff if second game

    Dim f As New fNewGame
    If f.ShowDialog <> DialogResult.Cancel Then

        Dim bGameOn As Boolean = True

        If f.rbComputer.Checked Then
            Player1 = New HumanReversiPlayer(f.tbPlayerName.Text, _
                Color.Red, Me)
            Player2 = New ComputerReversiPlayer("BorgBlue", _
                Color.Blue)
        ElseIf f.rbHuman.Checked Then
            Player1 = New HumanReversiPlayer(f.tbPlayerName.Text, _
                Color.Red, Me)
            Player2 = New HumanReversiPlayer(f.tbPlayer2Name.Text, _
                Color.Blue, Me)
        Else                 'network game
            If f.rbSrv0.Checked Then

                Dim fSrv As New fServerConnect(f.tbPlayerName.Text)
                If fSrv.ShowDialog = DialogResult.OK Then

                    oClient = fSrv.pClient

                    Player1 = New HumanReversiPlayer(f.tbPlayerName.Text, _
                        Color.Red, Me)
                    Player2 = New NetworkReversiPlayer(fSrv.pOpponentName, _
                        Color.Blue, oClient.GetStream)

                    oThread = New Thread(New ThreadStart( _
                        AddressOf CType(Player2, _
                        NetworkReversiPlayer).LookForTurn))
                    oThread.Start()

                Else
                    bGameOn = False
                End If
```

```
            Else
                Dim fCl As New fClientConnect(_
                    f.tbPlayerName.Text, f.tbIPAddress.Text)
                If fCl.ShowDialog = DialogResult.OK Then

                    oClient = fCl.pClient
                    Player1 = New NetworkReversiPlayer(fCl.pOpponentName, _
                        Color.Red, oClient.GetStream)

                    oThread = New Thread(New ThreadStart( _
                        AddressOf CType(Player1, _
                        NetworkReversiPlayer).LookForTurn))
                    oThread.Start()

                    Player2 = New HumanReversiPlayer(f.tbPlayerName.Text, _
                        Color.Blue, Me)

                End If
            End If

        End If

        If bGameOn Then
            AddHandler Player1.IsMyTurn, AddressOf TurnNotify
            AddHandler Player2.IsMyTurn, AddressOf TurnNotify

            Game = New ReversiGame(Me, Player1, Player2)
            AddHandler Game.BadMove, AddressOf BadMoveNotify
            AddHandler Game.PlayerWon, AddressOf PlayerWonNotify
            AddHandler Game.TieGame, AddressOf TieGameNotify
            AddHandler Game.RepeatingTurn, AddressOf RepeatTurnNotify
            AddHandler Game.UpdateScore, AddressOf ScoreUpdateNotify

            Player1.MyTurn = True
            Me.Invalidate()
        Else
            sb0.Text = "game cancelled"
        End If
    End If

End Sub
```

About half of this routine displays the Start New Game dialog box and then sets up ReversiPlayer instances of the appropriate subclass based on the type of game being played. If the player selects a network game, then one of two new forms, either fServerConnect or fClientConnect, will display to establish communication. Once the computers have established communication, the program creates one human and one network player class.

The bottom third of the code instantiates the ReversiGame class variable (named Game) and passes the two player class instances to it. A series of event handlers on the game class are also attached so that the game can report what the score is and who the eventual winner is when the game gets that far.

Setting Up the Network Server

When specifying a network game, it's necessary that one of the two players selects the Wait for Someone to Connect to Me option and the other selects the Connect to Someone Else option on the Start New Game dialog box displayed in Figure 7-1. For the purposes of setting up the game, the person who selects Wait for Someone to Connect to Me is the server. Once a user specifies that she is the server, the program waits in a loop until being contacted by the other machine (the client) or until the player hits the Cancel button. This wait loop happens inside of a form named fServerConnect, as shown in Figure 7-2.

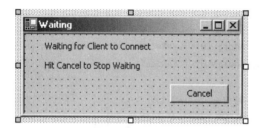

Figure 7-2. The server connect form displays when the server is waiting for another machine to contact it

The code behind the server connect form, displayed in Listing 7-7, uses the TCPListener class instance and a TCPClient class instance to perform the communication with the other machine. The TCPListener class is a .NET Framework class that listens for connection requests from other machines. To begin listening, the class is instantiated by passing in the local Internet Protocol (IP) address (known as *localhost*) and a port number. This program is hard-coded to communicate on port 8878.

Listing 7-7. Server Connect Form

```
Public Class fServerConnect
    Inherits System.Windows.Forms.Form
```

```
Private THEPORT As Integer = 8878
Private FPlayerName As String
Private FOpponentName As String

Private FThread As Thread
Private FListen As TcpListener
Private FClient As TcpClient

Sub New(ByVal cName As String)
    InitializeComponent()
    FPlayerName = cName

    Dim oIPA As IPAddress = Dns.Resolve("localhost").AddressList(0)

    Try
        FListen = New TcpListener(oIPA, THEPORT)
        FListen.Start()
    Catch oEx As Exception
        MsgBox(oEx.ToString)
    End Try

    FThread = New Thread(AddressOf LookForIt)
    FThread.Start()

End Sub

Private Sub LookForIt()

    Dim oStream As NetworkStream
    Dim oRead As StreamReader
    Dim oByte() As Byte
    Dim cSend As String

    FClient = FListen.AcceptTcpClient

    lbOut.Text = "Connecting..."
    Application.DoEvents()

    Me.Cursor = Cursors.WaitCursor
    Try

        'open the stream, read the name of the opponent.
        'Send your name back
```

```
                         oStream = FClient.GetStream
                         oRead = New StreamReader(oStream)

                         FOpponentName = oRead.ReadLine
                         FThread.Sleep(500)

                         'add crlf so READLINE works
                         cSend = FPlayerName & Microsoft.VisualBasic.vbCrLf
                         oByte = System.Text.Encoding.ASCII.GetBytes(_
                           cSend.ToCharArray())
                         oStream.Write(oByte, 0, oByte.Length)

                         FListen.Stop()

                 Finally
                         Me.Cursor = Cursors.Default
                         Me.DialogResult = DialogResult.OK
                         Me.Close()
                 End Try
         End Sub


         Private Sub cbCancel_Click(ByVal sender As System.Object, _
             ByVal e As System.EventArgs) Handles cbCancel.Click

             FThread.Abort()
             FListen.Stop()

         End Sub


         ReadOnly Property pOpponentName() As String
             Get
                     Return FOpponentName
             End Get
         End Property


         ReadOnly Property pClient() As TcpClient
             Get
                     Return FClient
             End Get
         End Property


   End Class
```

Once the form sets up the TCPListener class, the form calls its Start method, which instructs the class to begin looking for incoming requests. In this code, a new thread then begins and spawns to handle those requests. Putting the request handler in a new thread is necessary because the TCPListener class's AcceptTCPClient method is a blocking method—it halts code execution in the current program thread. If you called this method on the main thread, there would be no way for the player to hit the Cancel button to abort the process.

Setting up a new execution thread is almost trivial in Visual Basic .NET, but the syntax is a bit convoluted. You instantiate a Thread class, which is passed a delegate routine that the thread executes. The routine takes no parameters. In the server connect code, the thread executes the LookForIt routine:

```
FThread = New Thread(AddressOf LookForIt)
FThread.Start()
```

This spawned thread will terminate either when the routine LookForIt completes or when the thread's Abort method executes. (The Cancel button on the form calls the Abort method on the thread, as shown in the method cbCancel_Click in Listing 7-7.)

The routine LookForIt begins by calling the AcceptTCPClient method on the TCPListener class. As stated before, this is a blocking method, so this code won't end until a client connects to the TCPListener class or until the client clicks the Cancel button to abort the thread running this code. When a client does connect, the AcceptTCPClient method returns an instance of a TCPClient class. This class enables sending and receiving data on a network. All the game communication from this point forward will use this class instance.

The client begins the communication by sending her name to the server. The server code that reads this name is part of the LookForIt method shown in Listing 7-7:

```
oStream = FClient.GetStream
oRead = New StreamReader(oStream)
FOpponentName = oRead.ReadLine
```

Data is read from the TCPClient client by using a *stream*. A stream is an abstract concept that you can think of as any stream of bytes being read or written from one source to another. You use streams for reading/writing files. The StreamReader class used in this method allows for the line-by-line reading of text information. The previous three lines of code attach a StreamReader class instance to the TCPClient variable named FClient, read a single text line from the stream, and place it into the string variable named FOpponentName.

Once the server reads the opponent name, it sends its own player's name back to the client:

```
cSend = FPlayerName & Microsoft.VisualBasic.vbCrLf
oByte = System.Text.Encoding.ASCII.GetBytes(_
    cSend.ToCharArray())
oStream.Write(oByte, 0, oByte.Length)
```

The regular string of characters must be encoded into a byte array to be sent correctly through the stream. Also, a carriage return/line feed is appended to the player name, which allows the client to use the ReadLine method on her own end to get the name as a single line of text.

Once the names are exchanged in this way, the server dialog box closes. One final thing to notice is that the TCPClient class used to exchange the names on this dialog box (held in a variable name FClient) is actually passed back to the main form of the game via a property on the fServerConnect dialog named pClient so that this same variable can be used for communication during actual game play. You'll see a parallel setup for the client code listed next.

Setting Up the Network Client

The fClientConnect dialog code, displayed in Listing 7-8, contacts the server game across the network.

Listing 7-8. Client Connect Dialog Box

```
Public Class fClientConnect
    Inherits System.Windows.Forms.Form

    Private THEPORT As Integer = 8878

    Private FPlayerName As String
    Private FServerName As String
    Private FOpponentName As String

    Private FThread As Thread
    Private FClient As TcpClient

    Sub New(ByVal cName As String, ByVal cServer As String)

        InitializeComponent()
```

```
        FPlayerName = cName
        FServerName = cServer

        FThread = New Thread(AddressOf LookForIt)
        FThread.Start()
End Sub

Private Sub LookForIt()

        Dim oStream As NetworkStream
        Dim oRead As StreamReader
        Dim oByte() As Byte
        Dim cSend As String

        FClient = New TcpClient(FServerName, THEPORT)

        lbOut.Text = "Connecting..."
        Application.DoEvents()

        Me.Cursor = Cursors.WaitCursor
        Try

            'open the stream, Send your name to the server.
            'read his name back
            'this is in the opposite order of the server
            oStream = FClient.GetStream

            cSend = FPlayerName & Microsoft.VisualBasic.vbCrLf
            oByte = System.Text.Encoding.ASCII.GetBytes(cSend.ToCharArray())
            oStream.Write(oByte, 0, oByte.Length)

            FThread.Sleep(500)

            oRead = New StreamReader(oStream)
            FOpponentName = oRead.ReadLine

        Finally
            Me.Cursor = Cursors.Default
            Me.DialogResult = DialogResult.OK
            Me.Close()
        End Try
End Sub
```

```
Private Sub cbCancel_Click(ByVal sender As System.Object, _
    ByVal e As System.EventArgs) Handles cbCancel.Click

    FThread.Abort()

End Sub

ReadOnly Property pOpponentName() As String
    Get
        Return FOpponentName
    End Get
End Property

ReadOnly Property pClient() As TcpClient
    Get
        Return FClient
    End Get
End Property
End Class
```

The client code is similar to the server code in that it spawns a separate
thread to handle the communication. The client must know the name (or IP
address) of the server to which its trying to connect. Because it's initiating communication, the client simply creates a direct instance of the TCPClient class,
passing the server name and the desired port number:

```
FClient = New TcpClient(FServerName, THEPORT)
```

Assuming the server is listening, this client creation should come back right
away, allowing communication to begin. The sending and receiving of the names
happens in the same way as by the server class, but in the opposite order. The
client sends its name first, then waits to receive the server name. Once the name
exchange is complete, the form closes. As in the server connect dialog box, the
TCPClient variable used to exchange names passes back to the main form so that
intragame communication can continue.

Sending Game Data

The lines of communication are open, so all that remains is to send and receive
data back and forth. You can send the data a number of ways. For example, you
could send two integers that represent the x, y coordinate of the piece to which
the player is going to move. Although this might work fine for this game, you

want to implement a solution that you can easily extend to a more complex game. You'll find that it isn't too hard to send *entire class instances* over the wire from one program to the other.

To do this, you first have to *serialize* the class instance into some type of format that can easily be sent through the TCPClient object. Visual Basic .NET makes it pretty easy to use XML as that format, as shown in Listing 7-9.

Listing 7-9. The SendMyTurnToOpponent *Method, Found in the* NetworkReversiPlayer *Class*

```
Public Sub SendMyTurnToOpponent(ByVal aP As ReversiPiece)

    Dim oSer As New XmlSerializer(aP.GetType)
    Dim oSW As New StringWriter
    Dim oWriter As New XmlTextWriter(oSW)
    Dim oByte() As Byte
    Dim cSend As String

    oSer.Serialize(oSW, aP)
    oWriter.Close()
    cSend = oSW.ToString
    cSend = cSend.Replace(Chr(10), "")
    cSend = cSend.Replace(Chr(13), "")
    cSend &= Microsoft.VisualBasic.vbCrLf
    Try
        oByte = System.Text.Encoding.ASCII.GetBytes(cSend.ToCharArray())
        FStream.Write(oByte, 0, oByte.Length)
    Catch oEX As SocketException
        MsgBox(oEX.Message)
    End Try
End Sub
```

The SendMyTurnToOpponent method takes a ReversiPiece object as a parameter, converts it to XML format, and then loads that XML into a string variable named cSend. Listing 7-10 shows the contents of this variable.

Listing 7-10. XML-Serialized Version of a ReversiPiece *Object*

```
<?xml version="1.0" encoding="utf-16"?>
<ReversiPiece xmlns:xsd="http://www.w3.org/2001/XMLSchema"
xmlns:xsi="http://www.w3.org/2001/XMLSchema-instance">
```

```
<Location>
  <X>192</X>
  <Y>240</Y>
</Location>
<Size>
  <Width>48</Width>
  <Height>48</Height>
</Size>
<Value />
</ReversiPiece>
```

As you can see, all of the public properties of the ReversiPiece class and their values are represented as elements in the XML file.

One additional problem exists when sending this XML data across to the other computer. The easiest way to send it is all on a single line. This allows the TCPClient class in the receiving program to use the ReadLine method, which retrieves one whole line of text. The XML created by Listing 7-9, however, is broken up into several individual lines. No big deal, though—it isn't too difficult to remove the carriage returns and line feeds from the XML string and then add one final carriage return/line feed to the end:

```
cSend = cSend.Replace(Chr(10), "")
cSend = cSend.Replace(Chr(13), "")
cSend &= Microsoft.VisualBasic.vbCrLf
```

Now the cSend variable contains one XML line that represents one class, and this data can travel over the wire. You do this the same way that the player name traveled over the wire when the communication was established—you encode the string variable to a byte array and then write it to the TCPClient variable FStream:

```
oByte = System.Text.Encoding.ASCII.GetBytes(cSend.ToCharArray())
FStream.Write(oByte, 0, oByte.Length)
```

Receiving Game Data

The LookForTurn method, which is part of the NetworkReversiPlayer class, loops continuously in its own thread looking for data from the other player (see Listing 7-6 on how to set up this separate thread). Listing 7-11 shows how this method looks for data and then converts it into a ReversiPiece class instance.

Listing 7-11. Deserializing Data from the TCPClient *and Rehydrating Back into a* ReversiPiece *Object Instance*

```
Public Sub LookForTurn()

    Do
        If FStream.DataAvailable Then

            Dim cPiece As String
            Dim oPiece As New ReversiPiece
            Dim oSer As New XmlSerializer(oPiece.GetType)
            Dim oRead As StreamReader

            oRead = New StreamReader(FStream)
            cPiece = oRead.ReadLine
            oPiece = oSer.Deserialize(New StringReader(cPiece))

            RaiseEvent MyMoveLoc(Me, oPiece.Location.X, oPiece.Location.Y)
        End If
        System.Threading.Thread.Sleep(250)
    Loop Until False

End Sub
```

This method reverses the process found in the SendMyTurnToOpponent method. It first uses the ReadLine method of the TCPClient class to retrieve a complete line of text from the network connection (remember, the XML class definition exists in a single line of text because you removed all of the carriage return/line feeds). This string is stored in the string variable cPiece. Then, an XMLSerializer class instance converts the string variable back into a ReversiPiece instance named oPiece.

After retrieving the ReversiPiece object, the code raises the event that moves the current player, MyMoveLoc. This event handler requires the player moving and the x, y coordinate of the piece to which the player is moving. The coordinates from the ReversiPiece object that were sent over the wire are the coordinates sent to the event handler.

Debugging Network Code

Debugging the network version of a game is a bit trickier than debugging other games. The network version of Reversi requires two instances of the game to be running: the client instance and the server instance. Visual Studio .NET will of course only let you debug one version of the program at a time, so you'll have to decide which version you want to run in debug mode and which version to run straight from Windows. This usually depends on what part of the code you want to debug at the time. Say for the sake of example that you want to debug the server code; follow these steps:

1. Compile the program.

2. Set desired breakpoints in the source.

3. Run the program from Visual Studio.

4. Select New Game, specify Network Game, and specify Wait for Someone to Connect to Me. Change the machine name or IP address (127.0.0.1 should always work if the client and server are running on the same machine).

5. Click OK.

6. Navigate to the project folder in Windows Explorer.

7. Go to the Bin directory.

8. Double-click the executable to run it. This will be the client instance.

9. Select New Game, specify Network Game, and specify Connect to Someone. Change the machine name or IP address if necessary.

10. Click OK.

11. Play the game. You'll have to switch between the client and server boards to make your moves.

12. Your breakpoint in the server program should trigger normally.

Moving Forward

You've seen two different Reversi solutions. The first focused on creating a set of generic class interfaces for implementing a two-player game but made the assumption that one player was controlled by the computer. In this chapter, the second solution allowed for both human and computer opponents, and it supported network play.

Moving forward, you could refactor these two solutions into one, all-things-to-all-programmers, two-player game engine. It could use interfaces to describe necessary functionality and include generic player classes that support mouse functionality and network communication. In the course of developing such a solution, if you find that your classes are getting too dependent on one another, look into decoupling them using event handlers. The final product would be nothing short of a two-player game-developing "toolkit."

CHAPTER 8

Using DirectX

YOU MAY NOT HAVE NOTICED, but the drawing speed in some of the previous games was a bit slow—okay, maybe more than a bit slow. The slowdown was most noticeable in the NineTiles game from Chapter 3, "Understanding Object-Oriented Programming from the Start." In fact, I was originally going to add an opening animation sequence that showed all the tiles flipping over simultaneously, but this turned out to be too slow.

If you do some Google research on speed issues, you'll find that the bitmap rendering in the Graphics Device Interchange, Plus (GDI+) classes isn't quite ready for prime time. There are reports of unnecessary palette and color transformations going on behind the scenes when using the GDI+ classes for drawing. Trying to correct the problem by changing the color depth of the source bitmaps does nothing to speed up the drawing to any great degree.

Fortunately, for most of the games discussed to this point, blazing-fast bitmap rendering speed isn't necessary. The games should run at an acceptable speed. If you continue on the game-development track and create bigger and more complicated games, this speed will most likely become a barrier at some point, though. You have three ways to get around the graphics speed trap:

- Stop writing games until Microsoft addresses some of the GDI issues.

- Drop back down to the Win32 application programming interface (API) for graphics drawing (bitblt, stretchblt, and so on).

- Move over to DirectX drawing.

Obviously, the first option is no fun at all (plus, the book would have to end right here!). The second option is possible, but don't you get a slight feeling of failure when you have to stop using a cool new language and return to old habits? Plus, using the bitblt function could get tricky with all the device handles and such.

The third option sounds like the best choice by default. DirectX is a huge set of multimedia functionality built into the Windows operating system. It has gotten both bigger and better with each new release, and the latest release, DirectX 9, is no exception. DirectX 9 includes a managed class interface for the .NET developer. In other words, drawing using the DirectX classes is scarcely more difficult than drawing using the GDI+ classes. Thus, you'll break the speed barrier.

Installing DirectX 9

A version of DirectX is installed with every version of Windows, but the erstwhile developer needs the DirectX software development kit (SDK) to program to the DirectX libraries. You can find the SDK at http://www.microsoft.com/windows/ directx/default.aspx. After downloading and installing it, you'll find a DXSDK folder on your C: drive packed full o' DirectX goodness. The huge help file might be the first thing you want to peruse, or you can dig right into the sample programs, which are available in Visual Basic .NET, C#, or C++.

NOTE *DirectX 9 is a large enough API that one could write an entire book about the library. In fact, someone has. Check out .NET Game Programming with DirectX 9.0 by Alexandre Santos Lobao and Ellen Hatton (Apress, 2003).*

This chapter focuses on one aspect of DirectX, known as *DirectDraw*. This functionality creates fast bitmap graphics, which is what needs to improve in the old games. In this chapter, you'll learn about DirectDraw through two example programs. The first is a "do-one-thing" program that simply introduces the concepts and renders a bunch of graphics to the screen to prove the speed of the DirectX library. The second program puts the concepts together to create the bulk of an arcade game.

Understanding DirectDraw Basics

The sample solution DirectXDemo demonstrates displaying bitmap images to the screen using the DirectX API. In a good display of conservation, it recycles one of the graphics from a prior project, the three-dimensional die. To demonstrate the speed of the DirectX API, this demo displays 250 spinning dice in random locations on the screen, as shown in Figure 8-1.

Press escape to exit

Figure 8-1. Spinning dice aplenty

DirectX drawing is based on the concept of *surfaces*. A surface is both a source for bitmap data and a destination. The DirectXDemo application utilizes three surfaces:

- The source bitmap

- The "screen" surface (also called the front surface)

- The back buffer surface, or back surface

DirectDraw achieves smooth animation by performing all drawing to a hidden surface, the back buffer, and then swapping the position of the front and back surfaces once rendering is complete. As a developer, you don't need to keep track of which surface is being displayed, however—all drawing always happens on the back buffer.

DirectX 9 encapsulates all of the functionality of a DirectDraw surface inside a .NET Framework managed class called (obviously enough) Surface. This class resides in the Microsoft.DirectX.DirectDraw namespace, which becomes available in Visual Studio .NET after installing the DirectX 9 SDK.

The other important class you'll use in a simple DirectDraw application is the Device class. The Device class encapsulates the capabilities of the system upon which the program is running.

Initializing a DirectDraw Application

Getting a DirectDraw application ready for rendering using the DirectX 9 managed classes requires setting up a Device instance and the front and back surfaces used for rendering. Listing 8-1 shows some private form variables and the initialization routine used in the demo application.

Listing 8-1. Setting Up a DirectDraw Application

```
Private Const WID As Integer = 1024
Private Const HGT As Integer = 768

Private FDraw As Microsoft.DirectX.DirectDraw.Device
Private FFront As Microsoft.DirectX.DirectDraw.Surface
Private FBack As Microsoft.DirectX.DirectDraw.Surface

Private Sub InitializeDirectDraw()

    Dim oSurfaceDesc As New SurfaceDescription
    Dim oSurfaceCaps As New SurfaceCaps
    Dim i As Integer

    FDraw = New Microsoft.DirectX.DirectDraw.Device

    FDraw.SetCooperativeLevel(Me, _
      Microsoft.DirectX.DirectDraw._
      CooperativeLevelFlags.FullscreenExclusive)
    FDraw.SetDisplayMode(WID, HGT, 16, 0, False)

    With oSurfaceDesc
        .SurfaceCaps.PrimarySurface = True
        .SurfaceCaps.Flip = True
        .SurfaceCaps.Complex = True
        .BackBufferCount = 1
        FFront = New Surface(oSurfaceDesc, FDraw)
```

```
        oSurfaceCaps.BackBuffer = True
        FBack = FFront.GetAttachedSurface(oSurfaceCaps)
        FBack.ForeColor = Color.White
        .Clear()
    End With
  FNeedToRestore = True
End Sub
```

The `InitializeDirectDraw` procedure begins by creating an instance of
a DirectDraw `Device` class and sets what's known as the *cooperative level*. The
cooperative level specifies to the operating system the performance requirements
of your application. Intensive games will want to use the `FullscreenExclusive`
level used here, meaning that the application will create a full-screen window
(unrelated to any form in the application) upon which the drawing will happen.

Next, the `SetDisplayMode` method sets the resolution of the window. The sample program creates a 1024×768 window using 16-bit color.

The remainder of the procedure defines the device as having one back buffer
and then initializes the front and back surfaces. The front surface, `FFront`, is instantiated by calling the constructor and passing the `Device` variable to it. The back buffer,
`FBack`, is retrieved by calling a method on the front surface (`GetAttachedSurface`). The
last line within the `With` block clears the surface. Finally, a Boolean variable named
`FNeedToRestore` is set to `True`, which tells the class that all of the DirectX surfaces
require restoration before drawing can happen.

The program now has destination surfaces, but it still needs a source surface
to store the die bitmap that contains the animated frames. You need to import
the die bitmap into the solution as in Chapter 1, "Developing Your First Game."
Listing 8-2 contains the code that loads this bitmap into a DirectDraw surface.

 TIP   *Don't forget to change the* Build Action *property on any
bitmaps in your solution to* Embedded Resource.

Listing 8-2. Loading Bitmaps into Surface *Instances*

```
Private FDieSurf As Microsoft.DirectX.DirectDraw.Surface

Public Sub RestoreSurfaces()

    Dim oCK As New ColorKey
    Dim a As Reflection.Assembly = _
      System.Reflection.Assembly.GetExecutingAssembly()
```

```
FDraw.RestoreAllSurfaces()

If Not FDieSurf Is Nothing Then
    FDieSurf.Dispose()
    FDieSurf = Nothing
End If

FDieSurf = New Surface(a.GetManifestResourceStream( _
    "DirectXDemo.dicexrot.bmp"), New SurfaceDescription, FDraw)
FDieSurf.SetColorKey(ColorKeyFlags.SourceDraw, oCK)

End Sub
```

The Surface class takes a resource stream as its first parameter. This is the same way that a GDI+ Bitmap class loads a resource that's embedded in the solution. The second parameter is a SurfaceDescription class instance. This class contains properties that can describe the surface (you can see another SurfaceDescription class being used in Listing 8-1 to describe some aspects of the front and back screen surfaces). For loading bitmaps, the surface description properties aren't needed because the attributes of the surface are retrieved from the attributes of the bitmap itself. Thus, the surface constructor in Listing 8-2 creates a blank, default SurfaceDescription with no specified properties.

The last line in Listing 8-2 sets the color key for the surface. A color key specifies one or more colors that are to be treated as transparent when rendering. Because no such color assignment happens in Listing 8-2, the ColorKey object named oCK declares pure black (RGB color 0, 0, 0) as the transparent color. This program uses black because the background of the dice bitmap is also black.

Note that the surfaces of your application may be "lost" and require restoration. This is especially true in windowed DirectDraw applications (as opposed to full-screen applications) that can lose focus. Because of this possibility, the main drawing loop of the program needs to check that the device is ready before it can actually draw. Once the device comes back from a "not ready" state, the source bitmaps need to be re-created. This is why the method in Listing 8-2 is called RestoreSurfaces as opposed to a name that connotes a one-time load such as LoadSurfaces.

Creating the Drawing Loop

The drawing in the sample program happens in a method named DrawFrame. Listing 8-3 shows the majority of this routine, along with the Form_Load and Form_KeyUp events.

Listing 8-3. The DrawFrame *Method*

```vb
Private Sub Form1_Load(ByVal sender As System.Object, _
  ByVal e As System.EventArgs) Handles MyBase.Load

   Me.Cursor.Dispose()
   InitializeDirectDraw()
   SetupDice

   While Me.Created
      DrawFrame()
   End While
End Sub


Private Sub DrawFrame()

   If FFront Is Nothing Then Exit Sub

   'can't draw now, device not ready
   If Not FDraw.TestCooperativeLevel() Then
      FNeedToRestore = True
      Exit Sub
   End If

   If FNeedToRestore Then
      RestoreSurfaces()
      FNeedToRestore = False
   End If

   FBack.ColorFill(0)
   < drawing code removed>

   Try
      FBack.ForeColor = Color.White
      FBack.DrawText(10, 10, "Press escape to exit", False)
      FFront.Flip(FBack, FlipFlags.DoNotWait)
   Catch oEX As Exception
      Debug.WriteLine(oEX.Message)
   Finally
      Application.DoEvents()
   End Try
End Sub
```

```
Private Sub Form1_KeyUp(ByVal sender As Object, _
    ByVal e As System.Windows.Forms.KeyEventArgs) Handles MyBase.KeyUp

    If e.KeyCode = Keys.Escape Then
        Me.Close()
    End If
End Sub
```

The Form_Load event runs the initialization method that has already been discussed and then calls the DrawFrame method over and over in a loop. The loop continues to run as long as the Created property on the current form is set to True. One other interesting thing that happens in the Form_Load event is the disposal of the form's cursor so that it isn't visible on the game surface. Getting rid of the cursor is as easy as invoking its Dispose method.

The DrawFrame method does some checking before any drawing happens to make sure everything is in the correct state for drawing. The first check makes sure the front surface exists. If it doesn't exist, then there would be no destination surface to display to the user, so the draw loop exits immediately. The next test happens by calling TestCooperativeLevel on the Device object. If this method returns False, then the device isn't ready to draw, so again the draw loop exits. In addition, a form-level Boolean variable named FNeedToRestore is set, which indicates that the dice source surface object needs to be re-created.

Once the TestCooperativeLevel method returns True, drawing is almost ready to begin. If the FNeedToRestore variable is True, then the source bitmaps are loaded (or reloaded) by calling RestoreSurfaces. With this, everything is ready for the drawing to commence.

The first task performed is clearing the back buffer to black and using the ColorFill method on the Surface object. The code immediately after the ColorFill method is where the actual dice drawing takes place (but I've removed that code so that the focus is on the structure of the drawing loop itself).

The remainder of the DrawFrame method happens inside of an exception handler so that any errors are dealt with in a graceful manner. First, some text is drawn into the upper-left corner of the back buffer, indicating that the user can hit the Escape key to stop the application. Then, the back buffer is copied to the front buffer by calling the Flip method on the Surface class. Flip is actually an inaccurate description inherited from previous versions of DirectDraw, where two surfaces were in fact actually swapped, serving as back buffers and then front buffers in alternate frames. The method actually copies the contents of one Surface class to the other.

The Catch portion of the exception handler writes the error to the Debug window so that the developer can inspect it later, and the Finally portion calls an Application.DoEvents so that Windows messages can process normally. Without this DoEvents, the application wouldn't be able to intercept keystrokes, including the keystroke meant to shut down the application.

Finally, the KeyUp event handler for the form detects the pressing of the Escape key and closes the main form when detected. This stops all drawing and exits the application.

Setting Up the Dice Drawing

Taking a quick inventory, the program now has the capability to set up a full-screen DirectDraw surface and draws a black screen with the text *Press escape to exit* in the upper-left corner. A dice bitmap also loads into a Surface instance, but it isn't actually drawn anywhere yet. All that remains is the code to track a bunch of dice and to draw them onto the screen.

Create a class named SimpleDie, shown in Listing 8-4, to keep track of each die object. It's referred to as "simple" because the code contains no capability to move around on the screen; each die simply spins in place.

Listing 8-4. Class to Keep Track of One Die on the Screen

```
Public Class SimpleDie
    Private FLocation As Point
    Private FFrame As Integer

    Public Sub New(ByVal p As Point)
        FLocation = p
    End Sub

    ReadOnly Property pLocation() As Point
        Get
            Return FLocation
        End Get
    End Property

    Public Sub Draw(ByVal FDest As Surface, ByVal FSource As Surface)

        Dim oRect As Rectangle

        oRect = New Rectangle((FFrame Mod 6) * 72, (FFrame \ 6) * 72, 72, 72)

        FDest.DrawFast(FLocation.X, FLocation.Y, FSource, oRect, _
            DrawFastFlags.DoNotWait Or DrawFastFlags.SourceColorKey)

        FFrame = (FFrame + 1) Mod 36
    End Sub
End Class
```

This class stores only two pieces of information—a screen coordinate that's passed into the class constructor and a private Frame variable that's incremented as each frame is drawn. The sole method on the class is the Draw method, which takes two DirectDraw Surface instances as parameters: the source image and the destination. This Draw method calculates a source rectangle based on the current frame and then uses a DrawFast method on the DirectDraw Surface class to transfer that part of the source surface to itself. The DrawFast method takes as parameters a coordinate pair (the place the bitmap should be drawn on the destination), the source surface, a rectangle that represents the portion of the source surface to copy, and some flags that can specify some additional functionality. In this case, the flags specify to use the color key of the source surface when drawing to determine transparency and to draw as quickly as possible by indicating the DoNotWait flag.

The demonstration program shows the speed of DirectDraw as compared to GDI+ drawing, so it should display lots of dice on the screen at the same time. The program is written in such a way that the number of dice displayed is a constant that you can easily change. You can store the information for the 250 die object instances using an ArrayList to store as many class instances as you want. Listing 8-5 shows the SetupDice method and the modified DrawFrame method with the code in place to draw the dice.

Listing 8-5. Initializing 250 SimpleDie *Object Instances*

```
Private FDice As ArrayList
Private Const NUMDICE As Integer = 250

Private Sub SetupDice()

    Dim d As SimpleDie
    Dim r As New Random

    FDice = New ArrayList
    Do While FDice.Count < NUMDICE
        d = New SimpleDie(New Point(r.Next(0, WID - 72), r.Next(0, HGT - 72)))
        FDice.Add(d)
    Loop

End Sub

Private Sub DrawFrame()

    Dim d As SimpleDie

    <code removed>
```

```
        FBack.ColorFill(0)

        For Each d In FDice
            d.Draw(FBack, FDieSurf)
        Next

        Try
            FBack.ForeColor = Color.White
            FBack.DrawText(10, 10, "Press escape to exit", False)
            FFront.Flip(FBack, FlipFlags.DoNotWait)
        Catch oEX As Exception
            Debug.WriteLine(oEX.Message)
        Finally
            Application.DoEvents()
        End Try
End Sub
```

As you can see, you can modify the number of dice shown by altering only the constant definition NUMDICE. For instance, I cranked it up to 1,000, and it was still much faster than my GDI+ experiments in the early days of designing the NineTiles game. The SetupDice method creates random locations in the horizontal range of 0 and the width of the screen, minus the width of the die frame, and the vertical range of 0 to the height of the screen, minus the height of a die frame.

 CAUTION *DirectDraw doesn't effectively handle drawing "off the edges" of a surface, so you'll have do some math to keep from trying to draw at coordinates less than 0 or greater than the width of the destination surface.*

Finally, the bitmap data for the die *isn't* stored in the die class. When it's time to draw the die, the source surface data is passed into the class for drawing. You would obviously not create an identical surface instance for each die class—it would be random access memory (RAM) suicide to store the die frames bitmap in memory 250 times. The next example also uses this approach, where sprites with the same appearance look outside of themselves to get their sprite data.

Building an Arcade Game

With DirectDraw capabilities so easily within the grasp of the Visual Basic programmer, you'll now write an arcade game and get some sprites interacting on the screen. The arcade game is called *SpaceRocks*, and it involves a little spaceship floating around on the screen and shooting at some asteroids. (Sound familiar? Not to me, either.) Figure 8-2 shows a stirring game of SpaceRocks in action.

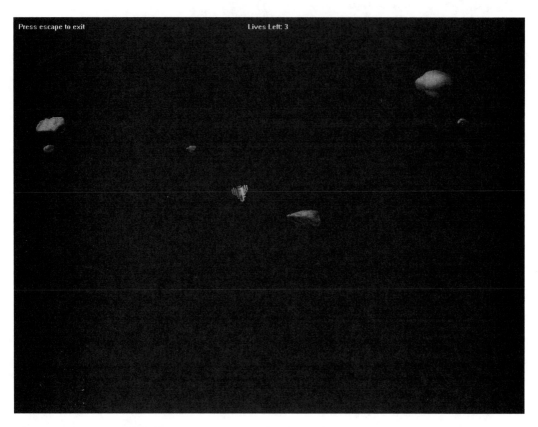

Figure 8-2. SpaceRocks, ahoy!

The structure of this game isn't unlike the structure of the DirectXDemo program previously described, but there's one further level of abstraction between this program and the last. In the previous program, much of the coding happened at the form level, such as the storage of the DirectDraw Device and Surface variables and the Dice object array. In SpaceRocks, a reusable class named dxWorld sets up the DirectDraw surface and device objects and handles the basic functions such as clearing the back buffer to black and flipping the back buffer to the front. Think of this as the generic game class; any future games you write will be subclasses of this class. Listing 8-6 shows portions of the dxWorld class (with some already-discussed elements removed).

Listing 8-6. The Ancestor Class for Future Games, dxWorld

```
Public MustInherit Class dxWorld

    Private FFrm As Form
    Private FNeedToRestore As Boolean = False

    Protected oRand As New Random
    Protected oDraw As Microsoft.DirectX.DirectDraw.Device
    Protected oFront As Microsoft.DirectX.DirectDraw.Surface
    Protected oBack As Microsoft.DirectX.DirectDraw.Surface
    Protected oJoystick As Microsoft.DirectX.DirectInput.Device

    Public Sub New(ByVal f As Form)
        MyBase.New()

        FFrm = f
        FFrm.Cursor.Dispose
        AddHandler FFrm.KeyDown, AddressOf FormKeyDown
        AddHandler FFrm.KeyUp, AddressOf FormKeyUp
        AddHandler FFrm.Disposed, AddressOf FormDispose

        InitializeDirectDraw()
        InitializeJoystick()
        InitializeWorld()

        Do While FFrm.Created
            DrawFrame()
        Loop
    End Sub

    Protected Overridable Sub FormDispose(ByVal sender As Object, _
      ByVal e As System.EventArgs)

        If Not (oJoystick Is Nothing) Then
            oJoystick.Unacquire()
        End If

    End Sub
```

```
ReadOnly Property WorldRectangle() As Rectangle
    Get
        Return New Rectangle(0, 0, WID, HGT)
    End Get
End Property

'override for better keyboard handling
Protected MustOverride Sub FormKeyDown(ByVal sender As Object, _
    ByVal e As System.Windows.Forms.KeyEventArgs)

'override for better keyboard handling
Protected Overridable Sub FormKeyUp(ByVal sender As Object, _
    <similar to prior discussion, removed>
End Sub

Private Sub InitializeDirectDraw()
    <similar to prior discussion, removed>
End Sub

'override to set up your world objects
Protected MustOverride Sub InitializeWorld()

'override when bitmaps have to be reloaded
Protected Overridable Sub RestoreSurfaces()
    oDraw.RestoreAllSurfaces()
End Sub

Private Sub DrawFrame()
    <similar to prior discussion, removed>
End Sub

'override. put all your drawing in here.
Protected Overridable Sub DrawWorldWithinFrame()
    Try
        oBack.ForeColor = Color.White
        oBack.DrawText(10, 10, "Press escape to exit", False)
    Catch oEX As Exception
        Debug.WriteLine(oEX.Message)
    End Try
End Sub
End Class
```

The constructor for the dxWorld class takes a form as a parameter, and this form is dynamically assigned event handlers for its KeyUp, KeyDown, and Dispose events. The form used as the parameter for this class needs to have almost no code in it at all, except for the code that sets up an instance of this dxWorld class (actually, an instance of a descendant of the dxWorld class because dxWorld itself is declared MustInherit). As shown in Listing 8-7, creating an instance of this game on the form happens in four lines of code on an empty form.

Listing 8-7. Creating a New dxWorld *Instance*

```
Public Class fMain
    Inherits System.Windows.Forms.Form

    Dim FWorld As dxWorld.dxWorld

    Private Sub fMain_Load(ByVal sender As System.Object, _
        ByVal e As System.EventArgs) Handles MyBase.Load

        FWorld = New dxWorld.dxSpaceRocks(Me)
    End Sub
End Class
```

All of the important variables in the dxWorld class are declared as protected so that they'll be accessible in the descendant classes. This includes the Surface variables for the front and back surface and the DirectDraw Device object. There's also a Random object instance set up so that random numbers can be generated from anywhere inside the class or its descendants.

Setting Up a Joystick

You might also notice a variable named oJoystick, which is of type Microsoft.DirectX.DirectInput.Device. Yes, the new game class will be able to handle joystick input as well as keyboard input. Getting the joystick ready happens in the InitializeJoystick method on the dxWorld class, as shown in Listing 8-8.

Listing 8-8. The InitializeJoystick *Method*

```
Private Sub InitializeJoystick()

    Dim oInst As DeviceInstance
    Dim oDOInst As DeviceObjectInstance
```

```
        'get the first attached joystick
      For Each oInst In Manager.GetDevices( _
        DeviceClass.GameControl, EnumDevicesFlags.AttachedOnly)

          oJoystick = New Microsoft.DirectX._
            DirectInput.Device(oInst.InstanceGuid)
          Exit For
      Next

      If Not (oJoystick Is Nothing) Then

          oJoystick.SetDataFormat(DeviceDataFormat.Joystick)
          oJoystick.SetCooperativeLevel(FFrm, _
            Microsoft.DirectX.DirectInput. _
            CooperativeLevelFlags.Exclusive Or _
            Microsoft.DirectX.DirectInput.CooperativeLevelFlags.Foreground)

          ' Set the numeric range for each axis to +/- 256.
          For Each oDOInst In oJoystick.Objects
            If 0 <> (oDOInst.ObjectId And _
              CInt(DeviceObjectTypeFlags.Axis)) Then

                oJoystick.Properties.SetRange(ParameterHow.ById, _
                  oDOInst.ObjectId, New InputRange(-256, +256))
            End If
          Next
      End If
  End Sub
```

InitializeJoystick retrieves the first game control device that it finds attached to the machine and then sets the range of all Axis objects within that joystick to have a range from –256 to +256. The standard game pad will have an x-axis and a y-axis; some three-dimensional controllers, such as SpaceBall, may have an x-axis, y-axis, and z-axis to be defined. Based on Listing 8-8, all axis objects associated with the joystick will be found and have their range set.

You'll see the code that shows how to poll the joystick for data and use it to update the game state later in the section "Setting Up the Ship Control Code." You first need to see how to set up the game elements themselves.

Creating the dxSprite Class

The base information to keep track of an object on the screen is stored in a class named dxSprite, as shown in Listing 8-9. This class is somewhat similar in structure to the SimpleDie class defined for the DirectXDemo project.

Listing 8-9. The dxSprite *Class Interface*

```
Public MustInherit Class dxSprite

    Public Event GetSurfaceData(ByVal sender As dxSprite, _
        ByRef oSource As Microsoft.DirectX.DirectDraw.Surface, _
        ByRef oRect As Rectangle)

    Property Location() As PointF
    Property Size() As Size
    Overridable Property Frame() As Integer
    ReadOnly Property BoundingBox() As Rectangle
    ReadOnly Property WorldBoundingBox() As Rectangle
    Property pShowBoundingBox() As Boolean
    ReadOnly Property Center() As PointF

    Public MustOverride Sub Move()
    Public Sub Draw(ByVal oSurf As Microsoft.DirectX.DirectDraw.Surface)
End Class
```

Much of the definition of this class is straightforward and doesn't require explanation. There are a few members, however, that do require a bit of clarification. The GetSurfaceData event is used as a callback so that the sprite class doesn't have to store surface (source bitmap) data directly. The reason you might not want to store surface data with the sprite was hinted at in the DirectXDemo application earlier. First, a game might contain dozens (hundreds?) of instances of the same sprite, and you certainly don't want to store multiple copies of the same bitmap data in each individual sprite instance.

Second, a single object may have several bitmaps to represent it depending on the state in which it might be. For the SpaceRocks game, for example, the ship object has three possible sprites: a ship with a fire trail, a ship without a trail, and an exploding ship for when it gets hit by a rock.

Using an event to retrieve the proper sprite based on the state of the object in question helps to decouple the sprite class from the game class. Note that there's nothing directly relevant to an arcade space-shooting-rock-type game in the class definition shown in Listing 8-9. The goal is to keep the dxSprite class generic enough to reuse in different projects (but you'll be creating SpaceRocks-specific subclasses for this game).

The Draw method of the sprite class is also nonstandard. As mentioned earlier in the chapter, DirectDraw doesn't take kindly to copying surfaces off the edge of the destination surface. The copy fails miserably, in fact, and crashes the program. Even if this crash is handled gracefully with a structure exception handler, the sprite "winks" out of existence as it reaches the edge of the destination surface instead of smoothly scrolling off the screen.

You must do some nasty rectangle manipulation to fix this problem. If you want to draw a ship partially off the left side of the screen, for example, then the program has to clip off the left side of the sprite and draw only the right portion of the rectangle on the left side. If the ship sprite is moving left, then each frame will clip more and more of the left side of the ship until it disappears. Figure 8-3 shows a sprite off the left side of the screen. The gray area is the area to be clipped.

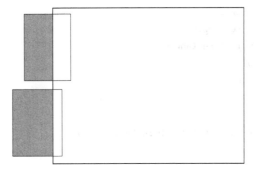

Figure 8-3. Two sprites partially off the left side of the screen. The gray area must be clipped, and only the white area should be drawn.

The nasty clipping math must also adjust the *bounding boxes* of each sprite. The bounding box represents a rectangle that surrounds the sprite and helps to test for collision between two sprites that might hit each other (the ship with a rock, for example). There are two representations of the bounding box stored for each sprite. One is declared in *sprite coordinates*, meaning that the upper-left corner in this bounding box is usually 0, 0. The second bounding box representation is stored in *world coordinates*, meaning that the upper-left corner is usually the same as the sprite's Location property (the location on the screen). Listing 8-10 shows a portion of the Draw method.

Listing 8-10. A Portion of the Draw Method

```
Public Sub Draw(ByVal oSurf As Microsoft.DirectX.DirectDraw.Surface)

    Dim oSource As Microsoft.DirectX.DirectDraw.Surface
    Dim oRect As Rectangle
    Dim oPt As Point
    Dim iDiff As Integer
```

```
RaiseEvent GetSurfaceData(Me, oSource, oRect)

If oSource Is Nothing Then
    Exit Sub
Else
    Try
        FWBB = Me.BoundingBox           'start w/ normal bbox

        'start at the location
        oPt = New Point(System.Math.Floor(Location.X), _
            System.Math.Floor(Location.Y))

        If oPt.X < 0 Then
            'draw partial on left side
            oRect = New Rectangle(oRect.Left - oPt.X, oRect.Top, _
              oRect.Width + oPt.X, oRect.Height)

            If oPt.X + FWBB.Left < 0 Then

                FWBB = New Rectangle(0, FWBB.Top, _
                FWBB.Width + (oPt.X + FWBB.Left), FWBB.Height)

            Else

                FWBB = New Rectangle(FWBB.Left + oPt.X, FWBB.Top, _
                    FWBB.Width, FWBB.Height)

            End If
            oPt.X = 0
        End If

        <lots of other rectangle-clipping code removed>

        'should never happen, just in case
        If oRect.Width <= 0 Or oRect.Height <= 0 Then Return

        'offset the bounding box by the world coordinates
        FWBB.Offset(oPt.X, oPt.Y)

        'draw the sprite
        oSurf.DrawFast(oPt.X, oPt.Y, oSource, oRect, _
         DrawFastFlags.DoNotWait Or DrawFastFlags.SourceColorKey)
```

```
                  'draw the bounding box
                 If Me.pShowBoundingBox Then
                     oSurf.ForeColor = Color.Red
                     oSurf.DrawBox(FWBB.Left, FWBB.Top, FWBB.Right, FWBB.Bottom)
                 End If

             Catch oEx As Exception
                 Debug.WriteLine("-------------------------------------")
                 Debug.WriteLine(oEx.Message)
             End Try
          End If

      End Sub
```

Creating the dxSpaceRocks Class

The SpaceRocks game is implemented in the class named dxSpaceRocks, which is
a descendant of the dxWorld class. This class contains the classes that store all of
the game objects, including the ship, the rocks, and any bullets currently flying
around. The rocks and bullets are stored in a different way because there can be
multiple instances of these classes in the game at one time. The player's ship is
always a lone instance, so the class that contains the ship information has
a much different structure.

Setting Up the Game Class

Listing 8-11 shows the declaration of the game class and the instantiation of the
private variables that track all the game objects.

Listing 8-11. The dxSpaceRocks *Class with the Game Object Class Definition and
Initialization Code*

```
Public Class dxSpaceRocks
    Inherits dxWorld

    Private FShip As dxShipSprite
    Private FRocks As dxRockCollection
    Private FBullets As dxBulletCollection

    Protected Overrides Sub InitializeWorld()

        Dim oRand As New Random
```

```
        FShip = New dxShipSprite
        FShip.Location = New PointF(100, 100)
        FShip.Size = New Size(96, 96)
        FShip.pShowBoundingBox = False

        FRocks = New dxRockCollection
        FRocks.pShowBoundingBox = False

        FBullets = New dxBulletCollection
        FBullets.pShowBoundingBox = False

    End Sub

    Protected Overrides Sub RestoreSurfaces()
        MyBase.RestoreSurfaces()

        FShip.RestoreSurfaces(oDraw)
        FRocks.RestoreSurfaces(oDraw)
        FBullets.RestoreSurfaces(oDraw)
    End Sub

    <code removed>

End Class
```

The rock and bullet storage classes are collections, and their class names refer to them as such. The ship class, however, is a direct descendant of the dxSprite class, so its initialization is a bit different from the other two.

The procedure RestoreSurfaces, if you'll recall, is called when bitmap surface objects have to be re-created. Because the game class itself isn't storing any source surface objects, each game class has its own RestoreSurfaces method, and this method is called from the game's method of the same name. This procedure was originally declared as protected and Overrideable in the base dxWorld class, which gives you the ability to access it and override it in the subclass.

Setting Up the Game Class Drawing and Movement

Drawing for all descendants of the dxWorld class happens by overriding the protected method DrawWorldWithinFrame. Listing 8-12 shows that method.

Listing 8-12. The `DrawWorldWithinFrame` *Method*

```
Protected Overrides Sub DrawWorldWithinFrame()

   Dim p As New Point((WID / 2) - 40, 10)

   MyBase.DrawWorldWithinFrame()

   'joysticks don't generate events, so we update the ship
   'based on joystick state each turn
   UpdateShipState()

   FShip.Move()
   FRocks.Move()
   FBullets.Move()

   FBullets.Draw(oBack)
   FShip.Draw(oBack)
   FRocks.Draw(oBack)

   FBullets.BreakRocks(FRocks)

   oBack.ForeColor = Color.White
   Select Case FShip.Status
      Case ShipStatus.ssAlive
         oBack.DrawText(p.X, p.Y, "Lives Left: " & _
           FShip.LivesLeft, False)
          If FRocks.CollidingWith(FShip.WorldBoundingBox, _
            bBreakRock:=False) Then
              FShip.KillMe()
          End If

      Case ShipStatus.ssDying
         oBack.DrawText(p.X, p.Y, "Oops.", False)

      Case ShipStatus.ssDead
         If FShip.LivesLeft = 0 Then
            oBack.DrawText(p.X, p.Y, "Game Over", False)
         Else
            oBack.DrawText(p.X, p.Y, _
               "Hit SpaceBar to make ship appear " + _
                  "in middle of screen", False)
         End If
   End Select

End Sub
```

The DrawWorldWithinFrame method runs once per every "clock tick" of the game engine. It controls both object movement and object drawing. At the start of the method is a call to a procedure named UpdateShipState. This procedure (described next) changes the state of the ship based on what joystick buttons are being pressed. Then, the program calls a Move method on the ship class and the rock and bullet collections. The Move method updates the position of every game object based on its current location, the direction it's traveling, and the speed at which it's traveling.

Once all the game objects have been moved, the Draw method of the three game class objects is called, passing in the variable that holds the back buffer DirectDraw surface. You've already seen the Draw method for the dxSprite class (with all the rectangle clipping logic), and the Draw method on the collection classes simply calls the Draw method for each dxSprite in their respective collections.

The remainder of the DrawWorldWithinFrame method handles the drawing of a text message at the top of the screen based on the current state of the player's ship. The game will report the number of lives the player has left, report a simple *Oops* as the ship explodes because of collision with a rock, give instructions on how to make the ship reappear if the user has lives left, or report *Game Over* if no lives remain. One other task is handled within this Case statement, and that's the collision check between the ship and the rocks (the CollidingWith method on the FRocks variable).

Setting Up the Ship Control Code

The remainder of the dxSpaceRocks class handles ship movement via keyboard or joystick. Listing 8-13 shows this code.

Listing 8-13. Ship Movement Code for the dxSpaceRocks *Class*

```
Public Class dxSpaceRocks
    Inherits dxWorld

    Private FLeftPressed As Boolean = False
    Private FRightPressed As Boolean = False
    Private FUpPressed As Boolean = False
    Private FSpacePressed As Boolean = False

    <some code removed>

    Protected Overrides Sub FormKeyDown(ByVal sender As Object, _
      ByVal e As System.Windows.Forms.KeyEventArgs)
```

```vb
        Select Case e.KeyCode
            Case Keys.Left
                FLeftPressed = True
            Case Keys.Right
                FRightPressed = True
            Case Keys.Up
                FUpPressed = True
            Case Keys.Space
                FSpacePressed = True
            Case Keys.B
                FShip.pShowBoundingBox = Not FShip.pShowBoundingBox
                FRocks.pShowBoundingBox = Not FRocks.pShowBoundingBox
                FBullets.pShowBoundingBox = Not FBullets.pShowBoundingBox
        End Select
End Sub


Protected Overrides Sub FormKeyUp(ByVal sender As Object, _
    ByVal e As System.Windows.Forms.KeyEventArgs)

    MyBase.FormKeyUp(sender, e)

    Select Case e.KeyCode
        Case Keys.Left
            FLeftPressed = False
        Case Keys.Right
            FRightPressed = False
        Case Keys.Up
            FUpPressed = False
        End Select
End Sub


Private Sub UpdateShipState()

    Dim oState As New JoystickState
    Dim bButtons As Byte()
    Dim b As Byte

    Dim p As PointF

    If Not oJoystick Is Nothing Then

        Try
            oJoystick.Poll()
```

```
    Catch oEX As InputException
        If TypeOf oEX Is NotAcquiredException Or _
          TypeOf oEX Is InputLostException Then

            Try
                ' Acquire the device.
                oJoystick.Acquire()
            Catch
                Exit Sub
            End Try

        End If
    End Try

    Try
        oState = oJoystick.CurrentJoystickState
    Catch
        Exit Sub
    End Try

    'ship is turning if x axis movement
    FShip.IsTurningRight = (oState.X > 100) Or FRightPressed
    FShip.IsTurningLeft = (oState.X < -100) Or FLeftPressed
    FShip.ThrustersOn = (oState.Y < -100) Or FUpPressed

    'any button pushed on the joystick will work
    bButtons = oState.GetButtons()
    For Each b In bButtons
        If (b And &H80) <> 0 Then
            FSpacePressed = True
            Exit For
        End If
    Next

Else
    FShip.IsTurningRight = FRightPressed
    FShip.IsTurningLeft = FLeftPressed
    FShip.ThrustersOn = FUpPressed
End If
```

```
            If FSpacePressed Then
                Select Case FShip.Status
                    Case ShipStatus.ssDead
                        'center screen
                        FShip.BringMeToLife(WID \ 2 - FShip.Size.Width \ 2, _
                                            HGT \ 2 - FShip.Size.Height \ 2)
                    Case ShipStatus.ssAlive
                        p = FShip.Center
                        p.X = p.X - 16
                        p.Y = p.Y - 16

                        FBullets.Shoot(p, FShip.Angle)
                End Select
                FSpacePressed = False
            End If
        End Sub
End Class
```

Keyboard state is stored in Boolean variables named FLeftPressed, FRightPressed, FUpPressed, and FSpacePressed. These variables are set to True in the KeyDown event and to False in the KeyUp event (if the appropriate key is indeed being pressed, that is). By storing the variables in this way, the game allows for object movement as long as the correct key is down. For example, once a user presses the up arrow, the ship should have its thrusters on until the key is released. The Boolean FUpPressed will stay True as long as the arrow is down.

The B key is the last key that affects the game—it turns the bounding boxes on and off for debugging purposes.

NOTE   *This was especially useful to me as I slowly coded the "sprite-half-off-the-screen" code in the* dxSprite's Draw *method (see Listing 8-10 to relive the pain).*

The function UpdateShipState, called once per drawing frame, polls the joystick and keyboard Boolean variables for their states and updates the state of the ship accordingly. For example, if the joystick's x-axis has a value that's greater than 100, then the ship is turning clockwise. A move in the negative y direction on the joystick is the cue to turn on the thrusters. Pressing Button 1 on the joystick (or pressing the spacebar) either fires a bullet or brings a dead ship back to life.

Setting Up the Ship Class

The dxShipSprite class is a descendant of the dxSprite class discussed earlier. This class controls the player's ship as it cruises around on the screen. There are three graphics required for the ship—one for the ship with thrusters off, one with thrusters on, and one for an explosion sequence for when the ship is biting the dust. Figure 8-4 shows one frame of each of the bitmaps.

Figure 8-4. The first frame of the each of the three ship graphics

Drawing the Ship

The two ship graphics consist of 24 frames. Each frame represents a different rotation of the ship in a circle. There are 15 degrees of rotation between each frame (360 degrees / 24 frames = 15 degrees per frame). The explosion sequence is only six frames and was designed by hand (and not very well; bear in mind that I don't consider computer graphics design among my talents).

Drawing the correct graphic at the correct time is a function of what state the ship is in at the moment. There's an enumerated type declared called ShipStatus that defines whether the ship is currently okay, in the middle of exploding, or dead and gone. If the ship is gone, then the program obviously doesn't have to draw it at all. If the ship is in the middle of exploding, then the explosion graphic is chosen for display. If the ship is okay, then one of the two ship graphics are displayed, either with or without the thruster fire. The ship control code in Listing 8-13 hinted at the fact that the ship sprite has a property named ThrustersOn, and this property determines which of the two ship bitmaps to draw. Listing 8-14 shows the portion of the dxShipSprite class that loads the three bitmaps into DirectDraw Surface variables and the code that selects the correct surface to draw in a given frame.

Listing 8-14. Ship Sprite State and Graphics-Related Code

```
Public Enum ShipStatus
    ssAlive = 0
    ssDying = 1
    ssDead = 2
End Enum

Public Class dxShipSprite
    Inherits dxSprite

    Private FShipSurfaceOff As Microsoft.DirectX.DirectDraw.Surface
    Private FShipSurfaceOn As Microsoft.DirectX.DirectDraw.Surface
    Private FShipSurfaceBoom As Microsoft.DirectX.DirectDraw.Surface

    Public Sub New()
        MyBase.new()
        AddHandler Me.GetSurfaceData, AddressOf GetShipSurfaceData
    End Sub

    Private FStatus As ShipStatus
    ReadOnly Property Status() As ShipStatus
        Get
            Return FStatus
        End Get
    End Property

    'we can keep surfaces in the ship
    'sprite class because there's only one of them
    Public Sub RestoreSurfaces(ByVal oDraw As _
      Microsoft.DirectX.DirectDraw.Device)

        Dim oCK As New ColorKey

        Dim a As Reflection.Assembly = _
          System.Reflection.Assembly.GetExecutingAssembly()

        If Not FShipSurfaceOff Is Nothing Then
          FShipSurfaceOff.Dispose()
          FShipSurfaceOff = Nothing
        End If

        FShipSurfaceOff = New Surface(a.GetManifestResourceStream( _
          "SpaceRocks.ShipNoFire.bmp"), New SurfaceDescription, oDraw)
        FShipSurfaceOff.SetColorKey(ColorKeyFlags.SourceDraw, oCK)
```

```
      If Not FShipSurfaceOn Is Nothing Then
          FShipSurfaceOn.Dispose()
          FShipSurfaceOn = Nothing
      End If

      FShipSurfaceOn = New Surface(a.GetManifestResourceStream( _
         "SpaceRocks.ShipFire.bmp"), New SurfaceDescription, oDraw)
      FShipSurfaceOn.SetColorKey(ColorKeyFlags.SourceDraw, oCK)

      If Not FShipSurfaceBoom Is Nothing Then
          FShipSurfaceBoom.Dispose()
          FShipSurfaceBoom = Nothing
      End If

      FShipSurfaceBoom = New Surface(a.GetManifestResourceStream( _
         "SpaceRocks.Boom.bmp"), New SurfaceDescription, oDraw)
      FShipSurfaceBoom.SetColorKey(ColorKeyFlags.SourceDraw, oCK)

End Sub

Private Sub GetShipSurfaceData(ByVal aSprite As dxSprite, _
   ByRef oSurf As Surface, ByRef oRect As Rectangle)

   Dim aShip As dxShipSprite = CType(aSprite, dxShipSprite)

   Select Case aShip.Status
      Case ShipStatus.ssDead
          oSurf = Nothing

      Case ShipStatus.ssDying
          oSurf = FShipSurfaceBoom

      Case ShipStatus.ssAlive

          If aShip.ThrustersOn AndAlso _
            oRand.Next(0, Integer.MaxValue) Mod 10 <> 0 Then

              oSurf = FShipSurfaceOn
          Else
              oSurf = FShipSurfaceOff
          End If

   End Select
```

```
        oRect = New Rectangle((aShip.Frame Mod 6) * 96, _
            (aShip.Frame \ 6) * 96, 96, 96)


    End Sub
End Class
```

The `RestoreSurfaces` code is similar to what you saw in the DirectXDemo application, except that there are three surfaces to load instead of one. The routine `GetShipSurfaceData` is special because it serves as the event handler for the `GetSurfaceData` event for this object. If you'll recall, the `GetSurfaceData` event is raised from within the `Draw` method of the `dxSprite` class (see Listing 8-10 if you need a reminder). When the `Draw` method is ready to draw, it raises this event and expects the event handler to pass back the correct source `Surface` object that needs to be drawn, as well as a `Rectangle` object that indicates which portion of the source bitmap to draw. The routine `GetShipSurfaceData` does all of that work for the ship class. Based on the state of the ship and whether its thrusters are on or off, the appropriate bitmap is returned. The last line constructs a source rectangle based on the value of the `Frame` property, based on the knowledge that all of the ship graphics are 96-pixels wide and high.

 NOTE *The game uses one additional trick when selecting a bitmap to display. Ten percent of the time, the* `GetShipSurfaceData` *routine returns the ship graphic without the thruster fire, even when thrusters are on. This gives the fire a little "flicker" effect.*

Moving the Ship

The ship's current location is stored in the `Location` property defined on the ancestor `dxSprite` class. The trick is figuring out how to move the location based on the current angle of the ship, whether the thrusters are currently on, and how long they've been on.

Properties control the velocity of the ship, which is how many pixels it moves per frame in both the x and y directions, and its acceleration, which controls how fast the velocity is increasing.

Listing 8-15 lists the `Move` method of the ship class, which is called once during every frame by the `dxSpaceRocks` game class.

Listing 8-15. The Move *Method of* dxShipSprite

```
Public Overrides Sub Move()

    Dim dx, dy As Single

    'we're only moving every x frames
    FSkipFrame = (FSkipFrame + 1) Mod 1000
    If FSkipFrame Mod 3 = 0 Then

        Select Case Me.Status
            Case ShipStatus.ssAlive
                Turn()

                If ThrustersOn Then
                    Acceleration += 1

                    dy = -Math.Sin(FAngle * Math.PI / 180) * Acceleration
                    dx = Math.Cos(FAngle * Math.PI / 180) * Acceleration

                    Velocity = New PointF(Velocity.X + dx, Velocity.Y + dy)
                Else
                    Acceleration = 0
                End If

            Case ShipStatus.ssDying
                Frame += 1

                Velocity = New PointF(0, 0)
                Acceleration = 0

                'we're done drawing the boom
                If Frame >= 6 Then
                    FStatus = ShipStatus.ssDead
                End If

            Case ShipStatus.ssDead
                'nothing
        End Select

    End If

    Location = New PointF(Location.X + Velocity.X, Location.Y + Velocity.Y)

End Sub
```

Note that there's a "governor" of sorts on the Move class in the form of an integer variable named FSkipFrame. This variable updates in every execution of the Move method, but it allows actual velocity and acceleration to change in every third execution. Without this governor, the ship's controls are far too touchy and hard to control.

The Acceleration property is an integer that keeps increasing as long as the ship's thrusters are turned on. (Actually, there's maximum acceleration defined in the property, so it does max out eventually.) The Acceleration variable, along with the current angle the ship is facing and some basic trigonometry, help determine the speed of the ship during this turn in both the x and y directions. This speed is stored in the Velocity property.

At the bottom of the Move method, the calculated velocity is added to the current location, which yields the new location of the ship.

Setting Up Rocks and Rock Collections

The rocks are simpler structures than the ship because they move at a constant speed and in a constant direction, and they aren't (directly) affected by the game player's control. This simplicity is counteracted by the fact that the game has to keep track of an undetermined number of them, however. Thus, a "manager" class keeps track of each rock.

The (rather cool) rock graphics themselves were created courtesy of POV-RAY models from Scott Hudson. The models represent digital representations of actual "potential earth-crossing" asteroids. Please visit the Web site http://www.eecs.wsu.edu/~hudson/Research/Asteroids for further information.

 NOTE *You can find information on POV-RAY and raytracing in Appendix B, "Using POV-RAY and Moray."*

Creating the Rock Class

The rock class itself keeps track of the size of the rock (there are three possible sizes), the direction it's moving, which of the two graphics to use, which direction it's spinning, and how fast it's spinning. Listing 8-16 shows the public interface for this class.

Listing 8-16. The dxRockSprite *Class and Enumerated Type for Determining Rock Size*

```
Public Enum dxRockSize
    rsLarge = 0
    rsMed = 1
    rsSmall = 2
End Enum

Public Class dxRockSprite
    Inherits dxSprite

    Public Event RockBroken(ByVal aRock As dxRockSprite)
    Property pAlternateModel() As Boolean
    Property pSpinReverse() As Boolean
    Property pRockSize() As dxRockSize
    Property pRotSpeed() As Integer
    Property Velocity() As PointF
    Public Overrides Sub Move()
    Public Sub Break()

End Class
```

Details of this class are mostly trivial and unworthy of you (who by this time is a nearly expert game programmer). The pRockSize property is mildly interesting in that the bounding box of the rock is different depending on the size of the rock.

Creating the Rock Collection Class

The dxRockCollection class is much more interesting than the rock class. This class keeps track of the six different DirectDraw Surface objects that store the rock graphics (two rock shapes in three sizes each). It also keeps the pointers to each individual rock class and handles all of the interaction between the game and the rocks (you can think of this class as a sort of "rock broker"). To that end, several methods on the collection class simply perform functionality upon each rock in the collection. The Draw method is one such method, shown in Listing 8-17, which merely calls the like-named method on each object in the collection.

Listing 8-17. The Draw *Method (and Some Others)*

```
Public Sub Draw(ByVal oSurf As Microsoft.DirectX.DirectDraw.Surface)

    Dim aRock As dxRockSprite

    For Each aRock In FRocks
        aRock.Draw(oSurf)
    Next

End Sub
```

Another interesting piece of functionality in the rock collection is the pair of overloaded AddRock methods, shown in Listing 8-18. These methods add a new rock to the collection. It also includes the code that runs when a rock is shot and split in two.

Listing 8-18. Adding a New Rock to the Game in One of Two Ways

```
Private Overloads Function AddRock()

    Dim oPt As PointF
    'start location along the edges

    Select Case FRand.Next(0, Integer.MaxValue) Mod 4
        Case 0
            oPt = New PointF(0, FRand.Next(0, Integer.MaxValue) Mod HGT)
        Case 1
            oPt = New PointF(WID, FRand.Next(0, Integer.MaxValue) Mod HGT)
        Case 2
            oPt = New PointF(FRand.Next(0, Integer.MaxValue) Mod WID, 0)
        Case 3
            oPt = New PointF(FRand.Next(0, Integer.MaxValue) Mod WID, HGT)
    End Select

    Return AddRock(dxRockSize.rsLarge, oPt)
End Function

Private Overloads Function AddRock(ByVal pSize As dxRockSize, _
  . ByVal p As PointF) As dxRockSprite

    Dim aRock As dxRockSprite

  aRock = New dxRockSprite
    With aRock
```

```
        .pShowBoundingBox = Me.pShowBoundingBox
        .pAlternateModel = FRand.Next(0, Integer.MaxValue) Mod 2 = 0
        .pSpinReverse = FRand.Next(0, Integer.MaxValue) Mod 2 = 0
        .pRotSpeed = FRand.Next(0, Integer.MaxValue) Mod 3
        .pRockSize = pSize
        Select Case pSize
            Case dxRockSize.rsLarge
                .Size = New Size(96, 96)
            Case dxRockSize.rsMed
                .Size = New Size(64, 64)
            Case dxRockSize.rsSmall
                .Size = New Size(32, 32)
        End Select

        .Location = p

        Do   'no straight up/down or left/right
            .Velocity = New PointF(FRand.Next(-3, 3), FRand.Next(-3, 3))
        Loop Until .Velocity.X <> 0 And .Velocity.Y <> 0

        .Move() 'the first move makes sure they're off the edge

        AddHandler .GetSurfaceData, AddressOf GetRockSurfaceData
            AddHandler .RockBroken, AddressOf RockBroken
    End With
        FRocks.Add(aRock)
End Function


Private Sub RockBroken(ByVal aRock As dxRockSprite)

    Select Case aRock.pRockSize
        Case dxRockSize.rsLarge
            AddRock(dxRockSize.rsMed, aRock.Location)
            AddRock(dxRockSize.rsMed, aRock.Location)

        Case dxRockSize.rsMed
            AddRock(dxRockSize.rsSmall, aRock.Location)
            AddRock(dxRockSize.rsSmall, aRock.Location)

        Case dxRockSize.rsSmall
            'nothing
    End Select
    FRocks.Remove(aRock)
End Sub
```

The first AddRock function is the one that's used when a new, large size rock is to be added to the game. It takes no parameters. Its job is to select a random point along one of the four edges of the screen, and then it calls the second AddRock method, passing along the size of the new rock (always large) and the location it has selected.

The second AddRock method actually creates the new instance of the dxRockSprite class, sets up all of its properties, and then adds it to the ArrayList that holds all of the rock objects. This second AddRock method is used when a rock is shot and splits into two smaller pieces. You can see this code in the RockBroken routine, which serves as the event handler for the rock class event of the same name. When a large rock is broken, two medium-sized rocks are spawned at the same location of the large rock, and then the large rock is removed from the ArrayList named FRocks (and thus from the game). When a medium rock is broken, two smaller rocks are spawned in the same location, and the medium rock is removed from the ArrayList.

The last interesting function in the rock collection class is the CollidingWith function, which determines if an outside agent has crashed into a rock and whether that rock should break as a result (see Listing 8-19).

Listing 8-19. The CollidingWith *Function*

```
Public Function CollidingWith(ByVal aRect As Rectangle, _
    ByVal bBreakRock As Boolean) As Boolean

    Dim aRock As dxRockSprite

    For Each aRock In FRocks
        If aRock.WorldBoundingBox.IntersectsWith(aRect) Then
            If bBreakRock Then
                aRock.Break()
            End If
            Return True
        End If
    Next

    Return False
End Function
```

The collision code in the game relies on the bounding boxes of all of the game objects (ship, rocks, and bullets). The bounding boxes are all represented by .NET Framework Rectangle objects. One of the most useful methods built into the Rectangle class is the IntersectsWith class, which returns True if the current rectangle overlaps another passed-in rectangle parameter. The function shown in Listing 8-19 checks to see if the bounding box for each rock in the collection intersects with the rectangle that's passed into the function. If it finds an intersection, the function returns True and the rock involved in the collision either breaks or doesn't break, depending on the value of the bBreakRock parameter (collisions with bullets break the rock, and a collision with the ship leaves the rock intact).

Setting Up Bullets and Bullet Collections

Keeping with the pattern of discussing things in decreasing order of complexity, the bullet class is the simplest of the three major game elements. The bullet has only one graphic (with only a single frame) and can move in a single direction at a fixed speed. Like the rocks class, a "manager" class keeps track of multiple bullets on the screen.

Creating the Bullet Class

The bullet class is simple and short enough to list here in its entirety, as shown in Listing 8-20.

Listing 8-20. The Bullet Sprite Class

```
Public Class dxBulletSprite
    Inherits dxSprite

    Private FFrameAliveCount As Integer

    Sub New()
        MyBase.New()
        FBoundingBox = New Rectangle(10, 10, 12, 12)
    End Sub

    Private FVelocity As PointF
    Property Velocity() As PointF
        Get
            Return FVelocity
        End Get
        Set(ByVal Value As PointF)
            FVelocity = Value
        End Set
    End Property
```

```
    Public Overrides Sub Move()
        Location = New PointF(Location.X + Velocity.X, _
            Location.Y + Velocity.Y)
        FFrameAliveCount += 1
    End Sub

    ReadOnly Property pFrameAliveCount() As Integer
        Get
            Return FFrameAliveCount
        End Get
    End Property
End Class
```

The bullet class keeps track of velocity and a property known as
FrameAliveCount. This property determines when a bullet has traveled far enough
and should be removed from the screen. The Move method is extremely simple. It
changes the location of the sprite by the value of the Velocity property in both
the x and y directions.

Creating the Bullet Collection Class

The collection class that keeps track of multiple bullets shares many features
with the rock collection class already discussed. It uses an ArrayList to store
multiple instances of the dxBulltetSprite class. Listing 8-21 shows the Shoot
method, which brings a new instance of the bullet class into the world.

Listing 8-21. The Shoot *Method*

```
Public Sub Shoot(ByVal p As PointF, ByVal iAngle As Integer)

    If FBullets.Count >= 4 Then Exit Sub

    Dim dx, dy As Single
    Dim aBullet As dxBulletSprite

    aBullet = New dxBulletSprite
    With aBullet
        .pShowBoundingBox = Me.pShowBoundingBox
        .Location = p
```

```
        dy = -Math.Sin(iAngle * Math.PI / 180) * 6
        dx = Math.Cos(iAngle * Math.PI / 180) * 6

        .Velocity = New PointF(dx, dy)
        .Move()

        AddHandler .GetSurfaceData, AddressOf GetBulletSurfaceData
    End With
    FBullets.Add(aBullet)
End Sub
```

The Shoot method first checks that there are fewer than four bullets already floating around in space. If four bullets are already on the screen, then the method returns without firing. If this check succeeds, though, then a new dxBulletSprite object is instantiated, properties are set (including the Velocity property, calculated from the angle parameter pass into the function), and the bullet is added to the ArrayList.

The method BreakRocks, shown in Listing 8-22, is called once in each drawing loop to see if the bullet has found its target.

Listing 8-22. The Method BreakRocks

```
Public Sub BreakRocks(ByVal FRocks As dxRockCollection)

    Dim aBullet As dxBulletSprite
    Dim i As Integer

    'check each bullet to see if it hits a rock
    'have to use a loop so you don't skip over when deleting
    i = 0
    Do While i < FBullets.Count
        aBullet = FBullets.Item(i)
        If FRocks.CollidingWith(aBullet.WorldBoundingBox, _
            bBreakRock:=True) Then

            FBullets.Remove(aBullet)
        Else
            i = i + 1
        End If
    Loop
End Sub
```

The method BreakRocks uses the CollidingWith function discussed in Listing 8-19 to determine if any of the bullets in this collection have collided with any rock in the game. A slightly tricky loop is employed in this method that requires some explanation. Whenever a collection is iterated and the possibility exists that elements in the collection will be removed during that iteration, then the program should never use the standard For..Each method to iterate, or the result is that items in the collection will be skipped. Instead, you should use a loop such as the one shown in Listing 8-22. This loop uses an integer counter to keep track of the place in the iteration. The trick is that if an element in the collection is deleted (in this case, a bullet), then the loop counter *isn't incremented*. Say the loop is an element 5 in a collection of 10, and this element is removed from the collection. After the removal, all of the elements after element 5 have "slid down" one place in the order, meaning the former element 6 is now element 5. By not incrementing the counter after a delete, the next iteration of the loop makes sure to check that next element.

Summary

Whew! What you may have thought was a reasonably simple game ended up being a complicated set of classes with some complex relationships. The result of this code, however, is a decent set of reusable classes for creating DirectDraw games. A "world" class encapsulates much of the DirectDraw setup code and surfaces for page flipping, a "sprite" class abstracts an on-screen object (which is generic enough for many uses because it doesn't attempt to store surface data within itself, instead employing an event to retrieve surface data from an outside source), and several examples of "manager" classes control several instances of similar game elements. You should be able to use this example and become the next Atari.

CHAPTER 9

Learning Other Object-Oriented Programming Topics

THIS CHAPTER COVERS A FEW important Visual Basic .NET topics that don't merit an entire chapter on their own but that represent some new features of the language and the underlying framework.

Understanding Structured Exception Handling

The sample projects that accompany this book contain numerous examples of structured exception handlers. This programming construct takes the form shown in Listing 9-1.

Listing 9-1. Exception Handling Syntax

```
Try
    <code block>
[Catch [e as Exception]]
    <exception handling block>
[Catch [e as Exception]]
    <exception handling block>
[Finally]
    <always-execute block>
End Try
```

An exception handler begins with a Try statement, followed by any number of statements. There may or may not be a Catch block. The Catch block, which may define a class of exception that it handles, runs if a runtime exception matching that class occurs in the previous Try block. The Finally block (also optional) is guaranteed to always run, regardless of any exceptions thrown or handled previously.

One caveat on the optional portions of an exception handler: Both the Catch clause and the Finally clause are optional, but the Try block must contain one or the other. For example, the following code block isn't legal:

```
Try
    <code block>
End Try
```

Not only is the previous code block illegal, it's also useless because it doesn't handle any exceptions that might occur within the code.

Exception handlers require a new way of error handling. The old-school Visual Basic programmer used to conceive of every possible error while developing the program and build tests into the code to handle every type of problem. Consider a program that writes a complicated data structure to disk (say a CAD program or a Doom level editor). Suppose that the code that writes the complicated data structure is several thousand lines of code. The process would be as follows: Open the file; write the header; write structure A; write substructure A1, A2, and A3; write structure B; write substructure A, B, and C; and so on. Now, consider all of the errors that might occur as this code runs:

- **Permission errors**: It's possible that the user would try to write a file to a read-only location, such as to a CD-ROM or an area of the network to which the user doesn't have write access. Or, the user might attempt to overwrite a file that's marked as read-only.

- **Media errors**: Perhaps there's a bad cluster on the destination media, and the write operation fails at some point.

- **Out of disk space errors**: The media may run out of disk space as the file is being written.

These are only a few of the problems that might occur while writing. So, how might the Visual Basic programmer handle these problems? The first problem, checking for write access on the destination drive, isn't too big of a problem. The program can write the header or a short portion of the file, check for any return codes or problems that might have occurred, and then stop the write operation at that point and exit the program cleanly.

The second and third problems are much more difficult to handle cleanly, however, because they could happen at any time during the data save operation. The save could get 5 percent through—or 50 percent or 95 percent—and then a failure could occur. Should the program be written in such a way that it checks after every write to disk that the write was successful? For example:

```
Write to disk
If WriteFailed then PrintErrorMessage, exit.
Write to disk
If WriteFailed then PrintErrorMessage, exit.
Write to disk
If WriteFailed then PrintErrorMessage, exit.
```

Ugh. Surely there's a better way. The most common way Visual Basic 6 developers handled errors such as running out of disk space or write errors was to not handle them at all and hope they never occurred.

One of the primary powers of structured exception handling is that the program doesn't have to check for errors after every line. Instead, the program designates that entire block of code should run, and if an exception happens on any of those lines, then execution jumps to the exception handler. Without focusing on exact .NET class names or file Input/Output (I/O) syntax, Listing 9-2 shows how you might write the complex data saver.

Listing 9-2. Pseudocode for the Complex Data Writing Routine

```
bError = false

Try
    Open File for Write
Catch PermissionException
    Print "Permission Error"
    bError = true
Catch AnyOtherException
    Print "Some other Error"
    bError = true
End Try

If bError then exit sub

Try
    Write Some Stuff
    Write Some More Stuff
    Write Still More Stuff
    Write An Incredible Amount Of Stuff
Catch MediaFailException
    Print "Bad Media"
Catch OutOfSpaceException
    Print "Media Out Of Space"
```

```
Catch AnyOtherException
    Print "Some other Error"
Finally
    Close File
End Try
```

This code is about a zillion times cleaner because it handles the three potential errors identified earlier, and it does so regardless of how much more code you might add to the writing block. You can identify two exception handlers in this code. The first makes sure the file can be opened for writing. If a permission exception occurs, the user is told as such through some mechanism (identified only as Print in the pseudocode), and the routine exits. For even more robust error handling, this code includes a second exception handler that will catch all exceptions except the permission exceptions already caught by the previous block.

The second exception handler looks for the specific errors discussed earlier, plus it includes the catchall for anything you haven't thought of to this point. It also contains a Finally block that makes 100-percent sure the file closes, no matter what errors may have occurred earlier.

I became grateful for one particular exception handler during the development of this book: the exception handler in the DirectDraw code for the dxSprite class discussed in Chapter 8, "Using DirectX." By default, a DirectDraw program with an unhandled exception locks up the machine to a degree because the DirectDraw window doesn't disappear to make way for Visual Studio to display any error that has occurred. Because of this, the best way to debug the drawing code is to place the DirectDraw code inside an exception handler and write any error that occurred to the Debug window. Listing 9-3 shows this exception handler.

Listing 9-3. Exception Handling in a DirectDraw World

```
Try
    FWBB = Me.BoundingBox              'start w/ normal bbox

    'start at the location
    oPt = New Point(System.Math.Floor(Location.X), _
        System.Math.Floor(Location.Y))

    If oPt.X < 0 Then
        'draw partial on left side
        oRect = New Rectangle(oRect.Left - oPt.X, oRect.Top, _
            oRect.Width + oPt.X, oRect.Height)
```

```
    If oPt.X + FWBB.Left < 0 Then

        FWBB = New Rectangle(0, FWBB.Top, _
        FWBB.Width + (oPt.X + FWBB.Left), FWBB.Height)

    Else

        FWBB = New Rectangle(FWBB.Left + oPt.X, FWBB.Top, _
           FWBB.Width, FWBB.Height)

    End If
    oPt.X = 0
End If

<lots of range checking code removed>

 'should never happen, just in case
 If oRect.Width <= 0 Or oRect.Height <= 0 Then Return

 'offset the bounding box by the world coordinates
 FWBB.Offset(oPt.X, oPt.Y)

 'draw the sprite
 oSurf.DrawFast(oPt.X, oPt.Y, oSource, oRect, _
    DrawFastFlags.DoNotWait Or DrawFastFlags.SourceColorKey)

 'draw the bounding box
 If Me.pShowBoundingBox Then
    oSurf.ForeColor = Color.Red

    oSurf.DrawBox(FWBB.Left, FWBB.Top, FWBB.Right, FWBB.Bottom)

 End If

Catch oEx As Exception
    Debug.WriteLine("------------------------------------")
    Debug.WriteLine(oEx.Message)
End Try
```

Understanding Garbage Collection

This book has barely discussed memory concerns at all, and that's by design. As you probably know by now, .NET programming languages feature an automatic "garbage collector" that cleans up memory automatically. Thus, the code snippet in Listing 9-4 is legal and even preferable, but an old C++ programmer might break out in hives just looking at it.

Listing 9-4. Allocating Objects and Never Freeing Them

```
Public Sub AllocateLotsOfStuff

    Dim a as new AReallyBigObject
    Dim b as new ASecondreallyBigObject
    Dim c as new AnInordinatelyLargeObject

    a.DoWork
    b.DoSomethingWith(c)
    c.ReportResults

End Sub
```

So, where's the code that deallocates the objects a, b, and c? The answer is of course that there isn't any, and in most cases there doesn't need to be any. This type of code is legal because the task of cleaning up "standard" objects—either those you've programmed yourself or those built into the .NET Framework—is left to the garbage collector. Think of the garbage collector as a little process running in the background looking for objects that your code isn't using anymore. Kind of a janitorial detail, no?

Although relying on the garbage collector works much of the time, there are times when your classes will utilize unmanaged resources. In these cases, you still need to think in "old-school" terms and clean up after yourself.

 TIP *An* unmanaged *resource is a non-.NET Framework or pre-.NET Framework resource, one that's usually part of the Windows operating system. Things such as files, database connections, or old-style Win32 Application Programming Interface (API) resources like window handles are unmanaged resources that must be freed explicitly if your program uses them.*

When your classes utilize an unmanaged resource, you can make sure the resource is cleaned up by implementing a Finalize method in the class. Finalize is a protected method that you can override in your class, and it's called by the garbage collector.

CAUTION *You shouldn't declare any* Finalize *method as public because this allows code outside of the class to access it. Leaving* Finalize *at the protected access level makes sure that only the garbage collector will call it.*

Listing 9-5 provides some code for a sample class that implements a Finalize method.

Listing 9-5. Implementing a Finalize *Method in a Class*

```
Public Class ResourceHog

    Private f As FileStream
    Private oRead As BinaryReader

    Public Sub New(ByVal cFilename As String)
        MyBase.New()

        f = New FileStream(cFilename, FileMode.Open, FileAccess.Read)
        oRead = New BinaryReader(f)
        Debug.WriteLine("file opened " & DateTime.Now)
    End Sub

    Protected Overrides Sub Finalize()
        MyBase.Finalize()
        oRead.Close()
        f.Close()
        Debug.WriteLine("file closed " & DateTime.Now)
    End Sub

End Class
```

This class, found in the example program GarbageDemoOne, opens a file for reading in the class constructor, and it holds that file open throughout the life of the class (this isn't something I recommend; I'm simply illustrating a point). As the author of the class, you have to guarantee that the file get closed at some point by this class, and the protected Finalize method is the hook you need to get that job done.

The Finalize method helps you make sure that resources get freed in your class, but they still give you no say as to *when* they'll get freed. The garbage collector works some strange hours and normally you don't know when objects will get cleaned up. This is the price you pay as a developer who doesn't have to worry about freeing objects, as demonstrated in Listing 9-4. The garbage collector is telling you the following: "Hey, if you want *me* to free your objects, fine, but I'll do it on my own time."

Sometimes, this simply isn't a good enough solution. Classes may require the frequent or heavy use of system resources, and the developer of the class wants to provide a way for his fellow developers to get rid of those resources on demand, as soon as their presence is no longer required. A class can provide this functionality by implementing the IDisposable interface. This interface, which consists of a single method named Dispose, provides the functionality required so that the outside user can explicitly instruct your class to free any unmanaged resources it used.

The presence of an implementation of the IDisposable interface in a class is your cue as the user of the class that you should call the Dispose method explicitly when you no longer require the resources within that class.

The sample GarbageDemoTwo illustrates a class that implements the IDisposable interface (see Listing 9-6).

Listing 9-6. A Class Implementing IDisposable

```
Public Class DisposableResourceHog
    Implements IDisposable

    Private f As FileStream
    Private oRead As BinaryReader
    Private FName As String

    Public Sub New(ByVal cFilename As String, ByVal cName As String)
        MyBase.New()

        FName = cName
        f = New FileStream(cFilename, FileMode.Open, FileAccess.Read)
        oRead = New BinaryReader(f)
        Debug.WriteLine(FName & " file opened " & DateTime.Now)

    End Sub

    Protected Overrides Sub Finalize()
        MyBase.Finalize()
        Dispose(False)
    End Sub
```

```
    Public Overloads Sub Dispose() Implements System.IDisposable.Dispose
        Dispose(True)
        GC.SuppressFinalize(Me)
    End Sub

    Protected Overridable Overloads Sub Dispose(ByVal disposing As Boolean)
        oRead.Close()
        f.Close()
        Debug.WriteLine(FName & " file closed " & DateTime.Now)
    End Sub
End Class
```

The Dispose method is overloaded, so it comes in two forms. The first form, with no parameters, implements the lone member of the IDisposable interface. This method calls the second overloaded version of Dispose and then runs an interesting line that reads GC.SuppressFinalize(Me). The GC variable, as you may have guessed, is the .NET Framework garbage collector. What this part of the program is saying to the garbage collector is "Hey, I've just been explicitly told to release my resources, so you don't need to run my Finalize method when you get rid of me." This improves the performance of your application because objects with Finalize methods are much harder and take much longer for the garbage collector to clean up than objects without Finalize methods. By calling SuppressFinalize on this object, you've just converted this object to a "non-Finalize" type of object. The second overloaded Dispose method is the one that actually frees the resources. The variable Disposing distinguishes whether the call to this method came from Finalize or from Dispose. If it came from Finalize (disposing = false), then this call has been made from the garbage collector (remember, only the garbage collector calls Finalize), and the method shouldn't try to access any managed objects because the garbage collector may have already collected them.

The sample program creates instances of the DisposableResourceHog class shown in Listing 9-6 in two different ways. The first instance is created when the form opens, yet the Dispose method is never called. The second way creates an instance of class inside a button's Click event and then calls the Dispose method right away, demonstrating how resources are freed as soon as the user wants.

If you study the debug console output when running the program, you'll notice that the resources of the long-lived DisposableResourceHog class never get freed. This is because the Dispose method is called via Finalize, meaning that the .NET Framework garbage collector calls it. Because the FileStream class and the BinaryReader class used by this class are both managed classes, you're forbidden from trying to execute their Close methods because it's quite possible that the garbage collector has already removed these classes from memory. Thus, the class is written in such a way that if the Dispose method isn't explicitly called, then the potential exists for objects to not get explicitly freed or for handles to be explicitly closed. For this reason, when a class implements the IDisposable interface, you need to make sure and use that interface when you're done with the class. Once good way to ensure that you call the Dispose method is to put it in an exception handler:

```
Dim o as new DisposableResourceHog
Try
    <do stuff>
Finally
    o.Dispose
End Try
```

This coding pattern removes all possibility of not freeing the resources used by the class and ensures efficient memory management by the garbage collector.

Understanding Object Serialization

The purpose of most computer programs, when described in an abstract way, is to manipulate data. Game programs are no exception—they embody a set of data and move it around in such a way as to create a diversion for the player.

Many times, programs need to save data to permanent storage for later use. Word processors, spreadsheets, email clients, database front ends—all of these programs store data permanently to disk for reuse whenever needed.

Game programs could have the requirement to store data permanently. Many games implement "save" and "load" features so that the player can leave the game and go back to real life for a while and then resume the game later.

This book hasn't spent any time discussing save/load features for the games for one main reason: Because the games are all short in play length, there really isn't much need for storing a game in the middle that takes less than five minutes to play in its entirety.

Programming save/load functionality in the past was a bit of a pain because developers had to settle on a file format and then write line upon line of code that saved each changeable part of the game to disk. Take the cellular automaton program discussed in Chapter 5, "Understanding Polymorphism," as an example. A good object-oriented developer would probably write a save and load function on each CellularAutomataCell class descendant and then call those methods for each cell within the CellularAutomataGame class. Of course, each descendant of the CellularAutomataCell class has different types of properties to store, so you'd probably have to write methods that could be overridden in each descendant class.

The .NET Framework has made this tedious programming task much easier, you'll be happy to know. Built into the .NET Framework is the ability to serialize any object into several different predefined formats and then write that formatted data to (and later read from) disk. Better still, you can do this serializing and reading/writing in a few short lines of code.

To demonstrate this functionality, I've made a copy of the source code for the CellularAutomata project and added the load/save functionality. You can find this new project in the folder CellularAutomataWithSave. To implement the load/save functionality, made the modifications described in the following sections.

Marking Classes As Serializable

Any classes that are going to be sent to disk must first be marked as such. To do this, you add the Serializable attribute to the CellularAutomataCell class and all its descendants. An *attribute* is a compiler directive that describes some aspect of your class to the .NET Framework. This particular attribute tells the compiler that this class can be serialized to disk. The syntax for the Serializable attribute is as follows:

```
<Serializable()> _
Public Class ConwaysLifeCell
    Inherits CellularAutomataCell
```

Note the code continuation character—attributes must reside on the same line as the class definition itself.

You can attach a number of attributes to both classes and class members, and you can create your own attributes to help describe your code in other ways. For example, you can create a special attribute that denotes the author of a class and the date it was last changed. You can then write special programs that actually rip through your compiled programs, extract this custom attribute information, and output it for documentation purposes. Consult the online help for further information on attributes.

Pointing to the Formatters

The next required step is to add Imports clauses to the top of the code module that will be implementing the serialization. In this case, the code module is CellularAutomata.vb:

```
Imports System.Runtime.Serialization.Formatters.Binary
Imports System.Runtime.Serialization.Formatters.Soap
```

Usually you'd choose to use only one data format and not need both of these references, both formats will be demonstrated here.

Writing the Save Code

The SaveToDisk method you add to the CellularAutomataGame class is laughably simple:

```
Public Sub SaveToFile(ByVal cFilename As String)

    Dim oFS As New FileStream(cFilename, FileMode.Create)
    Dim oBF As New SoapFormatter

    System.Windows.Forms.Cursor.Current = Cursors.WaitCursor

    Try
        oBF.Serialize(oFS, FCells)
    Catch oEX As Exception
        MsgBox(oEX.Message)
    Finally
        oFS.Close()
        System.Windows.Forms.Cursor.Current = Cursors.Default
    End Try

End Sub
```

All that's happening here is that a FileStream is opened, a special class named a SoapFormatter is created, and then this class is used to write the data to the stream. The data written in this case is the FCells object, which is an instance of an ArrayList that's used to store all of the little CellularAutomataCell objects that make up the current game.

Notice that you don't have to specify *how* to write out the data. All you've done is say "Please output the current state of the FCells object to disk." The SoapFormatter writes out the ArrayList and all of the objects contained within automatically.

Now, the Simple Object Access Protocol (SOAP) format is an Extensible Markup Language (XML) format used to send .NET classes back and forth across the Internet, and as an XML format, it tends to make rather large files. As an alternative, you can also use a BinaryFormatter class and your on-disk files will be much smaller. To use this class, simply replace the declaration to the new formatter:

```
Dim oBF As New BinaryFormatter
```

Writing the Load Code

The load from disk code is similar to the save to disk code but with the contents of the file loaded into the correct object. In this case, the ArrayList FCells is assigned to the contents of the file:

```
Public Sub LoadFromFile(ByVal cFilename As String)

    Dim oFS As New FileStream(cFilename, FileMode.Open)
    Dim oBF As New SoapFormatter

    System.Windows.Forms.Cursor.Current = Cursors.WaitCursor

    Try
        FCells = CType(oBF.Deserialize(oFS), ArrayList)
    Catch oEX As Exception
        MsgBox(oEX.Message)
    Finally
        oFS.Close()
        System.Windows.Forms.Cursor.Current = Cursors.Default
    End Try

End Sub
```

Adding Buttons and Test

Now that the class can support file loading and saving, all that remains is to add Load and Save buttons to the main form of the program and to call these methods. In the spirit of true laziness, I've hard-coded a filename just to test out the functionality:

```
Private Sub cbSave_Click(ByVal sender As System.Object, _
    ByVal e As System.EventArgs) Handles cbSave.Click

    oCell.SaveToFile("c:\fred.lif")
End Sub

Private Sub cbLoad_Click(ByVal sender As System.Object, _
    ByVal e As System.EventArgs) Handles cbLoad.Click

    oCell.LoadFromFile("c:\fred.lif")
    oP.Invalidate()

End Sub
```

To verify that the save/load works, fire up one of the automata variants, let it run through a few dozen cycles, then hit the Save button. You can take note of two or three patterns in specific spots on the board so that you can identify them later. Then, resume the current pattern and let it change drastically from the save point. Finally, hit the Load button and see the board state magically resume back to its saved state.

The ability to serialize complex objects to disk is a great quick way to implement a save/reload feature for your games without having to write line-by-line I/O code.

Understanding Threading

Chapter 7, "Creating Multiplayer Games," covered threading briefly when discussing the multiplayer Reversi game. Separate threads were used when looking for the second player across the network when setting up the game and also for the code that polled the open network connection looking for move data during the game.

In the first case, a separate thread was necessary because the method that waits for a TCP connection, the `TCPListener.AcceptTCPClient` method, is a blocking method that halts all code execution as it does its job. Without this code running in a separate thread, the game couldn't support the ability to cancel the game setup because there would be no way for the program to handle the `Click` event of a Cancel button if code execution was blocked while running the `AcceptTCPClient` method.

The thread used during the game play wasn't absolutely necessary, but it makes the game "feel" smoother because the main program thread isn't handling the polling/waiting for the player across the network to make her turn.

If you looked carefully, you might have noticed that two different Visual Basic syntaxes were used when setting up the threads in the two parts of the program. Let's look at that a bit closer. The following is the thread setup code that polls for in-game player turn data:

```
oThread = New Thread(New ThreadStart( _
   AddressOf CType(Player2, _
   NetworkReversiPlayer).LookForTurn))
oThread.Start()
```

and the following is the code that sets up the thread that looks for the other network player in the game setup phase:

```
FThread = New Thread(AddressOf LookForIt)
FThread.Start()
```

It might be difficult to tell because of the extra class boxing code found in the first example, but there are actually two different thread start syntaxes being used here. Broken down a bit, the two syntaxes are as follows:

```
FThread = New Thread(new ThreadStart(AddressOf <method>))
FThread = New Thread(AddressOf <method>)
```

Is there a difference in the syntaxes? Actually, Visual Basic .NET users get a little syntactic sugar on their cereal when using threads because the two thread constructors are identical. The ThreadStart class is a required parameter in the constructor of a Thread class; however, if omitted, the compiler adds it automatically.

Passing Parameters to a Thread

Threads can be useful for doing multiple tasks seemingly simultaneously. For example, you might write an adventure game where every computer-controlled element (monster, enemy, and so on) could "think" of its next move in its own thread. Or, your computer-controlled board game opponent might consider each possible move in its own thread.

One challenge that comes up when using threads is sending and retrieving information to a routine that's running in its own thread. You might have noticed that the method used as the parameter of ThreadStart must be a method that takes no parameters and must not return a value. So, how might you send or receive values to code that needs to run in its own thread?

One solution involves wrapping the thread code around a class and using class properties as the communication mechanism. The sample project ThreadParametersOne demonstrates such a strategy. This program creates a class that simulates some work and then creates many instances of this class, with each instance performing the work in its own thread. The program then collects the results from each class instance.

The class that wraps the thread handling code in the example is called MyThreadExecutor. This class takes three parameters in its constructor: a name parameter (so the classes can be identified from one another) and minimum and maximum integer values. The purpose of the code is to return a random integer that lies between the passed-in minimum and maximum values, but the code that generates the integer needs to run in its own thread. Listing 9-7 shows the MyThreadExecutor class for generating a random number within a separate thread.

Listing 9-7. The MyThreadExecutor *Class*

```vbnet
Public Class MyThreadExecutor

    Private FThread As Thread
    Private FMin As Integer
    Private FMax As Integer
    Private FReturnVal As Integer

    Public Event NotifyDone(ByVal sender As Object)

    Public Sub New(ByVal n As String, ByVal iMin As Integer, ByVal iMax As Integer)
        MyBase.New()
        FMin = iMin
        FMax = iMax

        FThread = New Thread(AddressOf RunMe)
        FThread.Name = n
        FThread.IsBackground = True
    End Sub

    ReadOnly Property pThread() As Thread
        Get
            Return FThread
        End Get
    End Property

    ReadOnly Property pReturnVal() As Integer
        Get
            Return FReturnVal
        End Get
    End Property

    Private Sub RunMe()

        Dim oRand As New Random

        'pause a random amount of time to simulate doing actual work
        FThread.Sleep(oRand.Next(1, 4) * 1000)
        FReturnVal = oRand.Next(FMin, FMax + 1)

        RaiseEvent NotifyDone(Me)
    End Sub

End Class
```

The majority of the class is simple setup code, declaring parameters for the elements needed outside the class (the name, the return value, and the thread object itself). The thread is instantiated in the class constructor and is declared to execute the RunMe method when the thread begins.

RunMe is where all the "work" occurs. To simulate a method that might actually take a long time (such as looking for a potential move in a two-player game), the thread first pauses a few short seconds and then returns the random value. The RunMe method also raises an event that can be used by the calling program as notification that the work has completed.

Listing 9-8 shows the code that creates and runs all of the thread-based classes.

Listing 9-8. Creating and Running Thread-Centered Classes

```
Private Sub cbGo_Click(ByVal sender As System.Object, _
  ByVal e As System.EventArgs) Handles cbGo.Click

    Dim iNumOf As Integer
    Dim iLoop As Integer
    Dim FThreads As ArrayList
    Dim oExec As MyThreadExecutor

    Cursor = Cursors.WaitCursor
    lbOut.Items.Clear()
    lbStatus.Items.Clear()
    Application.DoEvents()

    Try

        Try
            iNumOf = CInt(tbNum.Text)
        Catch
            iNumOf = 10
        End Try

        FThreads = New ArrayList
        For iLoop = 1 To iNumOf
            oExec = New MyThreadExecutor("Thread" & iLoop, iLoop * 2, iLoop * 3)
            AddHandler oExec.NotifyDone, AddressOf DoneNotification
            FThreads.Add(oExec)
        Next

        For Each oExec In FThreads
            oExec.pThread.Start()
        Next
```

```
        'wait for each thread to finish
        For Each oExec In FThreads
            oExec.pThread.Join()
        Next

        'output the results
        For Each oExec In FThreads
            lbOut.Items.Add(oExec.pName & _
                " generated value  " & oExec.pReturnVal)
        Next

    Finally
        Cursor = Cursors.Default
    End Try

End Sub

Public Sub DoneNotification(ByVal sender As Object)
    lbStatus.Items.Add(CType(sender, _
        MyThreadExecutor).pName & "  is done")
End Sub
```

The generator procedure reads a value in a textbox to determine the number of MyThreadExecutor classes to create. Each class instance is generated in a For loop and added to an ArrayList so that it can be accessed later. Note that the individual threads aren't started in this initial setup loop.

Once all the classes have been set up, a second For loop, this one of the For Each variety, launches the thread contained within each MyThreadExecutor class instance. After this, a second loop begins. This one executes the Join method on each thread. The Join method blocks the current process until that thread terminates. By executing each one in a loop, you can guarantee that all of the threads terminate before the code moves beyond this loop.

The final loop outputs the results and uses the parameter pReturnVal on each class to find out what random number is generated. You could use either return parameters on the class wrapper or an event handler to send information back to the calling program. Figure 9-1 shows a sample of the program after creating and running 25 class instances.

Try running the example program a few different times using a different number in the textbox each time. The interesting thing is that the program takes roughly three to four seconds to execute whether you're generating 10 class instances or 100. This is true even though every class instance has a several-second pause built into it. If the same program was written so that each class instance was executed one after the other, then the execution time would increase linearly with the number of objects created. This is a good example of the power of threaded programs.

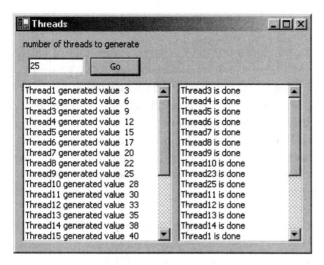

Figure 9-1. Threaded class example

Understanding Thread Safety

Most of the class definitions in the Visual Studio documentation describe the thread safety of the class. Obviously, having several threads simultaneously attempting to update a listbox or a collection class might produce undefined or undesired results.

The example shown that runs the individual classes and returns the results seems to work properly, but I've cheated in one place, and that's in the event callback named DoneNotification. This event simply updates a listbox when one of the threads is about to complete, and the program runs with no errors. However, a bit closer inspection points out that each call of the event handler happens in a separate thread. Because this event handler uses a listbox to update values, and listbox operations (like most Windows forms operations) aren't considered "thread-safe," this is a definite no-no.

To prove this point, you can add a single line into the notification handler and rerun it:

```
Public Sub DoneNotification(ByVal sender As Object)
    Debug.WriteLineIf(Me.InvokeRequired, "InvokeRequired!")
    lbStatus.Items.Add(CType(sender, _
      MyThreadExecutor).pName & " is done")
End Sub
```

The InvokeRequired method returns True if this code is executing in a different thread than the thread in which the control attached to it was created. You should see a number of InvokeRequired! phrases output to the Debug window if you run this code from Visual Studio, which is a warning that you're trying to access the calling form (and thus the listbox lbStatus) in a different thread from the one that created it.

So, does this mean you can't update any Windows Forms controls when writing multithreaded applications? Well, no, it's not quite that severe. What's required, however, is to instruct the program to run the user-interface-specific code back in the main thread, which is the same thread that created all the user interface elements. You do this using a rather complicated syntax with the Invoke method, which is declared on the Control object (thus, all Windows Forms controls contain this method). Listing 9-9 shows how you might use the Invoke method on a listbox. (You can find this code in the folder named ThreadParametersTwo (broken) with the source code that comes with the book.)

Listing 9-9. Using Invoke *to Run Code Back Up on the Main Program Thread*

```
Public Delegate Sub AddListBoxDelegate(ByVal cThreadName As String)

    'thread safe (but doesn't work in this program)
    Public Sub DoneNotification(ByVal sender As Object)

        Dim oExec As MyThreadExecutor = CType(sender, MyThreadExecutor)

        If lbStatus.InvokeRequired Then
            Dim oDel As New AddListBoxDelegate(AddressOf Me.AddListBoxValue)
            lbStatus.Invoke(oDel, New Object(0) {oExec.pThread.Name})
        Else
            AddListBoxValue(oExec.pThread.Name)
        End If
    End Sub

Public Sub AddListBoxValue(ByVal cThreadName As String)
    lbStatus.Items.Add(cThreadName & " is done")
End Sub
```

The Invoke method relies on the declaration of a *delegate*, which you might recall from Chapter 7, "Creating Multiplayer Games," is the declaration of a type of procedure or function. Once the delegate type is declared, you can create an instance of it and point it to an actual procedure or function in the program, and then this function can be invoked indirectly by using the Invoke method on any control. When Invoke is called, the code will run on the same thread from which the object attached to the Invoke was created. In this example, the listbox lbStatus is calling Invoke, so the main thread of the program will be where the called function (the function AddListBoxValue in this case) runs.

The second parameter to the Invoke method is an array of objects, which contains any parameters required by the function being invoked. The AddListBoxValue function requires a string parameter, so a single-element object array is created, and the desired string parameter is placed inside it.

This is all well and good, but if you run the project in the folder ThreadParametersTwo (broken), you'll find that the program hangs indefinitely when you try and run it. Can you figure out why it's hanging? (It took me awhile, let me tell you.)

What I've managed to do in this example is create a deadlock situation. Two parts of the program are each waiting for the other to execute. When Invoke attempts to run a process in the main thread, it has to wait because the main thread is running Thread.Join. This is a blocking method that's waiting for the subthread to finish. In other words, the main thread is waiting for the subthread to finish, and the subthread can't run anything because the main thread is being blocked. Holy deadlock, Batman!

The problem lies in calling the Join method on the subthreads. What I'm trying to do is have my cake and eat it, too. I can't block the main thread from running code until the subthread finishes, but then I expect the main thread to help the subthreads by running Invoked from them. I simply can't have it both ways. I must instead rework the program to either get rid of the Thread.Joins or get rid of the event handler called from the subthreads that require the use of the listbox and therefore Invoke. The third version of the program, found in the folder ThreadParametersThree, opts to implement the latter solution. It uses the notification and Invoke code to make sure that user interface access is thread-safe, but it doesn't use Joins to halt the main thread. Instead, as shown in Listing 9-10, it uses the IsAlive method on the thread to find out when it finishes and keeps the loop going until all created threads have completed.

Listing 9-10. Waiting for a Thread to Complete Without Using Thread.Join

```
Dim bDone as Boolean
'wait for each thread to finish. can't use JOIN

bDone = False
Do While Not bDone
    For Each oExec In FThreads
        bDone = True
        If oExec.pThread.IsAlive Then
            bDone = False
        End If
        Application.DoEvents()
    Next
Loop
```

This loop sets the Boolean `bDone` to `True` only after all the threads have completed. As long as one remains running, the loop will continue. The `Application.DoEvents` is necessary so that other parts of the program (in particular, the event notifications) have processing time to execute.

Writing multithreaded programs has become a simple process in Visual Basic .NET, and the technique can allow your programs to handle many tasks simultaneously. This can give you an edge when optimizing your games for speed.

APPENDIX A

The Basics of Visual Basic

MANY READERS OF THIS BOOK are former Visual Basic 6 developers who are moving on to the latest Microsoft flavor of the Basic language. If you're one of those users, then this appendix probably isn't for you.

Others, however, may be coming over to the Visual Basic language from some other development language. Perhaps you're a COBOL mainframe developer new to Windows development in general, or maybe you're a Java programmer unfamiliar with the syntax of Basic. This appendix serves as an introduction to the constructs used in the Basic language.

A third class of reader might be one who is new to programming altogether and wants Visual Basic .NET to become his first foray into the programming world. For that class of user, this book will help you ascend that mountain, but I also recommend some additional reading:

- If you're a beginner, check out *How Computer Programming Works* by Dan Appleman (Apress, 2000).

- Also by Dan Appleman is *Moving to VB .NET: Strategies, Concepts, and Code, Second Edition* (Apress, 2001). This book gets into some of the origins of the language and why some features are the way they are.

- If you're into the "learn-by-doing" style, I recommend *Karl Moore's Visual Basic .NET: The Tutorials* by Karl Moore (Apress, 2002).

- If you want to focus on Web development, *Programming the Web with Visual Basic .NET* by Constance Petersen, Lynn Torkelson, and Zac Torkelson (Apress, 2002) is worth perusing.

- If you have a background in mainframe programming, then *COBOL and Visual Basic on .NET: A Guide for the Reformed Mainframe Programmer* by Chris L. Richardson (Apress, 2003) will help you upgrade your skills.

- For more background on object-oriented programming concepts, *An Introduction to Object-Oriented Programming with Visual Basic .NET* by Dan Clark (Apress, 2002) will be of great help.

- Finally, if you're into short, quick example programs that demonstrate specific concepts or techniques, then my first .NET book *Visual Basic .NET Codemaster's Library* (Sybex, 2002) should prove useful.

Getting Started with Basic Programming

The following sections introduce the basic constructs of the Visual Basic .NET language.

Understanding Variables

A developer won't get too far in writing a program without using *variables*. The best way to think of a variable is as a little mailbox slot in the computer. The program can put something (a *value*) in the mailbox or look at the contents therein.

Variables also have a *type*, meaning that the mailbox can hold only a certain kind of value. An *integer* variable, for example, can hold numeric whole values, and a *string* variable can hold a sequence of characters. Table A-1 describes commonly used variable types. This list is by no means exhaustive—it's meant only to illustrate that you can use different variables in different ways.

Table A-1. Some Data Types

NAME	DESCRIPTION
Integer	Whole numbers
Boolean	Either special value True or special value False
String	A sequence of characters
Single	A floating-point number such as 1.41 or 3.3333333

When a variable is required in a program, it first has to be *declared*. Declaring a variable involves giving it a name and defining the data type that it'll hold:

```
Dim iNumber as Integer
```

The previous line of code declares a variable named iNumber and specifies that the variable will hold integer, or whole number, values.

NOTE *The keyword* Dim, *used when declaring variables, is a holdover from old versions of Visual Basic. It's short for* Dimension.

Placing a value into a variable is called *assigning* a value to the variable. You do this using the equals sign:

```
iNumber = 41
```

After the previous line of code runs, the iNumber mailbox will hold the value 41.

Understanding Operators

An *operator* is something that performs an action on one or more things. They're also grouped into separate categories. For example, the set of arithmetic operators perform mathematical functions. Even the nonprogrammer should recognize these examples of the plus and minus operators:

```
Dim x As Integer
Dim y As Integer
Dim r As Integer

x = 41
y = 35

r = x + y
Debug.WriteLine("answer is " & r)

r = x - y
Debug.WriteLine("answer is " & r)
```

To summarize what this program does, the first three integer variables (named x, y, and r) are declared. Then, the variables x and y are assigned values. The next line of code adds the values of the variables x and y together and stores the result in the variable r. The next line of code (the one that starts Debug.Writeline...) outputs the answer to a special window in Visual Studio called the *Debug window*. Finally, the value in the variable y is subtracted from the value in the variable x, and the result is placed in the variable r, which is output to the Debug window.

NOTE *The second assignment of the variable r in the previous code will overwrite whatever was held in the variable before. Consider variables as mailboxes that can hold only a single thing. Placing a second thing in the mailbox pushes whatever used to be there out the back of the mailbox and into the trash.*

Dozens of operators perform mathematical functions, combine strings of characters together, and compare the values within variables. Consult the Visual Studio online help for a complete list of operators.

Understanding If-Then

A program often has to perform some action only if some condition is true. The Visual Basic structure that fulfills this requirement is the If-Then statement. It has the following structure:

```
If <condition> Then
    <statements>
End If
```

The condition is evaluated and, if true, the code statements within the block execute. If the condition is false, these code statements are skipped. An alternate structure of the If-Then statement adds an Else clause:

```
If <condition> Then
    <statements>
Else
    <other statements>
End If
```

Like the first example, the condition is again evaluated, and the statements are run if it's true. If the condition is false, then the code denoted in <other statements> runs instead. A final variant allows for multiple conditions to be evaluated:

```
If <condition> Then
    <statements>
ElseIf <condition2> Then
    <other statements>
[ElseIf <condition3> Then
    <other statements>]
End If
```

The ElseIf clause allows you to test for more than one condition. You could, for example, execute one block of code if a condition evaluates a date as a weekday, a second block if the date is determined to be a Saturday, and a third if the date is a Sunday. There's no limit to the number of ElseIf blocks you can have, so you could execute one of seven blocks of code depending on each day of the week.

Understanding Loops

Many times, it's necessary for a program to perform the same function more than once. The Basic language supports different types of *loop* structures. One commonly used loop is the For loop, which runs a fixed number of times:

```
Dim iVal As Integer

For iVal = 1 To 10
    If iVal Mod 2 = 0 Then
        Debug.WriteLine(iVal & " is even")
    Else
        Debug.WriteLine(iVal & " is odd")
    End If
Next
```

This loop runs 10 times. The first time it runs, it assigns the integer variable iVal the value 1, then 2, then 3, all the way up to the value 10. Within the loop, the Mod (remainder) operator is performed against this variable. If the value of the variable divided by 2 has the remainder of 0, then the content of the variable is an even number, and the program outputs this fact. If the variable value divided by 2 has a remainder of 1, then the value is odd, and this is output.

Understanding Procedures and Functions

A programmer can break up code into smaller pieces of code known as either a *procedure* or a *function*. These smaller chunks of code can help to break up long stretches and make the code more readable. They can also reduce potentially duplicate code that needs to run from more than one place. Instead of having the same code in two places, the programmer can place the code into a procedure or function and then call it from those two places.

Listing A-1 performs the same function as the previous example, but it does so by using a function named IsAnEvenNumber that returns a True or False result.

The function requires a value be sent to it that it can evaluate. The act of sending a value to a function is called *passing a parameter.*

After the function evaluates whether the passed-in value is even or odd, a procedure named OutputResult writes the answer to the Debug window.

 NOTE *A procedure differs from a function from the standpoint that it doesn't return anything to the calling program.*

Listing A-1. Using Procedures and Functions

```
Dim iVal As Integer

For iVal = 1 To 10
    If IsAnEvenNumber(iVal) Then
        Call OutputResult(iVal, "even")
    Else
        Call OutputResult(iVal, "odd")
    End If
Next

Function IsAnEvenNumber(ByVal iVal As Integer) As Boolean

    If iVal Mod 2 = 0 Then
        Return True
    Else
        Return False
    End If

End Function

Sub OutputResult(ByVal iVal As Integer, ByVal cResult As String)
    Debug.WriteLine(iVal & " is " & cResult)
End Sub
```

Looking at an Example Project

The example Visual Basic .NET project named FirstApplication implements all of the code shown in this appendix in a project. You can start it by double-clicking the file FirstApplication.sln in Windows Explorer.

Using POV-RAY and Moray

SOME OF THE GRAPHICS IN this book probably caught your eye and made you think "Wow, that's pretty cool. How did he do that?" In particular, the dice from Chapters 1 and 2, the tiles that make up the NineTiles game in Chapter 3, and the asteroids from Chapter 9 were all created using a technique known as *ray tracing*.

 NOTE *Scott Hudson created the models of the asteroids, which were used with his permission. See* http://www.eecs.wsu.edu/ ~hudson/Research/Asteroids *for more information.*

Ray tracing is a technique where light waves are "traced" from light sources into the description of a scene, and the reflection of these light sources tells a computer program how to draw the scene. Put another way, a ray tracer simulates the way that the human eye decodes light waves into pictures. The input of a ray tracing program is the description of a scene. For example, a scene might consist of a light source and a geometric shape such as a cube. You can assign the cube surface properties such as color, bumpiness, ambience, and reflection. All of these properties will affect how the cube looks to an observer in the ascribed light conditions. The ray tracing program takes that scene description and turns it into a visual image of the cube.

Introducing Persistence of Vision

One of the most popular and long-lived ray tracing programs is the freeware program Persistence of Vision, or POV-RAY for short. I remember using this program before I was even using Windows ("Back in my day, we didn't even have Windows! We had to *type* in our commands!"), and the program has survived and even thrived with the explosion of the Internet ("Back in my day, there was no such thing as the Internet!"). You can find the Web site for the program at http://www.povray.org.

You can use POV-RAY to create truly amazing and lifelike computer graphics—if you have the patience to learn the scene description language, which is a fully blown programming language in its own right. Tons of sample rendering scripts come with the program, which can help you learn the language. If you're more visual in nature or find the programming language too unwieldy, you can use a shareware Computer-Aided Drawing (CAD) program such as Moray, which allows you to visually construct the three-dimensional scenes like you might do in AutoCAD and then export the scene in the POV-RAY scene description language for rendering.

Much of the rendering done in the POV-RAY community focuses on creating complex, realistic scenes. Indeed, the POV-RAY Web site highlights a random image from its Hall of Fame, and most of these images are amazing shots that look like they're straight from Industrial Light and Magic. Several years ago, I came up with the idea that the ray tracer would be equally useful in creating single, individual elements for simple games. The dice and tiles used in the NineTiles game are some examples of the game elements created using the POV-RAY program (and the Moray CAD program).

Trying to discuss the POV-RAY scene description language in an appendix wouldn't nearly do the program justice. This appendix shows a small sample of the Dice object used in the first chapters of this book to whet your appetite and introduce you to something new and cool you can do on your computer.

Creating the Ray-Traced Die

To create the ray-traced die, I used the Moray modeler to create the die "scene." The scene consists of a cube, the pips (the little white dots that make up the die's numbers), one light source, and one camera. I also grouped all of the pips for a given die side into a group in the modeler so that I could move each "pip set" as a group. Figure B-1 shows a wireframe shot of the die in Moray.

Figure B-1. The die in the Moray modeler

Understanding Materials

Each surface in a POV-RAY scene is described with one or more *materials*. The material is what gives each object its color, reflectiveness, and other properties. The die required two materials—the red, semitransparent body of the die and a bright white for the pips. After creating these materials in Moray and exporting them, their description in the POV-RAY language looks like Listing B-1.

Listing B-1. POV-RAY Pip Definition

```
#declare Pips =
   material  // Pips
   {
      texture
      {
         pigment
         {
            color rgb <1.0, 1.0, 1.0>
         }
         finish
         {
            ambient 0.258967
            brilliance 2.406
         }
      }
   }
```

The syntax of the POV-RAY language is somewhat like C or a C-language variant, with curly braces surrounding all of the blocks. The #declare specification indicates that this material is being defined but not yet used anywhere.

The material Pips is pure white, with ambient and brilliance values that make the white stand out quite a bit, even when a given side of the die is in shadow. I can't tell you I was smart enough to know how to make the renderer work this way beforehand—I use a pure trial-and-error approach until my scene looks the way I want it to look. The material for the die body isn't declared because it's used in only one place, so its description lies within the die body object itself, as you'll see next.

Setting the Camera and Light Source

When defining a scene in POV-RAY, you need at least one camera and one light source (a scene can technically have zero light sources, but then there would be no rays of light for the renderer to trace).

Listing B-2 shows the code that declares the camera and a single light source.

Listing B-2. POV_RAY Camera and Light Source Declaration

```
camera {  //  Camera StdCam
    location   <      -3.000,       3.000,       4.000>
    sky        <     0.00000,     0.00000,     1.00000>
    up         <         0.0,         0.0,         1.0>
    right      <     1.00000,         0.0,         0.0>
    angle         39.60000
    look_at    <       0.000,       0.000,       0.000>
}


light_source {    // Light001
    <0.0, 0.0, 0.0>
    color rgb <1.000, 1.000, 1.000>
    translate   <-18.754392, -0.401769, 61.307308>
}
```

The components of the camera declare its location in three-dimensional coordinate space (coordinate <-3, 3, 4> in this case), the orientation of the coordinate system used (which way is up), and where the camera is looking (at <0, 0, 0>).

The light source is a point light off to one side and high above the scene. Note that the floating-point values within the translate clause are seemingly "random" because I was manipulating the location of the light visually by dragging it around within the Moray program. You also have the option of typing these values directly if you want more "rounded off" numbers.

Creating the Die Body

The body of the die is a simple cube, having a 1-unit size. You declare cubes in POV-RAY using the following box statement:

```
#declare Body =
    box { <-1, -1, -1>, <1, 1, 1>
        texture {
        pigment {  color rgbf <0.75, 0.0004, 0.0, 0.4> }
        finish {
            //phong 0.2
            //phong_size 10
```

```
        ambient 0.2
        diffuse 0.8
      }
    }
}
```

Note that the material is built right into the definition of the box statement instead of using the #declare statement first and then using that material later. Each method is identical—the #declare statement makes it easy to reuse a material in multiple places and to have that material in a single place in case you want to play around with it.

Note how I've commented out the phong and phong_size declarations. I did this after I was done designing the object in Moray. Moray is great for creating the initial layout of a scene, but it doesn't allow you to use the full capabilities of the POV-RAY language. Because of this, I usually get the layout of the scene pretty close to perfect, do a final export, and then tweak the final script by hand. This final tweaking is necessary in the end to get the animation working. The only thing to keep in mind is that Moray can't import these exported POV language files, you'll have to repeat any changes you make to the POV-RAY code if you decide to go back into Moray to change something and then reexport it.

Creating the Pips

The location of the pips was another thing I wanted to tweak outside of Moray. The position of each pip (which is in reality a little cone embedded in the die body) had to be perfect or it would stick slightly out of the die body or lie too far within it, which would obscure the bright white color. To do this, I set up two variables in the script and then altered them by hand. The script in Listing B-3 shows these declared variables and two "pip groups."

Listing B-3. The Pips (Gladys Knight Not Included)

```
#declare PIPX=0.475;
#declare PIPZ=0.801;

#declare Twos = union {
  cone { // Cone020
    <0,0,0>, 0.0, <0,0,1>, 1.0
    material {
      Pips
    }
```

```
      scale 0.2
      rotate <-180.0, -270.0, -180.0>
      translate  <0.0, -PIPX, PIPX>
   }
   cone { // Cone021
     <0,0,0>, 0.0, <0,0,1>, 1.0
     material {
        Pips
     }
     scale 0.2
     rotate <-180.0, 90.0, -180.0>
     translate  <0.0, PIPX, -PIPX>
   }
   translate  PIPZ*x
}
#declare Threes = union {
   cone { // Cone011
     <0,0,0>, 0.0, <0,0,1>, 1.0
     material {
        Pips
     }
     scale 0.2
     rotate -90.0*x
     translate  <PIPX, 0.0, -PIPX>
   }
   cone { // Cone010
     <0,0,0>, 0.0, <0,0,1>, 1.0
     material {
        Pips
     }
     scale 0.2
     rotate -90.0*x
   }
   cone { // Cone009
     <0,0,0>, 0.0, <0,0,1>, 1.0
     material {
        Pips
     }
     scale 0.2
     rotate -90.0*x
     translate  <-PIPX, 0.0, PIPX>
   }
   translate  PIPZ*y
}
```

This excerpt shows the definition of two sides of the die—the two side and the three side. Each face is defined with a union structure, which is the POV-RAY equivalent of a "group" in Moray. By grouping pips together, you can move them as a unit.

Each individual pip is a cone scaled down to 0.2 and rotated in some direction so that the flat side faces outward (the flat side is the side that shows up on the surface of the die). The PIPX variable specifies how far the pips are from the center of a face. Making this number smaller "bunches" the pips closer together on a face. The variable PIPZ moves the pips closer or farther away from the center of the cube. Making this number smaller places the pips inside the cube; making it larger extends the pips outside the boundary of the die body.

By setting up these variables and then using them in the declaration of each pip, I was able to change their values in a single place and then rerender the die to see how it looked. I repeated this, oh, about a zillion times until the die looked the way I wanted it to look.

Once again, note that all of the pip groups start with the keyword #declare. This means that a construct is being defined, but that construct isn't being placed in the world yet. This is somewhat analogous to defining a class in Visual Basic .NET. A recipe for something is being declared, but the something isn't being called into being yet. That happens next.

Declaring the Die Object

With all the components declared, it's finally time to bring them into the scene. Listing B-4 is the declaration of the Die object.

Listing B-4. Declaring the Die Object

```
union { // Die
  object { Twos }
  object { Fives }
  object { Sixes }
  object { Threes }
  object { Fours }
  cone { // PipOne
    <0,0,0>, 0.0, <0,0,1>, 1.0
    material {
      Pips
    }
    scale 0.2
```

```
    translate  PIPZ*z
  }

  object {Body}
  rotate <0,-clock*10-90,-clock*10>
}
```

The Die object is a union of the five declared "pip groups," one additional pip that represents the one face (no sense putting a single pip in its own group), an instance of the Body object (the box), and one additional specifier to rotate the whole thing by some amount. The amount rotated depends on the special variable clock, which is actually passed into the script like a parameter from the renderer.

Rendering and Animating the Picture

By default, POV-RAY will render a single picture representing the scene described in the POV file, but my goal is to render 36 frames of the die as it rotates around. You can control animated frames, as well as a number of other rendering options, by editing values in an INI file. The following fragment shows a piece of the INI file used to render the dice animation frames:

```
Initial_Clock = 0
Final_Clock = 35
Width = 160
Height = 160
Input_File_Name = dice.pov
```

The values in this INI file give the name of the input POV file, the size of the output bitmap, and the number of frames to render. Other options within this file can control the type of output file (TIF vs. BMP vs. GIF), the type and amount of anti-aliasing to use, and whether to display the rendering as it happens within the POV-RAY program (turning off the preview will make complex scenes render faster).

The Initial_Clock and Final_Clock values tell the renderer how many times to render the scene and what value to pass into the clock variable for each pass. Looking back at the definition of the die, you can see that the die object rotates along various axes by an amount of 10 degrees multiplied by the amount of the clock value. Because the clock value will loop from 0 to 35, the die will rotate from 0 degrees to 350 degrees in 36 frames. When these frames are displayed together, the die will appear to rotate through an entire 360-degree cycle.

Summary

POV-RAY is an amazingly complex program that can produce beautiful pictures. In using the program in this simple way, I was able to create some slick three-dimensional graphics for my simple board games. You may find other great uses for this freeware renderer in creating your game content.

APPENDIX C

Using the BMPStitch Utility

USING POV-RAY TO CREATE animated bitmaps (described in the previous appendix) introduces a minor issue: the need to convert many individual frame bitmaps into a single multicell bitmap. This isn't a required step for creating the games in this book, but it's much easier to manage one large bitmap (in code and in Visual Studio) than it is to manage 36 smaller bitmaps. Figures C-1 and C-2 show the task needed.

Figure C-1. Turning these individual bitmaps . . .

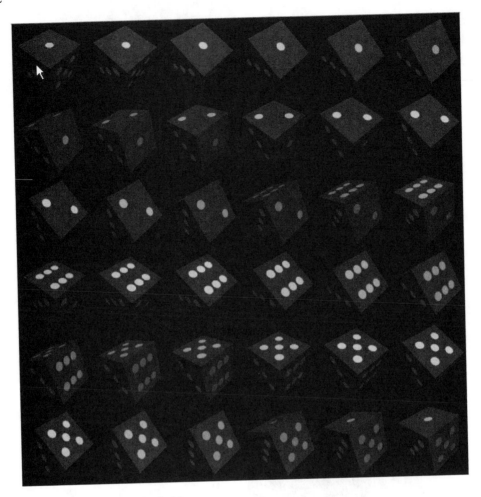

Figure C-2. . . . into a single bitmap

Smashing the 36 smaller images into one big one is nothing more than a cut-and-paste job. With a little patience and the Paint utility that comes with any version of Windows, you could, in time, create a large blank bitmap and copy each little bitmap into an appropriate place. This sounds a bit too much like real work, though—lining up images to single-pixel accuracy, dozens of copy-and-paste tasks—you can probably think of much better things you'd like to do with you time. It'd be much simpler if you had a program that could take the 36 images as input and smash them together for you.

Using BMPStitch

The BMPStitch utility is the solution to getting out of the tedious cut-and-paste job just described. In addition, this little utility lets you clip the individual bitmaps down, removing unneeded border space in each frame. This utility is useful enough that I've included it with the source code that accompanies this book so that you might be able to use it in your projects, should you find the need.

The program is a single-form solution that displays one of the images you intend to paste together. Clicking the Open button opens a standard dialog box so that you can select the first image in the intended animation sequence. Once selected, it displays on the form, as shown in Figure C-3.

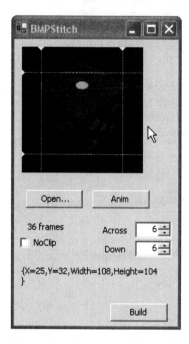

Figure C-3. Interface of the BMPStitch utility

The utility assumes you want to stitch together all of the image files found in the same folder as the first image you selected with the Open button. Thus, the best way to organize your art directories is such that all of the individual cells for a given animated bitmap reside in a folder by themselves.

The preview picture box in the utility contains two horizontal and two vertical lines that can be arranged on the bitmap. These lines serve as a clipping area within each bitmap. The text at the bottom of the form shows the clipping rectangle that will be used based on the orientation of the clipping lines. (Knowing the rectangle height and width of each cell is useful in the game program that's going to use the final bitmap in an animated sequence because this is the same height/width that will be needed to display one of the cells.)

You can preview the animated sequence by clicking the Anim button. This loads each bitmap found in the folder into the picture box. This feature is useful for making sure your clipping rectangle doesn't cut off any of the image as it moves.

Once you've loaded a bitmap, adjusted the clipping region, and made sure it all looks the way you want it, you build the final bitmap by choosing the number of rows and columns to create using the across/down selectors and then clicking the Build button. The utility then performs the tedious copy/paste job and saves the final bitmap as `c:\BMPStitch.bmp`.

 NOTE *I didn't want to save the final bitmap into the same folder as the cell bitmaps because then the utility, if run a second time, would use this bitmap as one of the cells, which would in turn produce undesired results. This could be fixed if the cell-reading code were perhaps "smarter" and chose only those bitmaps with the same height and width as the first selected bitmap or perhaps those with a name similar to the first selected bitmap, but this is a quickie in-house utility, so perfection isn't necessary. It saved enough cut-and-paste work for me that I didn't mind taking the final file, renaming it, and putting it into the Visual Basic .NET project folder.*

Using the BMPStitch Code

The BMPStitch utility contains a few code fragments worthy of discussion and study, especially for someone uninitiated with the .NET Framework. Some of the functionality may serve as a learning tool into this vast library.

Creating the ClipPictureBox Class

The most interesting part of the BMPStitch code is a class I developed for displaying the image and the clipping lines. This class is `ClipPictureBox`, and Listing C-1 shows the interface of the class.

Listing C-1. Public (and Protected) Interface of the `ClipPictureBox` *Class*

```
Public Class ClipPictureBox
    Inherits PictureBox

    Property ClipColor() As Color
    Property ClipDisabled() As Boolean
    Public Event ClippingRectChanged(ByVal r As Rectangle)
    ReadOnly Property ClippingRect() As Rectangle

    Shadows Property Image() As Image
```

```
Protected Overrides Sub OnPaint(ByVal pe As _
    System.Windows.Forms.PaintEventArgs)

Protected Overrides Sub OnMouseDown(ByVal e As _
    System.Windows.Forms.MouseEventArgs)

Protected Overrides Sub OnMouseMove(ByVal e As _
    System.Windows.Forms.MouseEventArgs)

Protected Overrides Sub OnMouseUp(ByVal e As _
    System.Windows.Forms.MouseEventArgs)

End Class
```

The ClipPictureBox class is an ancestor of the standard .NET Framework PictureBox class, meaning of course that it receives all of that ancestor's functionality "for free." This class extends the ancestor class by supporting the drawing and manipulation of the clipping lines. To that end, the OnPaint method and the three mouse-based methods OnMouseDown, OnMouseMove, and OnMouseUp are all overridden.

Another case of extended functionality occurs in the Image property, which is a property found in the base class. You can extend the functionality of the property so that you can initialize the location of the four clipping lines. You do this by using the Shadows keyword on the property, which indicates that this property replaces the functionality found in the base class. Listing C-2 shows the code for the Image property, as well as the private variables used to store the location of the four clipping lines.

Listing C-2. Shadowed Image *Property on the* ClipPictureBox

```
Private FClipInitialized As Boolean = False
Private FClipTop As Integer
Private FClipBottom As Integer
Private FClipLeft As Integer
Private FClipRight As Integer

Shadows Property Image() As Image
        Get
                Return MyBase.Image
        End Get
        Set(ByVal Value As Image)
            MyBase.Image = Value
```

```
        If Not FClipInitialized Then
            FClipTop = Height \ 4
            FClipBottom = (Height \ 4) * 3

            FClipLeft = Width \ 4
            FClipRight = (Width \ 4) * 3
            FClipInitialized = True
        End If
    End Set
End Property
```

What's interesting here is that you've specified to replace the Image property by using the Shadows keyword, but then you go ahead and use the base Image property to store the image. In effect, you're declaring that you want to replace the base property, but then you go ahead and use the property for storage anyway. You then add some functionality to the Set portion of the property. This new functionality initialized the four clipping line variables (only if they haven't already been set; the variable FClipInitialized acts as a flag to make sure the initialization happens only once).

This technique of shadowing a property and then using it anyway is a great way to "cheat" on a member that isn't declared Overrideable. The standard way of replacing or extended functionality on a class member is to override it, but you can't do this unless the base class explicitly declares the class Overrideable. You can shadow any member, though.

File Handling

The code within the utility's form has some base file handling functionality that's important. The first example of this functionality, shown in Listing C-3, occurs when the user clicks the Open button.

Listing C-3. Getting a File from the User, and Setting Up the ClipPictureBox *Control*

```
Public Class fBMPStitch
    Inherits System.Windows.Forms.Form

    Private FBaseFile As String
    Dim FFrames As Integer
    Dim pb As ClipPictureBox

    Private Sub cbFile_Click(ByVal sender As System.Object, _
        ByVal e As System.EventArgs) Handles cbFile.Click
```

```
        If oDialog.ShowDialog Then
            FBaseFile = oDialog.FileName

            If pb Is Nothing Then
                pb = New ClipPictureBox
                pb.SizeMode = PictureBoxSizeMode.AutoSize
                pb.Location = New Point(10, 10)
                pb.Visible = True
                AddHandler pb.ClippingRectChanged, _
                    AddressOf pb_ClippingRectChanged
                Me.Controls.Add(pb)
            End If

            pb.Image = Image.FromFile(FBaseFile)

            Call CountFiles()
        End If

    End Sub

    Private Sub CountFiles()

        Dim f As New FileInfo(FBaseFile)
        Dim d As New DirectoryInfo(f.DirectoryName)

        Dim cExt As String = f.Extension
        FFrames = 0
        For Each f In d.GetFiles("*" & cExt)
            FFrames += 1
        Next
        lbFrames.Text = FFrames & " frames"

        nudAcross.Value = Math.Sqrt(FFrames)
        nudDown.Value = nudAcross.Value
    End Sub
```

The variable oDialog is an instance of the .NET Framework class named OpenFileDialog. As shown in Listing C-3, the method ShowDialog opens the dialog box that requests a file from the user and returns True if the user does indeed select a file (the method returns False if the end user selects Cancel).

If the user selects a file, the code initializes a ClipPictureBox variable and adds it to the form. You could've done this by putting the ClipPictureBox into its own project and adding it to the Visual Studio toolbox, but this method does it at runtime instead. Once the `ClipPictureBox` is added to the form, it's loaded with the image from the selected file.

The routine `CountFiles` is called next. This routine uses some .NET Framework file and directory handling classes to count the number of files in the folder of the user-selected file. The first class, named `FileInfo`, encapsulates the functionality of any on-disk file. In this code, the class is initialized with the file selected by the user. The next line initializes a class named `DirectoryInfo` using the directory of the user-selected file as the constructor's parameter. What this gives you is a representation of the folder in which the user-selected file lies. One of the things the `DirectoryInfo` class lets you do is loop through all the files in the represented directory, and this is exactly what the remainder of the code does. The purpose of this loop is to count the number of files in the folder that have the same extension as the originally selected file. Once the number of files is known, it's stored in the variable `FFrames`, and the across/down controls are initialized to numbers that are the square root of this value. This works great when there are 36 frames because there would be six frames across and six down, but it doesn't quite work with, say, 24 frames. It does provide a reasonable starting value for the across/down controls, though.

Creating the Bitmap Building Code

Listing C-4 shows the routine that takes the individual bitmap files, smashes them into a large single bitmap, and then saves the bitmap to disk.

Listing C-4. The "Meat" of the Bitmap Stitcher: The Stitching Code

```
Private Sub cbBuild_Click(ByVal sender As System.Object, _
    ByVal e As System.EventArgs) Handles cbBuild.Click

        Dim b As Bitmap
        Dim f As New FileInfo(FBaseFile)
        Dim d As New DirectoryInfo(f.DirectoryName)

        Dim x, y As Integer
        Dim h, w As Integer
        Dim iA, iD As Integer
        Dim cExt As String

        iA = nudAcross.Value
        iD = nudDown.Value
```

```vbnet
    If iA * iD <> FFrames Then
        MsgBox("across * down must = frames", _
            MsgBoxStyle.Critical + MsgBoxStyle.OKOnly, "Error")
    Else
        w = pb.ClippingRect.Width
        h = pb.ClippingRect.Height

        b = New Bitmap(w * iA, h * iD, Graphics.FromImage(pb.Image))

        Dim g As Graphics

        g = Graphics.FromImage(b)

        Try
            x = 0
            y = 0

            cExt = f.Extension
            For Each f In d.GetFiles("*" & cExt)
                pb.Image = Image.FromFile(f.FullName)
                pb.Refresh()
                Thread.CurrentThread.Sleep(100)

                g.DrawImageUnscaled(pb.Image, x, y)

                x += w

                If x >= w * iA Then
                    x = 0
                    y += h
                End If

            Next

        Finally
            g.Dispose()
        End Try

        b.Save("c:\BMPStitch.bmp", System.Drawing.Imaging.ImageFormat.Bmp)
        lbClip.Text = "c:\BMPStitch.bmp saved"

    End If

End Sub
```

The first thing this routine does is check that the across/down control values, when multiplied together, actually add up to the number of frames found in the `CountFrames` routine discussed previously. If not, then the routine displays an error to the end user and exits.

If the math all works out, though, the bitmap stitching can begin. First, a bitmap simply named b is created that has the width and height needed to store the frame bitmaps. The program then loops through all the image files in the folder again, just as in the routine `CountFrames`. This time, though, each file is loaded into the `ClipPictureBox` variable and then copied into the appropriate spot on the final bitmap. Finally, the bitmap is saved to the hard-coded filename `c:\BMPStitch.bmp`.

Summary

The BMPStitch program is a good example of how it's sometimes useful to write utility software that supports and aids your primary coding effort. I had no intention of writing something that combined animated image frames together into a single bitmap, but I ultimately decided that writing such a utility would save time and make the game development process easier. The code to manage 36 individual bitmap frames would probably include some type of `ArrayList` or other collection structure, and this would be more complex than having a single bitmap and some simple math that calculated x and y offsets. In the end, the extra utility code made the actual game code simpler.

Index